IN THE BEAR'S HOUSE

Also by Bruce Hunter:

Poetry:
*Benchmark,*1982
The Beeekeeper's Daughter, 1986
Coming Home From Home, 2000

Fiction:
Country Music Country, 1996

In the Bear's House

a novel

Bruce Hunter

OOLICHAN BOOKS
LANTZVILLE, BRITISH COLUMBIA, CANADA
2009

Library and Archives Canada Cataloguing in Publication

Hunter, Bruce, 1952-
In the bear's house / Bruce Hunter.

ISBN 978-0-88982-253-5

1. Scots—Canada—Fiction. I. Title.

PS8565.U578I5 2009   C813'.54   C2008-907694-X

We gratefully acknowledge the financial support of the Canada Council for the Arts, the British Columbia Arts Council
through the BC Ministry of Tourism, Culture, and the Arts,
and the Government of Canada through the Book Publishing
Industry Development Program, for our publishing activities.

In the Bear's House is a work of fiction with guest appearances by
real and imagined historical figures.

Published by
Oolichan Books
P.O. Box 10, Lantzville
British Columbia, Canada
V0R 2H0

Printed in Canada

This book is for my brothers and sisters, and is dedicated
to the memory of
Ted Plantos, people's poet,
and Helen Carmichael Porter,
storyteller, teacher.

As I catch myself
Catching myself listening to the conch
Without the shell: the one voice now
For my son coming naked from the ocean. . .

—"Conch" by James Dickey

I wanted to tell you what the forests were like
I will have to speak
in a forgotten language

—W. S. Merwin

Clare

He was my first-born, my blue baby, my water baby. Before all the others came, passing from me in a rush. At first there was no indication of anything wrong. I suspected nothing, although I'd heard things from my grandmother on my mother's side—Grandma Locke, "pronounced like lucky," she'd always say.

"Tha wee bairn," my grandmother cooed when she held him the first time, already a damp red curl on his head, "he's a bonny wee lad, wha's dead couthie an' greets a' thae while if he's nae cuddled." I had no idea what she meant, and my Uncle Jack shrugged, but Mom laughed, the three of them with me in the maternity ward that day. Mom translated, "He's cute and cuddly, but if you don't hold him, he's gonna cry on you." Grandma Locke had warned me too of the mark of Cain. And she told ghost stories, which as a girl I laughed at, although I told her nothing of the ghosts I'd seen. As if admitting made them real, and the old country our family left, no longer old or far behind. His was not the mark of Cain, but another, as we would soon come to know. For a family named Locke, like lucky, we often weren't.

I'm not sure whether water was drawn to him or he to it. But as the doctor held him up for the first time, and the nurse cut the cord and whisked him from my sight, his blue skin, congested face and maybe most of all, his silence, terrified me. Through the daze of his birth, I could hear the quick clipped smacks on his bottom, the hiss of the oxygen tank behind the

9

curtains, and then his wailing, high-pitched screams, broken by gurgles and little gulps. He was breathing—and I would never again be so happy to hear a baby cry. He was born at 5:29 in the middle of the third week of May 1952, just as the sun sent its first dusty light through the corridors of Calgary General and the city below stirred in its final hours of sleep. Will was my first, and for the rest of his life, he woke before the sun.

Only my mother, her oldest brother Jack, and my grandmother came to see me in the maternity ward. My dad left a long time before and my husband was in prison. Mom had two outfits on the go made from some baby blue lambswool her boss had given her—she worked as a housekeeper and seamstress for a Jewish family in Mount Royal and sometimes she helped out in one of their stores. She made all our clothes. We lived in a rented farmhouse in Homepatrick, six blocks past the end of the Killarney bus line, out on the prairies near the Sarcee Indian reserve.

Lowell and I had gotten married the previous November at old city hall. I was seventeen. He was two years older and neither of our mothers approved, but I'd already miscarried once, and this time there was going to be a baby. And we knew Lowell was going to jail. He'd committed a serious crime. I was two months pregnant so his mother and mine had no choice but to let us marry. Lowell's mother wanted nothing to do with me and blamed me for everything that had happened to him, though his troubles started long before I came along.

At the end of the week, I carried my baby home.

Mom gave up her room with her treadle sewing machine, button boxes and bolts of fabric. We had a furnace but no running water. There was a hand pump by the kitchen sink and a privy in the backyard. Those old houses had only horsehair or newspaper insulation and that winter, when I got up to feed Will, I dusted off the thin layer of snow that had blown in across the covers of our bed. That year snowbanks covered the Banff Coach Road winding up the hill past the country radio station Mom listened to, all the hurting and mournful songs I hated. My grandmother assured me it's not the curse, but how we live. How you stand up when you fall down, she'd say. I scoffed when I first heard that.

The cursed know their lot, she claimed. The scattered thoughts of an old woman, I thought. It was certainly not what I believed as I shook the snow from my son's blankets. I wondered what we'd do, this baby and me. Not what would happen to my husband. That had been decided by the judge. For two long years, he'd been sent away. I wondered what would become of us.

This was the place he'd hide, the deaf boy named Trout. A broad band of aquamarine all around him, whiffs of sand, shreds of net, two bright glass floats, hand blown and carried across the current from the nets of Japanese fishermen. There, the dry delicate carcasses of seahorses, noble heads reined by invisible riders. Here, the warrior's helmet of a glossy Nautilus shell, beside the pink whorls of the conch, its knobby crown chipped and its peak gone. Several dried starfish, their arms lifted slightly, like the roofs of marine pagodas beached in the sand. The mottled cowry, the fragile whelks, the coolies' hats of limpets, the service station logo of the scallop, the bright Sanskrit wrapping the cone shells alongside the baroque curves and flutters of giant clams. The only living fish swam nearby, a dozen blue-banded barracudas and a pair of guppies in separate tanks where life-giving bubbles burbled unheard to the water's surface. His private sea.

Not the real sea, but a semblance of one, seven hundred and thirty-three miles due west. A blue room in a basement. A white ceiling over it, this inland and imagined place Trout and his mother conspired to create. Paint, sand and shells, their placement necessary illusions. The sand and the fishes were her ideas. "Just like the ocean," she'd said. A silent room jammed with a bright noisy language of his own, a jumble of colours, shapes, and dimensions, which he escaped to.

And the deaf boy endlessly rearranged, counted, and named each of the seashells. And then he started again. Each shell, each a particle, a promise of a language he longed to comprehend. They allowed him to assemble all the half-sounds, imagine the words that ended just beyond his reach. He knew sound must accompany the tree's movement in the wind, or the twitch of a bird's beak. He could see and feel them. And he had read the words for this. But he did not hear the sounds.

Above him, a small window and outside, the green laving of the lawn. Past the end of the street, the first farms on the edge of the city and behind them the raw bristle of brome, all that remained of the pale blonde prairie. Beyond the rising dunes of the foothills, the blue slopes of the Rockies, their edges snapped and jagged at the "moment" of upheaval, some twenty million years long. Themselves the wreckage of the Devonian seabed heaving thick plates of shale and limestone into the sky. In places, the shells and fossils of all the earlier seas littered some slopes with sea life so rich, it could be scooped up in delirious handfuls, like unburied treasure amongst the clouds.

Trapped six miles below his imaginary and silent ocean lurked the subterranean and tideless ooze of the Devonian Sea. Full of squashed marine life, darker and thicker than heavy syrup, toxic and exhilarating as any narcotic, pulled up in globular gulps by those mechanical tyrannosaurs, pump jacks, their obedient jaws smacking the ground. The domain of Trout at nine, and his future waiting to be lived and lost and escaped.

Whatever began first, the sea consuming him or his consumption of it, the obsession was nurtured by bimonthly arrivals of brown packages tied with string and postmarked Vancouver, packed in colourful boxes used for displaying tins of seafood. Gifts from a distant uncle, a ship's chandler, who sent along gold tins of salmon, packed with the dark flesh of Cohoes. All carefully rolled in the pages of the *Province*, along with the bright shells, sand and sea salt still on them. Trout was the kind of boy to whom people instinctively gave things. Often impromptu, whether out of pity or true generosity, it didn't matter. He never questioned them and offered thanks even when he already had dozens. The shells started that way.

The boxes came for several years, and soon his closet filled. Seashells covered his bookshelves, the windowsill, the floor, and more boxes were stuffed under his bed. He learned the Latin names: the conch, *Strombus giga Linnaeus*; the Nautilus, *pompilius Linnaeus; ficus gracilis Sowerby*; the Graceful fig shell with its lascivious pink curves and candour. Each he labelled with white tape and India ink, arranged carefully as a library full of treasure. By the time Trout was thirteen, there were two thousand shells, under the bed, in the closet, on top of the dresser. Many as small as a pearl, some as large as the Nautilus or the conch on the windowsill, basking beautiful and empty as a husk in the prairie sun.

By family, by order, by genus, Trout, who regularly failed Science, knew them by heart. His sweet secret language, all the colourful shapes, their names, light as a vowel, deft as a consonant, played over his awkward tongue. For a long time, he was happy among the remnants of the ocean floor. But sometimes, when he watched the adults talking around him, parts of words, skewed and sluiced, broke through the air. Incomprehensible bubbles came from their mouths as surely as from the aquarium above his bed. A glass separated him from others and most times he had his nose to it, feeling the weight of water and silence on the other side, a world that seldom made sense. Even when the bubbles snapped, leaving the casings of words all around him.

But it was not lonely here, on this side of that glass, not then. It seemed it must be so there. He'd pitied them. So much moving of mouths, the graceless flapping of arms and flipping of hands. Trying to convince each other, as the bubbles went one way and the movements of their owner another. Sometimes when he spoke, the bubbles came from his mouth. Some soundless, others jarring and jagged, crude vowels and chopped consonants, so that the faces of the others were etched in question marks. He learned quickly to be silent. And that the answer to most questions adults asked a child was probably yes. So, he smiled and nodded agreeably at nearly everything. And most of the time he was invisible.

He also learned somehow to love the words on the pages of the books he'd found in his grandmother's basement. He couldn't understand the words that escaped from the bubbles or the mouths of those around him. By the time he was seven, he learned not to trust the mouths, for most lied. Instead he read the faces, sometimes the lips, and always, the eyes. Somewhere in the fleeting difference between the eyes and lips was the truth.

Clare

That first year I wrote long letters to Lowell. I thought briefly of divorce. But this was 1952 after all and I was seventeen years old, with a baby. And I loved him. So I followed his instructions and sent copies of the marriage and the birth certificates to the parole board. He was a quiet man of very few words, which I liked. But I loved to write, letters, poetry, anything; and most of all, I loved to gab, enough for the both of us, he liked to tease me.

The spring I met him, I'd just turned fourteen and gotten the highest marks in the province for Language and Literature and received a certificate signed by the Minister of Education. My mom's bosses, the Singers, bought me a bound volume of the poems of William Butler Yeats. We're Scots, not Irish, but I soon fell in love with the rhythms and passion of the grey Connamara cloth of that fisherman who goes to a place upon a hill to cast his line as cold and passionate as the dawn. Mom, and in fact everyone in our family except me, fished, so I read that poem sometimes when we sat in the kitchen while Mom sewed and my grandmother baked—this was before everyone had television. We'd talked about my going to university. There were scholarships, she said, and Mrs. Singer told us she'd help if I finished grade twelve. Most of us didn't, in those years.

After school I would go to the Lido Cafe in Sunnyside. The night I met Lowell a girlfriend called and we went for Cokes. The week before, I'd had a fight with my boyfriend. Most of the kids in the Lido were older. One group of guys drove hot rods and on Saturday nights they'd come decked out in Zoot suits, with the wide shoulders and baggy pants that tapered tight around their ankles, watch chains drooping nearly to their knees. Some of them wore fedoras and swaggered like movie gangsters, and the place hushed when they came in and livened nervously when they got their orders and jammed the jukebox full of coins. They'd jive and jitterbug with their girlfriends to the Dorsey Brothers. Jimmy and Tommy, and Glen Miller and Les Brown and all the other big bands. There was nothing in this one-horse town and I was drawn to them.

Lowell wasn't the tallest or the handsomest, like in the movies, but he was raw and daring. The owner didn't allow dancing, but when the Zoot suit boys came in, he was quiet. And that Saturday night, a date night, Lowell came over to our table, nodded to my girlfriend, then me, held out his hand and extended the other towards the dance floor, all without a word.

At first we were careful, but soon I was dancing close and I could smell the whisky on him—unlike my boyfriend, Lowell was older. Everything about him—the smell of whisky, the car, the Zoot suit, and the casual way he offered me a cigarette—was dangerous. I was hooked even before I left the Lido on his arm that night. The summer before my girlfriend had smuggled a copy of *Lady Chatterley's Lover* up from the States and I hid it under my mattress. Like Lady Chatterley's love, it was all too newly true. Nothing happened, that night. He'd kissed me, but I turned my cheek as he let me out a block from our house, the rumbling muffler of his souped-up car pounding like my heart, my legs carrying me as fast as I dared through back alleys full of cottonwood fluff, hoping my girlfriend had covered for me.

And as I wrote to the parole board, I thought of that time and of the fathers who'd left us. Both Lowell and I had grown up without fathers, both of us only chldren, a lonely symmetry that drew us. It would have been odd if we hadn't found each other. My earliest memory of my father is of him in his uniform and the hat they wore, picking me up and taking me to get an ice cream cone. The delivery truck was full of laundry and when he wiped the ice cream from my chin, everything—his hands, his uniform and his hankie—smelled of dry cleaning, sweet and dangerous. Like cigarettes and whisky. I hadn't known much of anything let alone danger and I couldn't really see anything bad about it. Lowell was both sweet and dangerous. I couldn't believe my luck.

One night, when I was all alone, just after I'd started supper for Mom, and changed Will's diaper, I went back to the letters I wrote Lowell every other day. Then I heard a gasp and another and I rushed to the crib. Will's little arms stuck out in the air, as if trying to pull it in. He went red in the face. Mom wasn't home yet and I panicked. We didn't have a phone, so I scooped him up and ran next door. The neighbour drove me to the Holy Cross. Will had pneumonia. A lung collapsed, the doctor said, and he gave Will something I thought was penicillin. Years later I found out it was actually streptomycin, which might have done it. But all I wondered then was if he'd ever make it through that first year. I prayed like I'd never done before. With Lowell gone, the thought of my baby leaving me was too much to bear. I didn't think to ask them what this sickness and those pills might do, so grateful was I to have him.

Trout

While his room was safe, school, which began in order, soon turned to chaos. Comforting rows of yellowed wooden desks with pen slots and inkwell O's held apples or oranges. Worn and waxed hardwood floors with the full moons of lamps suspended by their chains. Trout counted an even number in each classroom. If First Grade had been a blur of tests and new routines he submitted to meekly, the beginning of the Second Grade made him cockier, familiar now with the rules. The new teacher's questions left him terrified, but if he followed the eyes of the others, their lips, the words on the board, the page, and caught the bubbles lifting from the teacher's quick lips and the broad hints in her hands, the emphasis of her body tilted towards or away, he could guess at what she said. But as she moved up and down the rows, coming up behind him, he shuddered. He was exposed. While he could almost hear the bland hum of her voice and knew the sharp hook of a question, he could not make out the words.

He had not yet learned that silence was insolence to some teachers. As he sat there, and silently shrugged, he saw all eyes looking at him. The bubbles, which lazily floated about his head and along the floor and over the windows, now popped. The teacher's hand on his shoulder propelled him from his desk, to stand in the corner, her breath blunt on his neck as she spoke. That tone, that heat, he could feel.

Outside the brown clapboard school with its sandstone porch, poplars had already yellowed. Green-headed mallards and Canada geese practiced their V's over the schoolyard, for fall comes early on the prairies. Trout stood in the corner, his neck at first stung red with shame. His back racked straight. His nose stuck to the plaster in that cold corner under the rueful smile and watchful eyes of Elizabeth II with her blue satin sash and dazzling jewellery. Below her hung two smaller pictures: to her right, a dour and pious Father Lacombe; to her left, an equally regal and darker Chief Crowfoot, perhaps the handsomest of the three. Over Trout's head, the letter Z of the practice alphabet pinned above the board: bravely last, the devil's halo, his friend Kenny claimed. A loser letter, always last, like Darcy Zack or Terry Zablocki in the lists of names, redeemed only by the flaming Z of Zorro's sword.

His neck and ears flushed in confusion, but shame gave way to curiosity. His mind busy in solitude began to enjoy itself, oblivious now to the teacher and the class going on behind him. The old school built in 1908, during the land rush at the discovery of oil fields in Turner Valley, had settled, and the blasting in the gravel quarry outside the schoolyard had cracked the old corner wide open.

Trout mapped the tributaries of fine cracks that led into one larger crevice that flowed towards the ceiling. Inside a plaster canyon was a solitary spider, an adolescent and dusty little house spider, as he would identify it later in his grandmother's books, among which he'd found a jar containing an ancient hairy tarantula pickled in formaldehyde. Eye-to-eye on the perpendicular, the spider scrabbled to look at him, and, startled at first, it hesitated. Then, although Trout was no threat, it began to fling silken threads from its back legs, making a web across the opening, just in case. But most of the time Trout and the spider engaged in a lop-sided staring match that left him cross-eyed.

Back in his seat, Trout now knew exactly what he was not supposed to do, and he did it anyway, so he could return to his corner. He even passed notes to Kenny Dawes. No one talked to Kenny, the strange elfin boy who'd moved from a town south of here weeks before and who lived on Trout's street. Who could prompt him by silently mouthing, fart. For there was no need to speak out loud to someone who could lip-read, Kenny had learned quickly. On cue, Trout ripped one and the wooden drawer of his desk rattled. A ripe windy riff set off a round of suppressed giggles from the children around him. Kenny Dawes sat in glee and the girl beside him smirked and pinched her nose as an invisible but gassy cloud passed between them.

Trout returned to the corner, smarting this time from a sharp rap to the back of his head that drew shocked stares. A schoolroom hero now, he watched the spider's web, which expanded and was covered with what looked like flecks of dirt. On his next visit, before the teacher realized that for Trout the corner was not punishment, those flecks had become many more little spiders. "It" was a she, and the flecks were cocoons of spider babies.

One day, encouraged by Kenny, Trout stopped

speaking altogether. He silently mouthed the answer to a question the teacher asked. If he couldn't hear her, she wouldn't hear him. Tit for tat, as his Grandma Dot said. Immediately he was sent out into the hall, to join the childless coats with mittens dangling from idiot strings from their sleeves above rows of red, white and brown rubber boots, each with their owner's name visible on the insides. On a ledge above the coats, bagged brown rows of sandwiches offered up the meatloaf smell of onion and ketchup, or punky blend of over-ripe bananas and peanut butter from the polka-dot bread bags Kenny's mother used. Surely the loneliest place on God's earth when classes were in and the soft light of the globes overhead was reflected in the polished oxfords of the principal as he bore down on Trout.

Trout made himself small and pressed into the corner beside a raincoat, wishing himself as plaid as its lining. The principal patted his shoulder, opened the door to the classroom, and motioned the teacher into the hall. Trout sat at his desk; the door closed, and the classroom hushed with tension. When the teacher returned, she was flushed but said nothing. Trout no longer found himself the object of questions. The next time the principal spotted him in the schoolyard during recess, he lifted Trout up to trip the switch for the buzzer that called the children back inside. It was an important job usually left to the principal or the captain of the school patrol. And in the days thereafter, Kenny and Trout walked home together, their mouths moving quickly and silently in their secret language.

Clare

Will was an affectionate and noisy baby at first, reaching out, laughing and grabbing at my hair, turning my face towards his when I cooed or sang to him. But when he was about a year old, mom said, "He's become a quiet one."

I ignored her, at first. I wanted one thing in my life, at least, to be perfect. And there were too many other things to worry about. Lowell's parole application, and I'd applied to train as a telephone operator. Which meant that between Mom and me, there'd always be someone with Will, as I'd have to work shifts. The money was terrific for those days and I'd be able to set some aside for when Lowell got out. Even his mother, Dot, had started to warm to her grandson, if not to me. She'd come over with bags of small gifts, little T-shirts and a striped baby blanket from the Bay and, when he was christened, a silver cup from Birks in the famous blue box. She never stayed long, arriving and leaving abruptly, never sitting down, as if her bottom would be rendered unclean by sitting on my mother's chesterfield. But I tried to be a good mother, reading *The Canada Food Guide,* Dr. Spock, and someone gave me *The Power of Positive Thinking* by Norman Vincent Peale—God knows, I needed it.

Sometimes Will seemed to understand me; other times he didn't. Near the end of his first year, I noticed he wasn't responding the way my cousins' babies had. One day I clapped my hands behind him and, when he didn't turn around, I knew something was wrong. I had so much to do that I didn't want to believe it. But if I smiled and opened my eyes wide and gestured, he seemed to respond normally. Time scooted by and I tried not to think.

Lowell's parole application was turned down. For a few weeks he didn't write even his usual short notes. Without a driver's license, I couldn't go down to Lethbridge for visitors' hours. So, one day, I went to see his probation officer to ask him what had happened. He told me about Lowell's record, stretching back to his teens. I hadn't known about that and thought of the picture I had of him, as a ten-year-old boy with short pants, wire-rimmed glasses. In his blazer, a student at the Lord Strathcona School for Boys, his two pals beside him in their school uniforms, all innocent and boyish, sissies even. Lowell had gone to school with the lawyers and crowns in the courtroom that day he was sentenced, but he had taken a different route.

The probation officer's office reeked of stale pipe smoke and carbon paper. There was a picture of the Premier, Ernest Manning, on the wall and a dusty copy of the Holy Bible lay closed on top of a bookcase. When he showed me the parole board's decision, that much I already knew. What caught my eye was a court report with the name of my old boyfriend, Roly Faro, under Assault. I thanked the man and left his office, with tears in my eyes, stumbling into the blinding sunshine. Lowell had been selective about what he'd told me. I now also knew why I'd never heard from Roly. Lowell was terribly jealous and at first I thought it a good thing. No one had cared enough about me before to be jealous or to fight for me.

In those days, a man would fight for a woman. And it seemed they were always fighting. It was so bad in the fifties that the Calgary police chief wanted the vets returning from Korea to sign in at City Hall, so he'd know where to dispatch the paddy wagon when the fight broke out. There were rumbles between the Southside boys and the North Hill or the boys from the Currie and Sarcee Barracks. Between the vets from the Second World War and the Korean vets and the boys left behind, too young to enlist, like Lowell, there was no shortage of angry men. There was a movie big around then, City Across the River, about a New York gang, the Amboy Dukes, starring young Tony Curtis, his hair all slicked back. Some said Elvis Presley copied his hairstyle from that movie. Greasers, people called them. The guys in Calgary acted out the movie, all cool and swaggering, fighting at the slightest provocation, real or not.

That was Lowell. That was who I'd married. I wondered what else he'd hidden from me. But I was determined he'd be a father to Will, and a good one.

"Oh, oh." Trout looked at Kenny Dawes, who tapped his shoulder and mouthed as they entered the room together. Black headsets covered their desks and wires ran to a large receiver at the front. The school nurse in her starched white uniform and winged hat, gangly and efficient, gave instructions for the hearing tests, as an elderly man sat behind the box apparently turning dials. Not hearing her, Trout watched the others for cues. His dandelion brushcut flattened under the large headphones, Kenny shot a blank look, crossed his eyes and shrugged. Trout didn't laugh as he might have, for he was completely alone. As each of his classmates pencilled their score sheets, he imitated them, curious as to exactly what he was supposed to be hearing. He couldn't see Kenny's answers.

Whatever the results of the test for his classmates, two weeks later Trout found himself with his mother waiting downtown in the Medical Arts building in the office of the contraption man, whose foyer contained a glass case full of gadgets. Some were odd and beautiful as seashells, like the long swooping black ear trumpet. Others were confusing and complicated, like the headset with its wire running into a cloth bag that held a Bakelite transmitter with a harness and a matching set of dry cells, like those in the science room. It was nearly as large as the walkie-talkies in the army surplus store.

The contraption man's office was full of more box-es, wires and cables, plasticky and rubbery smells, vials and jars. On a shelf above his head lay flesh-toned impressions of ear canals. Trout thought they looked naked and he was embarrassed by this. The contraption man, whose face sported a long wine-coloured birthmark that ran from below his left eye and along his cheek and ballooned to cover his Adam's apple and throat, sprayed saliva sometimes when he spoke, his spit full of Dentyne chewing gum. Trout was fascinated by the mark, but staring was rude he knew. So he looked instead at the huge schema of an ear canal on a chart behind the man, his head haloed by the hairy loop of the eustachian tubes. The only other free wall had a needlepoint: "The Meek Shall Inherit the Earth".

The contraption man held up the hearing aid for Trout and his mother. "This is the microphone," he pointed to a small gold object, "and this is the magic box that is listening for you." He put a hard plastic button in Trout's ear. "This is the speaker, so you can listen." Like the PA system at school, Trout understood, only the speaker was in his ear and the microphone on his chest. "You're listening to the listening," the contraption man laughed as he put Trout's finger on the volume dial and turned it. "You hear the echo?" A rasping scratched inside his ear and Trout winced, confused by the explosion of rippling static, but he nodded anyway at the contraption man. A body aid, the man called it.

Trout left the office with his contraption strapped to his chest in a white cloth sack. The size and colour of his dad's gold Zippo lighter, it had a thin cable that ran to the plastic button embedded in his ear. "That's quite the contraption," his father said, when Trout wore it at the supper table that night. "Let me see that." He held out his hand. "Small, but still pretty powerful," he said, handing it back carefully. There was awe and fear in his father's voice. Trout heard that. His father, who hammered metal for a living and loved fast cars. A tinbanger, Kenny Dawes called him.

His mother and sister took turns wearing it too. "Like a Japanese transistor radio," Pauline hooted and waved it side to side as she listened. "Dad," she pouted, "can I get one?"

"Stop it, Pauline," their mother's voice interrupted as she rapped the casserole dish with a wooden spoon. "If anything happens, it's a lot of money."

Trout could hear his mother's words now. His name, in her voice, had soft fur on it like the belly of his cat. And his sister's tones, flirty and stinging. But the sounds of the cars and trolleys and the rapping of the wooden spoon and his sister's jibes smarted harsh as a knee scraped on gravel. He wasn't sure if he wanted this. And on the trolley home, a woman had stared at him, looking past his eyes into his ear with the cable running from it. He could feel the cold prolonged stare.

His mother looked the woman in the eye and asked, "And how are we today?" He heard that. The woman turned away without saying anything and Trout felt his mother's arm around him, pulling him into her shoulder. But that night, Trout put his contraption to bed in its plush velvet box with its spring lid, like the ones watches came in. He slept with it under his pillow, opening and visiting it before he went to sleep and again in the morning when he woke.

At first he liked his contraption. At school he could now hear some of the words his teacher and Kenny said. Sometimes though, the bubbles floated by him and he was confused. But he learned to listen. And like the jigsaw puzzle laid out on his grandmother's card table, the colours and pieces of the words he heard filled in the spaces left by the ones he didn't. What he read, and he'd always read it seemed, now matched what the teacher said and the writing on the board. A month later, he got back a test with a perfect score. Higher even than Dicky Motherwell, who sat closest to the teacher and brought her a birthday cake.

Although somedays, his ears and head ached. Strapped to his chest, the golden box and its earpiece crackled and hissed in his ear, a simple microphone and receiver for which he was always grateful, although it was an unlovely approximation of an ear that failed him terribly at times. The words were closer now, but the sounds were still unrecognisable. And the wind roared static at him; its hissing tendrils lashed his head and ears. He told no one. He knew how much they wanted this to work, his grandmother and his mother. And although he loved even the screeching rumble of the gravel crusher and the staccato diesel roar of the earth scrapers in the gravel pit, sometimes he unplugged his contraption to let the bubbles wash over him again, for comfort. Always, though, he put it back to hear the words around him, because he wanted so badly to know them. He came to enjoy the wind's rush. It no longer frightened him and he'd come to crave it, all its crashing and snapping crackle.

Clare

Ours is a stubborn family of talkers—loquacious our middle name—not a dour Scot in the bunch. Will certainly was stubborn. When I took one of his toys from him, he'd snatch it back or howl. And although he had started already to walk little steps, he still wasn't talking other than to gurgle or howl. We were all concerned and I'd taken him to a bunch of doctors who all told me not to worry. One of them even patted me on the head. It's normal, he'd said, he'll grow out it,

I sang and talked to Will anyway. Only his eyes and smile gave me any clue he was aware. Until one day I was chopping vegetables in a rhythmic fury when I heard a matching thump, thump, thump to the sound of the knife on the cutting board. Will sat in the kitchen doorway looking up at me, his head a ring of red curls. I turned my back to him and thumped three times on the counter. He thumped his wooden block three times on the wall. I dropped to my knees and pounded my fists on the floor, dunt, dunt, dunt. He did the same with his toy and laughed at me, his eyes the clearest I'd ever seen. I took two spoons from the drawer and clapped them together. He looked confused at the high-pitched clicking, but when I banged them on the floor, he laughed again. I knew we had a secret language and a few days later, when a neighbour knocked on the door, Will looked up at me and repeated the knocking on the side of the cupboard, waiting for me to do the same.

By then I knew he could feel some sounds and not others, so when I talked to him or sang, I sat him on my lap facing me. I'd place his hands on my cheeks or on the side of my neck so he could feel the words or feel my humming to him. It took weeks, but one day, I heard him humming. We'd sit together, him on my lap with his hands on my neck. The two of us humming like a couple of bees. Other times, I'd make my lips vibrate like a tuba player and put his fingers to them. At first, he'd flinched, but then he'd reached out, curious, and I'd put my tuba lips to his forehead, his cheeks and his neck. He'd giggled until I had to stop, my lips hurting and my cheeks sore from laughing. He couldn't talk, but he could laugh and blubber and that wasn't a bad thing, Mom agreed.

She bought him a huge fluffy bumblebee with big eyes and stripes. We'll bathe him in sound, she said. So Mom and I would make buzzing noises, vibrating our lips close to his face and ears, making up nonsense rhymes, buzz-beee, buzzy-beee, buzz-bee, bee-bee, bay-bee.

With my cheque from the phone company, I got Will a tin drum for his second Christmas and sent Lowell a picture of the three of us in front of the tree. Lowell's mother Dot had gotten Will a blue sailor suit with one of those white sailor hats. I've lost that picture, but in a way it was one of the happiest times—we were a family, even though Lowell was still in Lethbridge.

As we cooked Christmas dinner, Will beat his drum, slipping into the knocking of a door, or the rhythms of the songs we made up for him, and we marched around the living room together.

"An unholy racket," Mom laughed, "but a lovely racket too," she said.

He learned in his own way to talk even if he couldn't say Mama.

"He's like his name, stubborn," she insisted. "He'll talk in his own time," she said, "don't you worry."

And for once I didn't.

Trout

Kenny's voice was sometimes carried off by the wind, but Trout could read his lips as he turned and called out, "We're almost there."

They followed the overgrown wagon ruts of the old Fort Whoop-up Trail, still visible beyond the gravel pit and the school. They stood on the cusp of the foothills and the wind pulled and rustled in the microphone of Trout's hearing aid as he and Kenny Dawes explored the grassy dunes that circled the small community where they lived. It never occurred to Trout to ask where *there* was.

Wherever it was, they usually never got to it, but always the promise lured them. *There* was the river, this time, but in Kenny's voice, *there* was like Montana in his auntie's voice, more promise than destination.

Kenny knew the foothills that lifted their tawny shoulders from the open prairie and dropped into grassy gulleys all the way to the blue slopes of the Kananaskis, eighty miles west. They followed the fence line of the last farm, with its sway-backed cows and rusting farm implements guarded by the old grizzened man who tended the school grounds and whose lethargic bull paced the fence line as they hiked towards the wolf willow henges on the sandstone bluffs above the Bow River. Trout loved the thrall of the river's wet rush in his new contraption and its damp updraft on his face when he lay on the sandstone, warm even on the coldest spring days, when ice saucers still floated on the pothole sloughs.

Other Saturdays, he went to his Grandma Dot's, where he sat at the feet of his old auntie. His great-great auntie, Martha Golding Worden, or Auntie as everyone called her, came west on an American construction train, before the C.P.R., and north by ox cart and stagecoach on the Whoop-up Trail, to meet the man she'd marry, having answered two newspaper ads in the *Toronto Telegram*.

A silver-rimmed crystal candy dish from Birks held Scotch mints on the marble-top table by his auntie's side in the Victorian parlour, with its floor-length ferns on wicker stands and its shadowy chintz curtains. In one corner stood an upright piano where his grandmother sometimes sang, "There's a Bluebird on My Windowsill," her stretched smile and arced eyebrows marking time with her hands on the keyboard. She was happy when she sang and Trout was grateful for that. In the other corner, in an ornate gilded cage, the ancient parrot, Joe, slept and squawked whenever a door slammed.

Her arms sun-spotted, Trout's white-haired auntie spoke slowly and deliberately to him. Never impatient like his Grandma Dot, she read the confusion in his eyes when he didn't hear. Often she'd gesture or sound out a word for him. Her quick card player's hands lifted and plummeted like a pair of birds. Often she told the story backward to its starting point, so Trout heard it twice.

"Papa came with me as far as Boston. All the way from Wickham, New Brunswick. On my own, by Northern Pacific from St. Paul's, Minnesota, and then by construction train carrying supplies to Helena, Montana, end of the line. No station there, just log buildings. Then I came overland to Fort Benton by stage coach and then north by open wagon and ox cart." She turned her head from east to west and opened her hands to express the vast distance, then levelled them to show the flatness of the land he knew.

Trout loved the word Montana as it called out in his auntie's voice. The word, after all those years, still filled with hope and light. Mon-tana. He could hear the promise.

His auntie pointed to the fireplace mantel, "Bring that to me, will you?"

Trout reached for the soapstone carving with clusters of angel wings and tiny catacombs on its side.

"No, no, bring me the sea shell."

He hefted the pink and white shell and lowered it gently into his auntie's sure grip as she placed it into her lap.

"That's a good boy." She tapped her ear, "You like the hearing aid?"

Trout nodded.

"Your Grandma Dottie will be pleased. Let me know if you can't hear me. Where were we?" For a moment, his auntie looked lost. Sometimes she would sit for hours in her chair, crunching Scotch mints in her jaws when conversation ended, a magnifying glass to a crossword puzzle in her lap, and her eyes elsewhere as he read beside her, reaching too for mints from the dish and crushing them loudly. His auntie never shushed him as his grandma did when he cracked a fresh one loudly in his teeth, enjoying the solid crunch ripping along his jaw.

"My, this is heavy. They weighed all my luggage. Paid by the pound. I almost threw this out."

Trout looked at her three white chin hairs that curled towards him as she talked.

She held up the conch. "But I kept it. I guess I had to. I knew someday there'd be a little boy to give it to."

His auntie winked and Trout laughed.

"It's a conch. C-H – con-SCH." She exaggerated the word for him. "Though I've heard it pronounced konk. Like a conk on the noggin." She rapped his head and they both laughed.

"Often, I was the only one on the coach. Part of the way, we rode in an open wagon. Oh, my, that was slow. Most of the freight came by bull trains pulling three wagons. Sometimes eight miles a day. Carried all my money and my gun in my purse. Papa gave me a little pearl-handled Derringer, a lady's gun. But when I arrived at St. Paul's, I went to a gunsmith and asked what a man would use and he showed me a Colt .45. Still got it and can still use it." His auntie set her lower lip and nodded. Trout reached for another mint and cracked it. He wanted that Derringer.

"1882 and I was eighteen years old. I knew what I was getting into. Women didn't travel alone." His auntie was defiant still, her chin up as she spoke.

"I carried this sea shell all the way from New Brunswick. The trip took nearly a month by way of Fort Whoop-up, Fort Macleod, and finally Fort Calgary, stopping every forty miles to rest the horses. I kept the Colt handy. Nearly nothing to see, in those days, north of Macleod. No fences, no bridges. The buffalo were all gone by then. We forded every creek and river. That was the first time I met your great-grandfather, Grandma Dottie's father. We dropped the mail at his ranch near Davisberg on the confluence of the Bow and Highwood Rivers. He'd came up the Missouri from St. Louis three years earlier on a paddle wheeler with his horses. My, Bob Begg was a handsome man with the handlebar moustache, and he was educated. You would have liked him."

"What was the gun for, Auntie?" Trout finally asked, wondering why she'd needed it if there was nothing north of Macleod. He knew it was rude to interrupt an old person, especially his auntie.

"Oh, well, I'd heard there were Indian troubles. And some of the men hadn't seen a woman in a long time. Your great-grandfather told me he'd had visitors. A Blackfoot raiding party in full war paint. He was alone on the ranch and he didn't know what to do. So he invited them in. His cabin had been a North West Mounted Police post, so they knew it. He boiled up a pot of water, throwing in handful after handful of tea. Oh my, he was scared. He was just two years older than me, straight from the agricultural college in Guelph, Ontario. But he sat cross-legged on the floor with the Blackfoot and after that they came by and were friendly to him. There'd been a massacre of a family south of Macleod, but when he told me the story of his visitors, I was glad I'd come. Oh, we knew we were all part of something then.

"And I was glad I had the gun. But really, I had no trouble. People were good to me. I stayed overnight in Macleod in a restaurant. The men slept on the floor with their bedrolls. Auntie Pearl, a tough little Negress, she was Colonel James Macleod's cook, let me share her bedroom for the night, a proper hostess. But, oh my," his auntie puckered her lips, "she was sharp with the men. Up at six o'clock poking them with a broom. When she started sweeping the floor at this end, the men at the other end had to be gone. There were a few Negroes. John Ware, of course, was the most famous. Bob Begg said he was one of the finest cowboys in Southern Alberta. They met at the Bar U when he went up to buy cattle. Some called him Nigger John Ware. There was a ridge named that. We don't say that anymore," she grunted. She jutted her chin and shook her head. "Bob Begg said, if people had ten miles to go to John Ware's place and five miles to someone else's, they'd gladly go the greater distance to John Ware's, he was so well regarded.

"Finally I got here. Took a room at Calgary House. Tarpaper and boards. Hadn't even been painted yet, but it had a bathtub and a laundry. It was in the old town beside the fort on the east side of the Elbow River on Ninth Avenue East in Inglewood. There were maybe a thousand of us then, in tarpaper shacks and a few tents and teepees outside the fort.

"I had answered two ads and written to both gentlemen. That first night I met one. Didn't like him. A handsome one, but slick. Made a fortune in land later. But I had my own money. My husband, your

Great-Great-Uncle Hiram, I met the next night. Hiram G. Worden, Esquire, was how he signed his letters to me." Auntie sighed and smoothed the lap of her sundress. Her toes curled as she talked.

Trout had never met his great-great-uncle or great-grandfather but in his auntie's voice they were alive.

"His new mail-order suit was a little too tight. But he smoked a cigar, which I liked. He wasn't as handsome as the other fellow, but he laughed with his belly. He wore a pinkie ring." She held up her hand and wiggled her little finger. "His hands were soft and white. He wasn't rough like many of the men. He always smelled good. He was a baker. We got married two weeks later. The railway came through the next year. We were certainly glad to see Engine No. 83. Everyone turned out to welcome the men building the line and to meet that first train.

"Oh my, we worked. But we did well." Auntie's brows arched in emphasis and flattened with sadness. "Then we lost everything in the fire in 1886. But, we started over, and in 1890 we opened my candy store right next to Hiram's new bakery across from the C.P.R. station.

"I brought my sister, your great-grandmother, out ten years later. Lavinia was the baby. There were four of us and I was the eldest. We all called her Bean. I introduced her to Bob Begg. He'd come out before me and he was one of the first people I met here. We got to know him later through the police chief, a friend of ours. We built this house at the turn of the century and held her wedding reception in the Alberta Hotel in 1902. It was quite the do. *The Cal-*

gary Herald called us the lovely Golding sisters in the society column. Bean was much prettier, like Mama. Your Grandma Dot's named for her." His auntie cradled the heavy shell. It was one he admired, wanted even. But at his grandmother's, the house of secrets, what was coveted would never be given.

"When I was a girl, we'd put it to our ears and hear the sea. I always thought it looked like an ear." She held it up. "See the pink lobe?" She tugged his ear. "Just like yours." She handed it to Trout. "It was Bean's. She said it would remind me of the sea. 'Never forget where you come from, Martha,' she told me. I want you to have it. You still have your collection, don't you?"

Trout nodded, his eyes on the prized shell. *Strombus giga Linnaeus.*

"People throw everything away nowadays," she sighed. "It's a conch from the West Indies. Mama's papa was a sea captain. Mama never talked about it, but Bean and I both wondered if he'd been a slaver, carrying those poor people over from Africa. I told her I'd keep it for her 'til she got here. And when she died I almost buried it with her. If it could speak, I wonder what would it say? What it might have heard.

"I never went home again." She shook her head slowly and peered down at Trout who was now sitting rapt on the carpet. She took off her gold wire glasses. "I never regretted it. Never." She breathed on the lenses and polished them with a linen hanky.

Trout wasn't sure. Her eyes didn't agree with her words. He stared at the conch in his hands and Auntie watched the traffic on 14th as the sunlight filtered through the chintz curtains onto the ferns. Her sun-spotted hand reached for a mint, and offered him the dish. The conversation was over.

Her stories sparked Trout's curiosity about treasures only a boy would covet in the house Auntie shared with Dot. The tarantula she'd found in a shipment of bananas, and kept in formaldehyde. Labelled in India ink, the jar with the furry banana spider sat on the highest shelf in her den, above the roll-top desk and pewter St. Bernard inkpot with a head that flipped open when she filled her fountain pen. Her stories didn't always make sense until later. The firebug who'd haunted the city in the '20s, so vivid, Trout was terrified for a week until he finally realized it was not an exotic bug, like the tarantula that crept into houses upside along power lines. A firebug, alas, was merely a man. When his grandmother Dot and his great-great-aunt Martha left him alone, he rifled the contents of drawers and cupboards, which took up whole walls.

One day he opened the bedside commode cupboard, and there, on the upper shelf, above the chamberpot, lay the short-barrelled Colt .45, with nickel plating and black gum handle. He recognized it from her stories. His mouth dry, he peered in the cylinder. Someone had removed the bullets. Trout slammed the cupboard shut and sniffed the gunpowder on his hands. He ran to the bathroom, washed his hands, and sank his nose in a book until Auntie and Dot came home. He never found the Derringer.

Auntie had told him about the burglar. "Mister, I

have a gun and I'll shoot. I can see that shiny top button on your shirt. I'm a pretty good shot, but I don't think you want to find out." Then she called the police. "The poor man was shaking, so was I," she said. "But I would have shot him. I was as scared as he was." Trout was not as surprised as he should have been.

Trout knew she was telling the truth—her voice was steady and her eyes were clear. His dad said, after Uncle Hiram died in the 'thirties, Auntie ran both the bakery and the candy store and kept the receipts in her bedroom.

Rummaging, Trout found white muslin bags of twenty five-cent bills, shinplasters, gold coins and paper money in denominations and colours he'd never seen before, hidden under the flannel nightclothes at the back of Auntie's closet.

"Martha Worden feared for her money after the Crash of '29," his dad had said.

Trout wondered exactly what had crashed and why grown men had jumped from the roof of the Palliser Hotel. But the woman thought to be the wealthiest, and oldest, in her family still did not trust banks.

When Auntie gave him the conch, she placed it in his hands as he imagined her sister Bean had once done. When he went out to the prairie, on those other Saturdays when he did not visit his auntie, he took the shell with him. Out there, with the school and the taunts of the older boys far behind, he and Kenny were free and happy. The conch, easily the heaviest thing in his pack, thunked against his back under his lunch and canteen. But he'd sit on the sandstone slab holding it to his contraption in its cloth sack, the river amplified twice now, once in the microphone and again in the conch, wrapping him in its noisy rush, listening to the listening.

Through the crackle of his contraption, he listened, not to the sea, but to the river, the hiss of water, and once more, to his auntie's stories. That Colt in her hands. The candlestick-phone at her bedside. A masked burglar against the wall. The wail of the Black Maria, the Paddy wagon hauling him away. History was not the olden days, or the turn of the century. It was now and forever in the coiled lobes of the conch.

One day at noon hour, when the older kids from the other school were in the playground, they came for Trout. The oldest one, the leader—a German boy Trout knew—stopped him. He was larger than the other kids, kept back two grades.

When he leaned into Trout's face, his breath smelled like raw meat. He plucked the receiver out of the cloth sack that hung on Trout's chest, and shouted into the receiver: "What it's like in there, retard?". Some of the other boys laughed. Retard was a word the physical education teacher used when they missed a pitch or fumbled a ball.

Out-numbered, Trout squirmed and didn't reply. Kenny Dawes ran towards them from the ball diamond.

"You dumb too, Deaf Boy?" asked the oldest boy. Only the bully laughed this time.

Then Kenny, with his dandelion tuft, stepped in

front of Trout. The older boy was a foot taller. Kenny poked his chin at the older boy, daring him.

"Fruit loop," the bully snarled. "What're you, a cop or somethin'?" Kenny's fists were clenched at his sides.

"Let's go, here comes Gover," one of the others said.

Trout could see the principal. His hand shielded his eyes from sun as he watched them from the porch of the school. The older boys separated and shuffled back towards the senior school.

Trout had watched once as the German boy rode his bike up and down in front of their neighbour, a quiet Dutchman, whose side yard was filled with long rows of tulips. Round and round the block he'd ridden in his father's army helmet, taunting. His father had been a sergeant in the German army, Kenny said. The S.S. Kraut, he called him.

English was a foreign language now for Trout. Hearing brought new words with sharp flint edges that sparked when they struck. The order and conjugations became confused. Trout knew that some words were sticks and stones and they were meant to hurt him. His mother had told him he was special. But not like the Special class at the school downtown. That *special* meant Dense or Thick, Odd or Different. As in Slow. The stones of adults were wrapped in cloth.

As they passed the older boys on the way home each night, he and Kenny Dawes ignored them. Trout mouthed silently to Kenny, "Don't." and they both crossed the street. Even then, he could hear their words and read their taunting faces. Each time a new word. *Hey, Deaf Boy, can you hear? You Mute? Hey Dozey. Hey Queer. Hey Idiot. Deaf and Dumb, Deaf and Dumb,* they chimed.

He told no one, not his mother nor his teachers. This was his shame. In his blue-walled room he picked up his shells, caressed them one by one: comfort, order and calm. He held up the conch with its pearled knobs crowning it. He put it to his ear. Nothing. He held it against the gold receiver, which hung above his heart. Noise. Not the sea, which he'd never seen. But a sound like it: washing, circling, hinting.

He shook the conch to see what was in it and a small piece of yellowed newspaper fluttered to the floor. Its torn corner said October 12, 1918 and there were a few words between the names of people: *Deceased, Survived by.* The shell had once belonged to his great-grandmother, a New Brunswick girl born on the sea, who'd come west to marry a rancher. Her letters home from the west spoke of the wind, the incessant wind over the river. That was the sound he imagined in the shell then. And the brittle newsprint, likely used to pack it after her death in the Spanish Flu epidemic of 1918, now lay in his hands like a scrappy note from a bottle tossed overboard.

He turned towards the mirror, which, like some of the books in his room, had once been hers. His fingers curled past the mother of pearl lip of the conch, reaching for more paper. But there was none. The fragment was all that was left. As he grasped the shell, he feigned a weighted punch towards his own face in the mirror. But he stopped short as a knuckle of the conch grazed the glass. He set the shell on his dresser. He took his ear plug out, coiled its cable neatly, put the gold receiver wrapped in its sack into the velvet case, and snapped it shut and placed it in his bottom drawer under his winter socks and his most guarded treasures. If this was hearing, Trout did not want it. Not now, not yet.

Clare

As the last months of Lowell's sentence neared, my life burned with brightness in what might otherwise have been a dark time. Working at the phone company, through my headset I could hear the homesick carillon call from the stone tower of the church across the street, and the start of evening traffic. It was, to me, the saddest time of day when the sun set and the supper hour began.

For nearly two years, I ended my day alone, watching others go home to their husbands.

My letters to Lowell increased in frequency and in passion. I began to plan for his release and bought a new dress. One of those off-the-shoulder numbers with swirls of red silk around a plunging neckline.

Mom was furious—she'd always made my clothes. "You're extravagant, Clare," she said. As if I was still more her daughter than my husband's wife.

She was right—the Lockes didn't complain, they made do. But I wanted something luxurious, just this once. I checked the local directories for a motel where we'd spend our first night. We'd never really had a honeymoon.

Will was walking now, climbing and getting into everything. He's a little drummer boy, Mom said, as we sang to him, stressing the ruppa bup, bup. Slapping his hands on our cheeks until he learned to do the same. And he'd look at the picture books we got him and make a cute kind of buzz when he saw the bee. And bark when he saw the dog. Saying "dog" without the hook on the *g* of the word. His little words lacked the hard sounds. All softened, like flannel. We thought it terribly sweet then, before we knew. He'd sit with the picture books, talking to himself in his own little language that at times made a sense of its own. At other times it was wonderfully close to ours, yet not. He was a hungry little boy, pulling the books from the shelves and the noise-making pots from the cupboards, as if he was trying to find one that would speak for him.

That Easter, the three of us caught the train up to Mom's sister's place in Olds. Mom had nine brothers and sisters and our family gatherings were always smoky and boozy then. There were tables full of pies and tarts, platters of beef from the ranch, bright jars of preserves and vegetables from their gardens. Aunt Meggie on her accordion and her son Alex on the fiddle, Aunt Shelagh on the guitar and my Uncle Jack recited Robbie Burns. His was a ragged voice, perfect for poetry, as he ranged through the half-sung strains of "The Young Highland Rover" and slapped the beat on his leg.

> "Loud blaw the frosty breezes,
> The snaws the mountains cover;
> Like winter on me seizes,
> Since my young Highland rover
> Far wanders nations over."

And when the party wound down, he picked up his bagpipes for the grand finale. Tanned and tough-hided men, my uncles, but sentimental just under the skin—their eyes watered easily. The rooms full of cousins and their babies and kids. Will made his way through them, smiling. His great-uncles played with him and his aunts scooped him up and twirled him around. He was unafraid and laughed, touching their cheeks and hair, taking them in, walking right up to his young cousins and peering into their faces. I'd worried about how they'd take him. He'll need lots of love, Mom said. Her brothers and sisters seemed to have known. Especially Uncle Jack, the gruff oldest brother, who put a new silver dollar in Will's little hand and he grabbed hold, not letting it go.

"Ay, he's one of us," Jack said. The others laughing, all of them old country Scots who'd sailed out of Glasgow with nothing at the start of the Dirty Thirties, for the prairies, and a homestead in the bush west of here. Going from worse to worst, Uncle Jack laughed. All of them started out poor—and all of them were generous. Our curse was certainly not stinginess of spirit. If I'd ever feared them not helping me, I didn't now. I also knew everything I had to give would never be enough and I hoped that Lowell could help me too.

When Lowell finally walked out of jail down in Lethbridge that fall, he was thin and grey in the skin, from lack of sunlight. He looked away when he saw me, as if it were too much at first, but he held me at arm's length in my new red silk dress and whistled. As he hugged me for the first time in nearly two years, his hands slid down my hips on the smooth fabric. But I knew that whatever man he'd been, another stood in his place now, for better or worse.

"Gordie, let's get us all a drink," he said, to the friend who'd driven me down to Lethbridge in Lowell's car, a hot rod he souped up from a Model T. "I know a guy." He spoke out of the side of his mouth now—something he never did before. It was hot and hazy that Sunday, the day of rest, and the only things open in those days were the churches—and bootleggers. I wasn't yet old enough to drink.

Doc Baldry's shack was out on the edge of the dry coulees near the high level bridge we'd passed on the way into town. An old rounder, a bootlegger, with a dwarf hand in a black leather glove, that always had a cigarette in it, he seemed to know we'd be coming and poured us a round of rye. The men played cards while I sat on the porch, looking out over the coulees and when we left, Lowell and his friend put two cases of whisky in the trunk of Lowell's car. When I frowned, Lowell said, "A favour for a friend." His eyes warned me not to ask.

That night at the Marquis Motel—the locals called it the Mar-kwiss—Gordie slept on the floor of our room. It wasn't the honeymoon I imagined. The two of them snoring, the smell of sour rye in the close air, my new dress on the back of a chair, Lowell turning in his sleep and moaning. As the first light came through the Venetian blinds, he pulled me onto him, without a sound. His arms clasped me, his chest to my back, his face buried in my neck, convulsing and then murmuring, all without waking.

I'd rented us the upstairs of the place Mom and I lived in back in Calgary. And Lowell was awkward with our son at first, not knowing what to do with either of us, but he was a builder. He got his tools out and built a toy box for Will and shelves for the kitchen of our new place. He'd found a job through the John Howard, working for a small construction company where only the owner knew about his record. But I knew it would be hard to keep anything quiet for long in this town with what the papers had done, the front-page stories, and The Albertan ran red headlines at that. Sometimes the police pulled us over and made us both get out. Lowell's car was easy to spot, a black 1923 Model T with a low frame and chopped roof. Lowell's fists curled, his face shamed red and taut.

In the car afterwards, he talked the hard con talk—out of the side of his mouth, which he covered with his hand while he talked. In the joint, he said, the bulls, the screws, beat the men if they talked. This was the man he'd become. Inside he was raging, I knew, but he said nothing to the cops, venting only when we got home. He'd uncap a bottle of rye and I'd join him after Will was asleep.

"I did the time," he'd say, and pace the small kitchen without looking at me.

I was frightened, at first. I'd read somewhere that prisons are the universities of crime.

When Lowell was sleeping one night, I found welts across his back and I knew he'd been lashed. They did that then in the jails. I knew not to ask. Lowell had come out of prison a changed man. That was then, he said, this is now, the only time I asked.

Eventually we settled into our life. He went off to work and I took two shifts on the weekend to help out, while Mom baby-sat. Most women didn't work then if they had kids, and Lowell was fiercely proud about me quitting. That happened soon enough when I was pregnant with our first daughter, Pauline.

It didn't occur to me—I was happy to have him there—to ask questions when he came back late. I was angry because his shift had finished hours before. But his was the greater rage, and we always seemed to have enough money. On payday, he'd bring home a bundle of T-bone steaks from the Bon Ton meat market, which was just around the corner from work, or a warm paper bag of meat pies, enough for my mom too. It felt like we were rich then. Some Friday nights we'd stop by the Cecil or the St. Louis. To see a friend, he'd say, usually a rounder or a bookie with "offices" in the downtown hotel lobbies. I didn't ask—he didn't encourage me, and it was exciting. I was nineteen, after all.

As a mother now, I look at my children and see how young nineteen really is. Breath-takingly young, our mothers must have thought. But I worried about that rage, and wondered what else that jail down there had done to him. I wondered too if he'd accept Will, if he'd be a father.

"Here you go, Sunshine. You can go warm her up for me." His father handed him the keys to the Pontiac. "You might want to put her in neutral." His father laughed. His mother looked worried, but his father's eyes met hers and she said nothing.

The year Trout turned thirteen, he started with his dad on the Saturday jobs. Usually he tore out old coal-burning furnaces and replaced them with new gas-burners, dirty work that paid hard cash under the table. His father was always working and Trout welcomed the time with him. In school, he had long since become invisible, keeping an agreeable but disengaged silence that saved him, his classmates and the teacher embarrassment at his only occasional hearing and often fumbled speech. He hid from questions by sitting nearest the teacher and nodding frequently. Kenny had meanwhile disappeared into the obscure middle rows.

After school, both of them took their curiousity and roamed the fast-diminishing prairie whenever they could. So Trout welcomed his father's offer and the chance to go elsewhere, often to the basements of the oldest houses in the city, with cellars as layered and rich as the ruins of faraway Pompeii, which he'd studied in school.

Early that spring Saturday, he and his dad drove downtown to the house his Grandma Dot and Great-Great-Auntie Martha shared. Dot hovered with a broom and cardboard boxes while Auntie waited anxiously at the top of the stairs, lest any of her treasures be lost. The light behind her made a fuzzy crown of her white hair, but she stayed put. Her arthritis confined her now to the main floor of the big house. His father fidgeted with a ring of skeleton keys, the cellar's padlock a flat medieval thing, older than any Trout had ever seen. An old coal-burner waited like a bandaged-up octopus in the centre of the room, its round ducts wrapped in asbestos frayed at the elbows. A door big enough to swallow a child marked the front, and its slatted vent smirked with a greedy set of teeth.

His father banged and hacksawed, cursing under his breath, his face red with exertion. Trout handed him tools. Trout's new gloves, smelling of fresh leather, protected his soft hands against sharp edges and grease. Dot swept, and piled old books and rags into boxes. She thwacked rugs on the clothes line with the wicker carpet beater, and twice hoovered the Persian carpet with her new electric sweeper, first one way, then another. When he was younger, Trout loved the Hoover's thrum reverberating through his toes, as his grandmother let him drive the vacuum, as she balanced him piggy-backed on her feet. The vacuum's low headlight poked under the clawed toes of the satin overstuffed sofa and chairs of Auntie's parlour.

Auntie was a Collector and a Saver. Stacked along the cracked cement walls, around the long arms of the grinning octopus, were dozens of wicker chests, metal footlockers, Gladstone bags and steamer trunks, some as old as the ones he saw tied atop stagecoaches in the T.V. Westerns. Behind his father were five-gallon wine jugs, of clay and wicker. When his grandmother moved a trunk, a black iron ball rolled across the floor and came to rest against the heel of his father's boot as he kneeled under the furnace.

"Oh, for God's sake, Mother." His dad's hair was coated in asbestos dust. "Jesus Murphy."

"No need to swear, and that stuff probably isn't good for you," she huffed.

"It's hardly swearing and I work with this every day." His father sighed. "Can you not wait?"

It was a cannonball. Dot placed it behind a wooden butter box so it wouldn't roll. The butter box held an old army canteen with a bayonet in a leather scabbard. Trout had never seen anything like it at Crown Surplus or Ribtor's. Everything there was World War Two. This was the Great War Auntie talked about, World War One, his Great-Great-Uncle Hiram's war. Trout wanted that cannonball. And the bayonet. He unsheathed it from its scabbard. The razor sharp blade was long enough to run a man through. When his grandmother went to another part of the cellar to stew, he hefted the wooden handle of the bayonet, his finger on the hilt, and he pushed the button where it locked on a rifle barrel. He knew he'd never get something so dangerous and knew not to ask. Those who asked, didn't get.

Trout thrust at a shadow on the wall, pretending it was the bully and he was defending Kenny. His finger followed the groove of the bloodslot in the blade that allowed the enemy's blood to escape. He'd read about that in one of Kenny's books on military weapons.

"That's not a toy." Dot stood in front of him, her

hand extended with the scabbard. She slapped the bayonet back in. The sharp pitch of her voice startled him.

"I was only looking," he said, angry, but emboldened now by his father's earlier cursing.

His grandmother looked hurt. She was frightened, he could tell. He'd never talked back to her before. "Maybe your father might want this?" she asked.

Trout's dad stared without saying anything; he was preoccupied with his work. White asbestos dust flecked his hair and shoulders.

When his father carried out the old furnace motor he'd replaced, Trout took the lighter boxes to the back alley, behind the old barn, which was now used as a garage. The garbage man would collect them from here. His grandmother's words were different than his parents'. Lane, not back alley, and ga-rawge. Too-may-to, tom-matt-o, his teachers said. Tomatto, his grandmother insisted. And traaw-sh, not garbage.

In the alley Trout saw books poking from boxes: dark, serious, not-for-children books, without the lofty clouds and simple drawings of the ones his grandmother allowed him to keep from her childhood and his father's books like *Tom Swift and His Incredible Rocket Sled.*

When his dad went back to the cellar Trout found a book in the garbage, *The Pilgrim's Progress.* A grown-up book for sure. He'd wanted in on those grown-up secrets: the low guarded conversations his dad and Dot had about Auntie. That his parents had at dinner when his dad threw down his cutlery and took off into the night, his car spraying gravel. Other times his mom sent his sisters and him out to play in the yard. Later his parents sat smoking at the kitchen table in their dressing gowns when Trout and his sisters came back in the house. This must be one of the sins of which the priest spoke at his grandmother's church. He didn't understand it a whit. It was a sharp word his grandmother used, with a stinger on the end.

It was a word odd and old-fashioned as the names of her friends, Hattie and Idabelle. Her church friends, sitting beside them on the wooden pews, their perfume wafting from them like too many lilac bushes. Those special Sundays when Auntie joined them, her throat was naked as a bird's, but not much sound came from it. Sometimes her hands were pale arthritic claws. But as Dot took to the pulpit for her solo, in a canary skirt and jacket that nipped her waist like Jackie Kennedy's, her white purse and matching shoes, she sang for both of them. Her soprano sounded sweet and clear in his contraption, even through the cranky public address system fussed over by the caretaker, Lawson Leggett, who beamed at Dot when she finished. Trout blushed, proud of his young grandmother. The look in the janitor's eyes was the same one his dad got when they drove down-town. "There's a looker," he'd wink and laugh. Then, catching himself, "Just like your Mom." Their secret. His grandmother too was a looker, he knew.

Although he was almost thirteen, Trout loved the old ladies, his grandmother and the great rumbling pipes of the church organ too, in St. Stephen's, of which she was parish clerk. When she returned from the pulpit, her head high and proud, her white gloved hands rested along the pew, as did Hattie McLay's and Idabelle Beck's. All of them with smart purses, wide-brimmed straw hats and trailing silk scarves.

"Oh, my," Auntie leaned towards him, and sighed in a voice everyone heard, "Dottie certainly can sing when she wants to." Trout couldn't sing a whit, he knew.

In music class, the teacher took away his recorder, although he had not played a note, but simply fingered silently along with the others, not playing what he couldn't hear. He knew then she'd not heard him and he'd been exposed for what he was. And now, even though he could not hear his own voice, he mouthed the words to hymns, put his lips and his heart into them, singing in silence. He imagined he could hear and it didn't matter anyway. For his grandmother now sang for the both of them, and the music travelled from the floorboards of the great old cathedral, across the summer air and through her gloved hand holding the hymnbook for him.

And when a pair of sparrows swooped in the choir loft windows and dive-bombed the priest, all the ladies smiled and he felt Auntie chuckle. Only Lawson Leggett, the caretaker, stuffed into his one Sunday suit, scowled at this momentary disruption in God's small, perfect kingdom.

The cellar door opened and his father waved him back. "C'mon, Trout. We haven't got all day." There was work to be done. Whatever this sin was about, he wanted in. Eager for its secrets, he slipped the dark-covered copy of *The Pilgrim's Progress* into his jacket, folded beside the toolboxes in the trunk of his father's Pontiac.

That night, Trout sat alone in his blue room surrounded by his shells, the pilfered *Pilgrim's Progress* open in his lap. His contraption bumped against his heart, and sputtered glips of meaning, in a code he seemed sometimes better able than others to crack.

History for Trout had already become a sixth sense, so when he opened the musty cover, he anticipated as he read. "From dear sister and daughter, Marth, your Prairie Pilgrim, love to Bean, Momma and Papa. Christmas, 1888." His neck hairs buzzed as he realized.

Marth was Martha, his beloved Auntie. And Bean, her sister, was the pet name of his great-grandmother. Momma and Papa were his great-great-great-grandparents. He rifled the pages and found a flat dried cluster of buffalo beans pressed in waxed paper. Up rose the smell of time, of cellar, prairie, sage, camphor and Old. He was grateful, as his dad put it, to have his auntie "still with us".

He found three photographs. The first showed a horse, and a woman who was no older than twenty. She was wearing black riding gloves gathered at the wrists. Two loops of rein crossed her lower hand, while the upper held the bridle. She wore a white satin blouse shiny with sunlight over a long skirt, with a buttoned flap along the hem, like it opened for riding. With her dark hair coiled on the back of her head she was, like his grandmother, a beauty. The horse's sleek head nuzzled her cheek.

A glossy bay or chestnut with white fetlocks and a

blaze on its forehead, the horse stood against her, the way Trout's cat leaned against his leg. In the background, a log barn, a cow in the corral and poplars lined the rise of the Bow valley.

He shivered even before he read. He knew. "Bean and her horse, Copenhagen. Davisburg, 1903." The flourishes were the light young handwriting of his Auntie. Calgary, Northwest Territories, the photographer's stamp read.

He flipped it again: Bean had died in the Spanish Flu of 1918. As he looked at her photo, he grieved her. Her presence alive and everywhere in his room, in her books, the coverlet on his bed, in the conch that was hers. The large oil painting of a New Brunswick river hanging in Auntie's house, painted by Bean. Those eyes, hair. And he too was hers. All that fierceness in a small body. A woman about whom no one spoke. And he knew not to ask. In his grandmother's house, the dead were done and gone.

He traced her chin and jaw, and the smooth lines over the ruffled collar. Her full lower lip, the upper one taut. He mimicked her, but it did not come easily to him, that smile

She squinted in the bright sun, but her eyes were happy. And she stood straight despite the big horse nearly wrapped around her. Neither faced the camera, as if the horse was her dance partner. Her cheeks tanned, she looked shy yet comfortable, with the blonde hills and the flagged leaves of poplars behind her.

The second photograph was a copy of one he had already seen hanging high in Auntie's bedroom, out of reach. Bean, this time, in a white high-necked blouse, with her husband Bob Begg. He was in a bowler and shirtsleeves, smiling under a handlebar moustache. Both were seated at opposite ends of the children's small table on the ranch house's porch.

In smaller chairs, his infant grandmother Dottie, her sister and brother, the Vancouver relatives who'd sent him shells, all dressed in white sailor suits with scarves, leggings and high-laced boots, looked down, fascinated by the dog eating from his bowl. Their faces were chubby, unlike Bean's, which was thin.

Her chin was tilted slightly to avoid the sun, which lit the curtains in the window behind her. Grass cropped up through the weathered porch boards. Her gaze, not on the children or the dog, was faraway. Her lips were relaxed, not a frown or a grin, enigmatic like the Mona Lisa, or perhaps just tired, like his mother. All those children, he wondered.

He read the back: "Dunbow Ranch, 1912. Bob Begg and Bean, their children, Lavinia (Dottie), Alexander, Norah. Her parrot Joe. Their dog Mike." Animals with real names like those of his friends' fathers. The same photographer's seal, this time stamped: Calgary, Alberta. No longer North West Territories. In seven years, three children and a province were born.

The parrot he hadn't noticed before. The same one in its cage beside the piano in Auntie's parlour. An Amazon, Joe was seventy, Auntie had said. Some lived to be a hundred. Trout had never understood its senseless squawking. Until now. Pretty Bean, Pretty Bean. The voice of Bob Begg. The scratchy cartoon voice of the parrot, Joe, was his great-grandfather's voice, speaking his great-grandmother's name, carrying on in the voices of the dead. Pretty Bean, Pretty Bean, echoed in his ears, as he remembered. Auntie and Joe had outlived them all.

Picking up the third picture, his hands trembled. A snapshot smaller than the others, as if taken with a small Kodak Brownie, it showed the front of Auntie's house, its twin turrets and verandah. Cars with tin fenders, cloth tops and running boards lined the street. A girl in black holding an umbrella peers over her shoulder at the photographer. Dottie. The camera looked past her. The wet street reflects the shadows of the crowd.

Trout smelled the cold rain. His uncle Hiram, Auntie and others. His great-grandfather Bob Begg, his moustache gone now. Together they carried a coffin to a high-topped hearse, white rubber tires shiny with rain. Trout stared at the lonely word on the back in faded ink: M*other*

The cramped child's printing was Dot's. He thumbed through the pictures and stared at her eyes. The too-soon beginning of darkness, a pinched sadness to her gaze in all the other pictures that came after. He jumped up off the bed. Tucked the pictures back in the book, and stashed it in his bottom drawer under all his secret stuff He could not tell his father. They'd hidden the past in pictures, trunks and butterboxes. But he would listen to Auntie and Joe for clues. What else, he wondered.

He felt the light steps of his mother and sisters in the kitchen above him as he breathed: saddle soap and harness leather, bay mares and buckboards, horseshit and wagon grease.

Bean—her name stuck in his throat, both longing and hurt. Her name wasn't stuffy, like Hiram or Norah. Unlike any other name in his family, except his.

Clare

Dot helped us buy a house, a bungalow, half an hour from downtown, near the Ogden Shops. There were only a few older houses on our street, from before the First World War, when the C.P.R. opened the Shops. And when we heard the news, I was shocked at first—she didn't make much as the parish clerk. But Lowell was subdued. I hadn't yet learned why— that his family, unlike mine, were conditional givers and Dot held the deed. I think now she was trying to make up to Lowell for the childhood he'd never had.

The house was small and needed finishing, and we couldn't have afforded it without Dot's help. Lowell traded work with a carpenter who lived across the park to add rooms in the basement when the twins were born. Behind us the prairies stretched towards the hills along the Bow River, and in front, the Salvation Army cultivated a market garden that supplied food to the single-men's hostel they ran across the tracks from the Shops.

Our first winter in the new house, when I was huge with Pauline, Lowell cleared a space in the backyard and watered in a rink where Will, in his snow suit, pushed his old high chair around, his ankles bent on the little hockey skates his dad got him. We saw deer and rabbits come up from the river and we'd leave bread crusts and leftover greens out for them. One night we heard noises in the side yard and next morning Lowell found bobcat tracks on the trail of a deer.

We didn't have much, but my kids always had lots to eat. The local farmers and Hutterites came around selling eggs and chickens. More houses were going up around us every day. All of them belonged to tradesmen and their wives, the Dutch, and Germans, Ukrainians, Poles, Latvians, lots of Scots and Irish. Some had large families, eight or nine kids. Many left Europe after the war. Some served overseas, and built houses on veteran's allowance. The women stayed home, except one or two who were nurses, or teachers at the school.

When our first daughter was born, there was no shortage of help. Our neighbours brought over huge casseroles to feed us: shepherd's pie, chicken paprikash, cabbage rolls, perogies and kielbasa.

From our front window we could see the homeless men working the Salvation's Army's garden plot. Some of the neighbours called them hosties. They rode the bus from downtown, red-faced from alcohol and living outdoors, clearly ill, in smelly cast-off dress coats from the Sally Ann. Some people got up in disgust when a hostie sat beside them and one of the bus drivers used to wipe down the hand rails and seats with a rag after they got off, cursing to himself. My kids were embarrassed when I talked to the hosties, but most of them smiled, grateful to be included.

Lowell was good with Will, although he didn't believe me, at first, when I told him our son was deaf.

"He can hear when he wants to," he said, one day after they'd been skating.

"Of course he can," I snapped, "when you talk right to him and he can see your face. He's lip-reading."

In my family, eventually we did talk about things—
his family didn't. Only Auntie talked about his father,
who died when Lowell was five. I knew more than
Lowell from talking to her. But I think Lowell was
afraid as I'd been at first, as if Will's deafness was a
reflection on him.

Lowell was a good provider. He'd sold the old hot
rod, after the police pulled us over the fifth time. It's
not practical, he told me that day. It wasn't. Loud,
with a single bench seat and a stick shift that banged
my knee. He brought home a sporty green Pontiac
coupe, more engine than car, with a cream-coloured
roof and stoic chrome Chief Pontiac rising from the
hood. I didn't ask how we'd pay for it, he was so proud
because it was nearly new.

All considered, his drinking didn't seem so bad in
those days—after the war, there was a lot of sorrow
to drown. And everyone drank, it seemed. Some of
our neighbours wouldn't talk to each other—not the
Germans to the Dutch—their hatred was still that
strong. But when they drank with Lowell in our little
kitchen or at the Legion, the stories came. Because
Lowell worked on the new Legion hall, they made
him an honorary member, so we went to their dances
and there were Christmas parties for the kids. I joined
the Ladies' Auxiliary, and made paper shamrocks and
cooked for St. Patrick's Day and Robbie Burns night.
No one had money, but we had fun.

Lowell bought a tent and a Coleman stove and
built a small trailer to haul everything. Auntie gave us
all the old camp gear from the ranch: cast iron stew
pots, fry pans, a tin coffeepot and enamel plates. We'd

go camping with my mom, my aunts and uncles, at Robinson's Corner near Bragg Creek and out to Water Valley.

Come fishing season, Mom's fridge had a tobacco can full of sawdust and maggots and she had a seasonal job at Manchester Hardware because she knew fishing tackle better than the guys. She bought Will a children's rod and tackle box for his birthday the year before he started school, so she could take him fishing on the Victoria Day weekend. The rest of us gabbed with my Uncle Jack and Aunt Shelagh who'd stopped by on their way back to the ranger station from a dog show, and we all watched my cousin's kids around the campfire. My family were storytellers, especially Jack who was a forest ranger. Pauline was a quiet toddler—she napped in the tent where I could hear her.

Mom came running back to camp at breakfast. Behind her, Will emerged from the bush carrying a fish straight out in front of him, like an offering. It wasn't a big one, but Mom was as excited as he was. Mesmerized, he kept saying, "Trout, trout," as he walked around showing everybody, his finger hooked through the gill the way Mom showed him. Trout was the clearest word I'd heard him say, until then, and I wondered if Lowell had a point—we hear what we want to. I knew then I had to make my son care enough to want to.

Over and over Will said "Trout", fascinated by the word. Mom told us how she hadn't caught a thing, when she saw Will's line bob, dropped her own rod and wrapped her arms around him when he'd frozen at the tug of the fish. She lifted him right off the ground and reeled in the trout before it got away.

When Uncle Jack tried to take the fish away to fry it for breakfast, Will wouldn't let go. Jack made him a promise. "From now on you can be our little fish—young Trout," he teased and showed Will how to fillet, flour and brown the fish in butter. In our family there's no higher affection than that for the wild, and Trout was the name they called Will by until the day they died.

Those were good years, I tell the kids. And they were. I put in hollyhocks and peonies, and Lowell planted a lilac that later bloomed outside our bedroom. We'd make love for a long time after the kids were in bed. His arms were strong, lifting my hips, and I muffled my cries in his neck, the smell of lilacs all around us when they bloomed for a sweet short interval in spring.

When Pauline was two and Will was four, Lowell and I took a trip to Las Vegas. He was making good money then, though I knew some of it came from card games. He looked as handsome as a lawyer in his new suit and he bought me a short turquoise summer dress with matching shoes, my favourite colour. Everything in those days was exaggerated: the shoulders of my dress, the grille on our nearly new car, my heels. Mom moved into our house for a week, while Lowell and I took the honeymoon we'd never had. Driving right on down through Lethbridge, we didn't stop until we hit the border, racing along the tops of the coulees, into Montana, west into Idaho. We spent the night in Nez Perce Indian country, near the site of a terrible massacre. The cemetery where the victims are buried was not far from our motel. Everything was so lush and green in Idaho, it seemed strange a massacre could happen there at all.

We headed south for Winnemucca, Nevada, and descended into the desert at Pleasure Valley, down the switchbacks, white crosses at the side of the road, a pile of broken cars at the bottom. The brakes smelled of hot metal and Lowell let the car cool while we drank beer in the shade of a billboard.

Everything about the States was new and exotic, like the beers, Budweiser and Pilsner, and cigarettes, Camels and Lucky Strikes. The cars were flashier colours, with more chrome, fancy mud flaps and white-walled tires. The people were friendly, demanding to know our names and introducing themselves. And every diner was full of pies and home cooking. I'd never travelled anywhere before and it was a boozy trip. I still have swizzle sticks and cocktail napkins and matchbook covers somewhere—I saved them all in an album, along with pictures of Lowell and me, with the other couple, George and Dorothy.

I've almost forgotten now, but my daughters loved the pictures of us around a table, our white smiles, our dark tans, drinks and cigarettes in everyone's hands. Nobody lives that way anymore. That picture shows Lowell squinting at the camera. He was happy and I was too. We'd sleep past breakfast until the heat in the motel room drove us out to swim in the pool.

In one of the pictures that my kids like so much, Lowell is perched on a diving board with his hands over his head, his knees bent, about to spring into the air. He'd won a trophy for diving off the Centre Street Bridge.

In Las Vegas every place had slot machines and a pool. Dorothy and I played the slots, while the boys worked the tables—Lowell knew the games and people back in Calgary who made a good living at crime. He seemed at home in Vegas. I think sometimes he should have become a professional gambler. For all his hard work, we often struggled, but we were young and scared, not daring to take a chance on him going back to prison even for a day.

We took in the shows at Caesar's Palace, and The Oasis, with Frank Sinatra, Dean Martin, Joey Bishop, Chris Hutsul and Peter Lawford, the Rat Pack, and Sammy Davis Junior at the Tropicana. At night the city rose up out of the desert, a mirage of pink and lime neon from the Riviera, the Hacienda, the Stardust, and the tail-lights of shiny convertibles cruising Las Vegas Boulevard. There were buffet tables loaded with every kind of fruit and meat. There was "too much" of everything, a phrase Grandma Locke used to utter. Las Vegas was an oasis for people like us, who'd never had too much before.

We'd go dancing and later tumble into our room, making love in the way we did then, young and tipsy, giddy with excitement. It was all so new. We'd have our clothes off before the door closed. Lowell was sleek and tanned from swimming, his shoulders burnished from the desert sun. He ordered a bottle of champagne and showered me with the American money he'd won. We'd be rich someday, I thought.

I always tell the twins I gambled in Las Vegas and doubled my luck. I asked for one baby and got two. The twins were conceived on that trip.

When we got home, Pauline and Will were so excited to see us, you'd have thought we'd been gone a month. For a long time, I felt guilty about Will. I'd been worried that Pauline would have trouble too, but she'd turned out just fine. I didn't know if the deafness was hereditary. For the first few years, when they played together, Pauline was patient, always turning her face to his when they talked, entering into his imaginary world in a way I couldn't. Except when I set the table for their imaginary friends that all kids have. For Will, they and his sister were his only friends. But he seemed to be content by himself, always thinking or daydreaming. Reading as if he swallowed a book whole more than read it—if he couldn't go into the world, it would come to him.

The neighbours' kids preferred to play with Pauline. It broke my heart that Will wasn't invited to their birthday parties and she was. If he minded, he didn't show it.

With Dot and Auntie's help, we had Will's hearing tested again in the second grade, after the school called to say Will was having trouble paying attention in class. The test results confirmed what I'd suspected all along—Will was nearly deaf. Now they have a name for children like him—profoundly hard of hearing. While the test finally told us what the problem was, it didn't tell us what to do. I didn't cry when we learned, but Dot did, and Lowell was silent.

When the school nurse called, she was blunt.

"You'll need to come in to discuss your son's hearing," she said. I was already angry and ready to fight for Will.

As I walked to the school, the special school bus zipped past and stopped in front of my neighbor's house. Every morning the Blue Bus, as the kids called it, came through our neighbourhood, taking them to the workshop for the mentally retarded. Some were. Like Dean Vandermeer, my neighbor's son, who'd play in his backyard and whose dog would pull tricks on him. Some were smart, like Ricky Dudek, who had hydrocephalus—water on the brain. His little cap sat flat on top of that head, huge as a globe, wobbling on top of his unsteady neck. I babysat for his mother, Maria, sometimes. Ricky was one of the smartest, sweetest boys I'd ever met. Maria said his I.Q. was well above normal.

Those kids were all gathered up like freaks and sent away. I'll never forget that bus. The kids with their lips and tongues flattened and sticky against the windows, others happy to be going somewhere and little Ricky looking bewildered in the middle of all of them. Nobody knew what to do with them, so we hid them away.

When the nurse sat down at her desk, I knew what was coming. I also knew she had something I didn't— an education, like my son's teachers, the principal, like damn near everybody in the school, and the doctor's office. Unlike nearly anybody in our neighbourhood. And they knew how to use it.

"At his teacher's request, we tested his hearing

again." She showed me the audiogram that sloped downward. "It's not good," she started to explain.

"We had it tested too."

"Oh." She seemed surprised. "Then you know."

I felt myself shrinking away from this woman, her words. Then something primitive in me snapped.

"He's going to need an education." I wrung my purse strap in my fists. "More than any of those other children out there." I nodded towards the schoolyard. "Did his teacher tell you how he's read everything in her classroom?"

"Mrs. Dunlop, I know this is hard."

"What are you going to do to help my little boy get an education? I don't want one more person telling me what he can't do." I started to cry, but they were tears of anger. "What are you going to do to help my son?"

She sat there embarrassed and handed me a Kleenex. I shook my head and took one from my purse.

"I'm sorry, it must be hard." She spread her fingers along the edge of her desk as if she might push it away. "I think I understand."

"How can you say that?" I stared at her.

"There's a residential school in Vancouver."

"I know, Jericho Hill."

In those days we pulled kids out of school, just like that. My friend Wanda's daughter, who was blind, was sent to the Jericho Hill residential school for the Blind and Deaf in Vancouver. The blind kids studied music—like they were all Ray Charles or something, just because they were blind. Besides, Wanda's daughter was tone deaf—all the music lessons in the world didn't help her one bit. The deaf kids were taught to make lawn furniture and sweep floors, as if that was all they could do.

"No." I thought of what Mom said about bathing him in sound. "No. He needs to hear music, poetry, laughter. Children learn to love by being loved. I want him here, with his sister, with his friends. And I especially don't want him going off to the Jericho Hill School."

"Let me finish."

"I already know."

She paused and looked at the audiogram in front of her. "There will be resistance from the board. And, I hate to say this, from some of the teachers."

"Do you really think I haven't thought about this?"

She hesitated and put the chart in a folder. "Will you come and talk to the principal?"

I nodded. "He needs to hear what I have to say." As I stood up to leave, she hesitated, and then said, "I do understand, Mrs. Dunlop, I think."

"Do you really? It's Clare, by the way."

She turned away for a moment towards the window onto the playground. "My son has polio." Her tone was soft now and she swallowed before she spoke. "There's nothing I can do for him. I'm a nurse, but Clare, I'm a mother too."

On my way in, there was a boy with braces on his leg and crutches. He was leaning against the chain link fence talking to Will and his friend Kenny. He'd seemed happy enough. Already he was tall, like his mother.

"Could you send him away?" I asked.

"Douglas?" She paused, then extended her hand. "No, I don't think I could, Clare. It's Barbara by the way. After I've made some calls, I'll phone you."

In the schoolyard, I watched the kids still at recess. Will seemed content there. He didn't see me and I was glad as I dabbed at my eyes. As I walked home, in some of the yards mothers sat out with their babies and small children were playing. In the prosperous years after the war, we seemed all in a rush to replace the lost, filling our houses and yards with young ones. It wasn't uncommon to see families of seven or eight then. I thought of what Maria Dudek told me. Fighting for Ricky. The best she could do for him was to let him ride the damned Blue Bus. And she was grateful. The doctors told her he might only live to be twelve or thirteen. I was lucky.

Without Mom, or Lowell's mother, what would I have done? And Lowell, although he didn't understand Will sometimes, helped me in whatever ways he could. Although he'd never had a father, he was learning to be one. Not having had a father isn't an excuse for being a bad father or mother, I told him. And I knew, it was still not enough. We needed that nurse, the principal, the teachers, both our families, and anyone else who could help. I would have to learn to trust them. Will was not just my son any more, he was everyone's child.

When he was little, I spent all the time I could with him reading, and talking, and Pauline seemed to know to do that too. As Mom said, we'd bathe him in sound. Together, Pauline, Will and I chattered to everything in the house, the cutlery, the food, the cat, even throwing in French sometimes: "Bonjour poulet," to the chicken when it came out of the oven. "Au revoir gateau," as the cake went into the dining room.

I got a book on teaching reading and taught all my kids. I showed them how to borrow books and we went once a week to the Bookmobile parked outside the school.

When Will was young I read him *Winnie the Pooh* and I'd lift his shirt and rub his tummy and he would rub Pooh's. Pauline, though, was a talker, enough for all of us actually. She still is. She understood Will's language and spoke it back to him. Will was a reader.

While Mom's family hadn't gone far in school, every one of them could and did read. When my Uncle Jack needed a house, he read up on it and built himself one, and a barn too. At our parties, he'd recite Robbie Burns and Robert Service and tease me in a mock Irish brogue. "Clare, will you not delight us with that lovely poem you do, by the Irishman, a Mr. William Butler Yeats?" The Scots love the word as much as the Irish, so there were always books and readers and stories around. When they started school, both Will and Pauline were already good readers, I made sure of that.

One day Will had come home from first grade upset because the other kids got books to take home and he didn't. I called up the school angry that Will was placed at a table near the teacher with the simple boy who lived down the street. The teacher told me the others needed help and Will had already read everything in the room.

He was a gentle boy then and when I had a birthday party for him, it was mostly with Pauline's friends, but he invited the simple boy, Jackie Epp, who came dressed in a pressed white shirt and bow tie, brought a card, and a nice toy car neatly wrapped. I'd been to his parent's place canvassing for the Legion. They were simple too, and poor. Their basement suite smelled of urine and rotting potatoes. A neighbour had seen the father at the dump, picking through garbage. Most people on our street shunned them. But Will invited Jackie and after that I always made an effort to speak to them no matter what the neighbours said.

But it broke my heart, when Will came home on the first day of Grade Two. The kids started the day by waiting in their Grade One class and the new teacher, the one he had trouble with, came to get them. His friend, little Jackie Epp, stayed behind, sitting at that table by the teacher for another year, maybe more. All Will said was, "Mom?" Caught in his throat, it came out as a moan and I started to speak, but he stared at me, and I knew he knew. He looked lost. I had no answer. I thought of how I fought for him and how Jackie's mother, who swept floors for a living, didn't stand a chance and neither did he. We were ignorant, all of us then, and afraid. I don't blame any of us now. Not my neighbours, that teacher, or the nurse.

But the school nurse called back and this time I went to see the principal, again prepared to fight. He was a small dapper man, with a quick temper I'd heard, who hucked books at the overgrown farm boys in the back rows, already kept back two grades, and used the strap when they lipped him. But I saw none of that, when he invited me into his office. Will's file with the jagged lines of the audiogram lay open on the principal's desk. He took off his jacket, offered me an ashtray and reached into his vest for a leather pouch of tobacco. "We will do," he nodded as he tamped his pipe, "whatever it takes."

Trout

On the Friday of the Victoria Day weekend, for he shared a birthday with Queen Victoria, Trout went to Auntie's house. Dot fried chicken in her electric frying pan, opening a can of white asparagus and another of mandarin oranges for a fancy salad. Her pantry was full of exotic foods, all in cans. Each time Trout visited her, there was a new appliance from the Sunbeam store, sprightly chrome and Modern. This time it was an automatic toaster. Unlike the one in Kenny's kitchen that flipped down at the sides, or his parents', that worked off the gas flame of the stove. There was a new stereo FM radio, and a portable colour television. His grandmother said Television, never T.V.—like a teacher, all four syllables crisp. And she cut her own lawn with her shiny red electric mower.

If Auntie was an Old Timer, a Pioneer, Dot was a Modern Woman. And slowly, Old Time moved to the basement, stored in trunks replaced with Modern. As much as Trout loved Auntie and her stories, he liked all the good things too that his parents would never buy and that came in cans. Out of a can, his mother sneered, and sniffed at the shiny new frying pan with its red light in the handle, although that Christmas his father got her one.

Dot had a store-bought cake, not a leaning angel food cake with pennies in it like his mother's, but a store-perfect creation of white and blue rosebuds, thirteen candles and a cowboy figurine in the centre.

She gave him a microscope, in a wooden box with glass slides, and a dissecting kit with a sinister razor-edged scalpel.

"You'll need that in high school next year," she said. Trout wasn't sure he would pass grade eight, let alone the Grade Nine departmental examinations. School was something he endured.

Auntie's gift was a book, a second-hand book. He was disappointed. So much of what his parents got was second-hand. Second hand was a curse. Nothing worse than being called a Second-hand Rose at school, the scourge of clothing from the Salvation Army Thrift Shop, Rod Warnock recognizing the striped sweater of many colours donated two years earlier. Even though most of their parents shopped there. Trout wanted New, Modern.

"It will be valuable someday," his practical auntie said. "Open it up. It's signed by the author himself." Trout looked at the hardcover, but without the plastic jacket, like the books from the Bookmobile. Inside was a signature, a dust dervish in black ink, and barely legible, "For Martha, Calgary, 1949".

"Bill was principal of the school at Castor. His wife Merna used to come into the store to buy candy. I liked Merna. Hiram and I met him at the Palliser Supper club one night. Bill and Merna were celebrating his book's publication by the *Reader's Digest*."

Auntie raised her eyebrows, impressed, and Trout knew he should be too.

"Merna had on a new gown and a tiara Bill had bought her with the cheque. They lived in High River. It was a lot of money then."

Trout's grandmother seemed impatient with his auntie, and whisked the dishes from the table with her pink rubber gloves.

"Oscar Petersen was playing that night. In those days, he wasn't allowed to stay at the Palliser even if he played the supper club," Auntie said.

Dot bristled and interrupted. "You should have gotten him the Hardy Boys books, he's a bit young for that stuff." She enunciated perfectly, her arched "stuff," like "rough," was how she referred to undesirable people. "Rough," she'd sniff. The past was always old news to her.

Auntie smiled slightly, like she'd stopped listening to her niece Dottie a long time ago, saying whatever she thought anyway. Trout tried to hide his disappointment, but it must have shown in his face because, when he cleared away her plate, Auntie's eyes were moist.

That night in bed, he opened the book, careful not to crack the spine. If it were treasure to his auntie, then it would be for him. As he read, he recognized the place. Though it was the Saskatchewan prairie, he knew the names: gopher, caragana, and crocus, wolf willow, bison, and Blackfoot, gulley, slough and Chinook. This was the place he and Kenny wandered, where *fort* was a secret hiding place from adults, and *river*, in a land where water was scarce and the wind nearly always fierce, magical as *oasis* in some other place.

And he became Brian Sean MacMurray O'Connal and the Saskatchewan prairie became the Ogden flats and the South Hill, and the river that entered the make-believe town of Crocus was the Bow River, that stretched all the way south and west in the land where he and Kenny roamed the sloughs and gullies, through the wolf willow and crocuses.

Kenny kept gopher tails for the mythical bounty of a nickel that no one they knew had ever collected. His father told them why, one day. They were a generation too late. There was no bounty anymore. But that promised nickel justified the flooding of too many gopher holes with endless buckets of water, the purchase of razor-head arrows and pump-action Daisy B.B. guns.

It was not the first book in which he recognized himself, but it was the first where he recognized the place in which he lived. He looked at the cover: *Who Has Seen the Wind*, by W.O. Mitchell. He wrote pretty well for a school principal, Trout thought.

Trout knew he'd hurt his auntie's feelings. His tongue had thickened and his neck had flushed in embarrassment, but he hadn't gotten out the words in time to apologize. But he would, as his grandmother had taught him, write Auntie a thank-you note. Hers was the gift of home.

That Monday, he wrote her a letter, signed with an ink-dervish signature and placed it in the stamped envelope his grandmother had given him as he left. He hoped his auntie hadn't seen his disappointment, although as he mailed his letter first thing Tuesday, he felt a twinge of guilt.

Later that week, Kenny, who'd already turned thirteen a month before, watched a hawk sailing over the prairie and smoked a cigarette. Off school property, he could smoke during lunch hour. Sitting beside him on the sandstone shelf above the river, Trout ate his sandwich, lost in his stolen copy of *The Pilgrim's Progress*. In which he became the pilgrim, and Kenny rafted on the Slough of Despond on a large tin Coca Cola sign like the one which blew off the billboard atop Waterfield's General Store, that they'd floated down the irrigation canal. His Valley of the Shadow of Death was populated by gophers puckering out warnings from nearby mounds, a sound he took for granted. But Kenny, his translator, heard them and imitated their high whistle for him in his contraption so he could hear. And he feared no evil because Bean rode beside him on her horse, her dog Mike behind her and her parrot Joe on her shoulder.

Parts of the Pilgrim's journey baffled him, while other parts struck quiet terror into his young heart and recalled the priest's Bible lessons and stern sermons to the families of the railway workers in the small Ogden church. Not an adult book after all, but a child's tale short on the juicier details of sin. The book was, however, not an unfamiliar place.

Moses's rod, Trout imagined carved of diamond willow gathered from the thickets where he and Kenny once built their forts along the river. The trumpet Gideon blew at the armies of Midian were like the one on which Bobby Ferguson across the alley practiced "The Saints Go Marching In", among skeletons of wrecked cars, while his snapping turtles dived in an old bathtub as Kenny and Trout spied on him in his parents' junkyard. School had long ago eluded their interest and they took their learning elsewhere.

The bully became Goliath of Gath, and Kenny was David, his slingshot full of seashells. At the gate to the Celestial City, beloved Auntie waited with a bowl of Scotch mints, and the skies were not cloudy all day and parrots flocked to the poplar trees. With a bayonet strapped to his belt, the conch under his arm, a World War One helmet on his head, and his knapsack full of sandwiches, Trout was not afraid to walk through the Valley of the Shadow of Death.

He read everything. If the hearing world left him out of its secrets, in reading, he didn't miss a word, profane or profound, sacred or sacrilege, from the *Classics Illustrated* comics and Kenny's Hardy Boy books, to his sister's Trixie Belden mysteries, and more recently, to the inky magazines and tabloids, *Men Only, Police Gazette* and *True Horror* that Kenny retrieved from a hole in the wall of his basement room. He read the science books in school, his textbooks, his mother's Bible and poetry, and the dusty books that belonged to his great-grandmother. From them Trout assembled the pieces of a vivid and oddly incongruent world that somehow fit together.

"Time?" Kenny tapped Trout's watch. Lunch hour passed quickly out on the prairie. "You coming over?"

Trout nodded, his eyes still heavy with daydreaming as the Pilgrim.

After school, they walked home. Kenny's room was more like a secret fort than a bedroom. Both Kenny's parents worked, and a year earlier his older sister had moved away. Often there was no one home. Unlike his own room, open to his mother and his sisters, Kenny's was full of secrets. There, his fingers greasy with black ink, Trout read in *True Horror* how the dead woke in their satin-lined coffins, buried alive, screaming to their death, alone and unheard by anyone. Until for some unexplainable reason, the grave was opened and revealed the coffin's padded interior tattered, and claw marks gouged into the wood by the grotesquely long nails of the dead. "Buried Alive," the ghoulish caption read, under a photograph of a scantily clad and busty woman lying in a coffin. Some of the skin magazines Kenny rescued from old Willie Harris's garbage can and squirreled away in his secret wall smelled of rotting fruit.

If Kenny's interest was trouble, and not getting caught, Trout's fascination was with the mysterious bodies of women. Some of the men's magazines had a black bar across where he knew the nipples were. Others for some reason, where the eyes were, as if they were something that shouldn't see or be seen. Monopoly money and Park Place had long lost their appeal and he read the rank magazines too many times, when Kenny suggested his club that day after school.

"It's about time. You're thirteen.

"What?"

"It's not your sin if someone else does it."

Trout stared dumbly. "What are you talking about?"

Kenny mimed holding a banana and whipped his hand up and down. "We'll call it The Masturbation

Club," he leered. Trout snapped his chin back, incredulous, but he didn't move.

"Way I see it, if you do it to me and I do it to you, one sin cancels out another," Kenny said. "Zero plus zero equals zero. Can't be a sin if someone else does it to you," he assured, with grim authority.

Then he reached into his shorts and pulled out his Bone; he called it, a Boner. A year before they would have laughed at the word. All their jokes then contained funny sounding swear words that shocked them silly.

Trout looked at the strange thing Kenny offered. He'd never seen anyone else's before. He had only sisters and once saw Pauline's blonde-covered slit when he'd accidentally opened the bathroom door and she'd shrieked. Kenny's was pale and white and as he put Trout's hand on it, it rose. It was warm.

"Mine looks like a bald guy standing up in church," Kenny laughed. "In praise of God."

Trout felt dumb. But since Kenny stood there with his pants down, Trout lowered his own and Kenny reached into Trout's shorts. His was hot, darker and redder, shorter and squatter, and as soon as Kenny's hand slipped up and down, it was angry. Kenny made his do tricks. It jerked back and forth on its own. Kenny shoved his hips forward in imitation of a dance he'd learned. "The Dirty Dog," he exclaimed. Trout was embarrassed, but it felt as good as it did in the dreams where he woke with a damp spot on his pyjamas.

In class, he daydreamed while Miss Boyle sat on her desk reading from *Pippi Longstocking*. Trout was fascinated both by the magic of the soda-pop tree and the fullness of the two round buns under Miss Boyle's cashmere sweater. He wondered if they were soft, like loaves of Wonderbread. He could feel his boner rise under his desk as he smelled her perfume, and he squirmed with uncomfortable pleasure. In the assembly hall, the solid music teacher with her grey beehive, whose cantilevered breasts poked out like fungi on a tree, pounded the keys of the piano, and Trout felt the hot mix of pain and pleasure. Kenny, who knew all about women's clothing, said Miss Suave wore a push-up bra.

Trout compared his and Kenny's. It had a mind of its own, unpredictable, and contrary, rising equally fiercely to the bass pounding of "O Canada" through the wooden floor of the gymnasium, to Kenny's hurried groping or the softness of Miss Boyle's breasts. He was more owned than owner of this new thing. Kenny moaned and closed his eyes as Trout's hand moved up and down. He first thought Kenny was acting.

"Faster," Kenny gasped.

A door slammed above them. His hand stopped on Trout's penis. Kenny's eyes flipped open and he drooped in Trout's hand.

"Jesus. My mom's home."

Both of them pulled up their pants as Kenny's mother yelled down the stairs. Trout hurried out the back door, before Mrs. Dawes could see him. He cut down the back alley and dawdled across the park, his neck and ears still red.

"Where have you been?" his mother exclaimed, when he got home. She brushed his hair away from his face and caressed his forehead. "You're sweating. Are you okay, Will?" He saw that she'd been crying and he turned away, but she tapped his shoulder. "Your Dad wants to see you." His pulse jumped. They knew.

His parents' bedroom door was partially closed. His father never came home early. He sat up in bed, with only his T-shirt on, his work boots and pants heaped beside the bed. There was an uncapped bottle of rye beside an empty glass on the night table. His cigarettes lay untouched.

He had never seen his father cry. Awkwardly his father pulled him into his arms as if he was taking comfort rather than offering it. "Auntie died." His father's words stung with the ether of rye and his stubbled face was wet and sandpapered Trout's neck.

"This morning." His mother dabbed her eyes with a tea towel. "She had a heart attack on her way to the store. There was nothing any one could do."

"She was so good to me," his father's voice choked and trailed off.

Trout was more stunned by his father's tears, which embarrassed him, than his auntie's death. Hs father never cried. And Trout had never known any one who'd died before.

This was the Valley of the Shadow of Death. And he wondered, if she ever got his letter, and he ached. Somehow he was responsible. He was being punished. She had seen his disappointment in her gift. He thought of his letter and he winced. It was too late. Better late than never. This was never. But he couldn't cry.

There was no supper that night. Neither he nor his father could touch the food his mother made. Later, with his bedroom light off, the streetlamp's glow caught in the hollow of the conch on the windowsill. He brought it to bed and cradled it beside his pillow. If it could speak, she'd said, what might it say. He lay there a long time, staring at the ceiling, exhausted by the stony ache in his chest. It would crush him and he dared not sleep lest he should not wake.

When he slept, finally, the confusion of the past week tumbled after him into his dreams. A dwarf Pilgrim, he dreamed the jawbone of an ass, Samson and Delilah, the damned cities of Sodom and Gomorrah, and the violence of fire, the test of the sword. His dreams were more vivid than any sermon or Bible lesson: firepits and one-eyed dragons flared along the Pilgrim's path. Kenny and his Bone with him in the Valley of Humiliation. The coffin lid slammed shut. First he, and then his auntie locked under the earth. The logic of dreams like Kenny's wavy logic, upside down and sideways. Zero plus zero equals zero. Zero and zero. Forever and ever, amen.

Earth crushed his chest, filling his nose and mouth. He choked and clawed, his nails scraping the stone lid of the sarcophagus. It wouldn't budge. He woke crying and the night was pitch black around him. For a moment he wasn't sure. He felt a mattress under him and his back began to sweat. If she had died or not. He could never go to Kenny's again. He was angry at his father's tears and there was a knot of terror in his chest, heavy and convoluted. He couldn't swallow. He got up and crossed to the bottom of the stairs and saw the light in the kitchen. His mother was up and he went to her.

"I wondered if you were ever going to cry. You loved her." His mother stroked his hair. "And she loved you." She touched one of his tears with her forefinger. "It's not a bad thing to cry."

He couldn't explain how afraid he was. Where are we going? he wanted to ask and couldn't, nor tell her of the fires burning along the dark roads in his dreams and the coffin that would not open.

"She was five months shy of a hundred. Ninety-nine years old." His mothers flicked a tear from the corner of her eye.

That Sunday, his parents went to the funeral. They didn't offer to take him and he didn't ask. He knew he could have. Instead, he went out alone to the prairies. He hiked farther than he had ever been before, past the first slough and the second, seven waves of gullies beyond the school and the gravel pit and farms. Like Moses, he would spend forty years in his wilderness of wolf willow and gophers.

When he had walked for two hours, he dropped exhausted on a boulder, and looked up at the sky. He found a rise past the South Hill, as close to the clouds as he could get without walking all the way to the mountains.

He bellowed the single most profane verb he knew, followed by God. Then he sat down and waited. The clouds streaked across the sky, mountainous and billowy, the wind crackled its static in the microphone of his contraption as it always did. The gophers stood up on their mounds like they did for Brian Sean MacMurray O'Connal, as they always had. As if they too were waiting for God's response.

But nothing changed out here. Nor had it since those earlier seas covered the Great Plains. The Pacific Ocean flooded from the Mackenzie down to Montana, he'd read. And great ancient reefs of spongy stromatoporoids, gelatinous tubes that rose ten stories from the bottom, munched on plankton, amongst fragile sea lilies, giant clams and upside-down cones of rugose coral and the armour-plated placoderm and sharks covered with spines sharp as bayonets. Where dreams and nightmares converged. Later came the dinosaurs and later again, the ice ages. This was just the beginning of eternity, he knew. Of Never Again. How far away his auntie was, and surely how great the distance now between him and Kenny. Eternity on earth.

The living sea was seven hundred miles west. Here, out on the prairie, itself a lonely golden trough with its waterless beaches and dunes, lay the Devonian Sea, six miles straight down under the grass-stained toes of his runners, a hundred and fifty million years away in time. Strangely, it comforted him to know the oozy plankton was still fermenting. He caught a gassy whiff, a ripe Devonian fart from the Esso refinery a mile west. Puff. Its cooked soup ran his father's lawnmower and Pontiac. Strangely wondrous and sad, all at once, like his auntie's death.

His auntie's life and his were pencil lines that ran a

hundred million million miles into the past and for-ever into the future. That was Eternity. Of that much he was certain, as he sat under a turquoise sky, an upside-down sea that could swallow him if gravity ceased. God did not respond to his incredible and daring curse.

Once more, he stood up, threw his head back and faced the sky. Bolder now, he unleashed a torrent of words, his words, Kenny's words. Words he had read in the skin magazines. Words he wasn't sure of, and words he knew. All the foulest words he'd heard his father use, aimed directly at God the Neanderthal, his stupid crown, his dark hair and beard and thick hairy arms, like Fred Flintstone, sitting there on his throne, high on a cloud, wearing a stern and pious expression. Trout knew his auntie wouldn't be there yet to hear him.

He waited again, out of breath, his face flushed with anger. He wanted to be smacked down. Even that would be better than this. Dwelling in the Val-ley of the Shadow of Death. But God was elsewhere that day. Only the wind rustled over the microphone of Trout's contraption.

God too was deaf, he was sure. Hoarse from more words than he had ever said at once, his eyes puffy, Trout reached into his pack for his sandwiches. Miracle Whip and Spam greased his raw throat. He wrapped the conch in his jacket. It would do as a stone, and he tried to sleep with his head on it.

But he was not Job, this was not the desert, and for that he was glad. He would go home to his parents, they would be waiting. When he got there, it would be suppertime. And so he ran through the Valley of the Shadow of Death, as if the Devil himself was chasing him. His pack thumped against his back, the weight of the conch reassuring him that he was, indeed, alive.

Clare

It's hard to believe now it could have been any other way, but Will stayed in a regular school and he went on to the junior high. The principal made sure of that and spoke to all the teachers. There wasn't any trouble that I was aware of. After that, the school nurse and I became—while not close friends—friendly, as she advised me on the girls. Lowell and I were very much in love. I was pregnant with the twins, after our trip. Then Emily came along—a phrase I've always found odd, as if she showed up on our doorstep in a pink snow-suit. But it was a golden time in our marriage, the bright plateau. We'd decided we wanted a big family, which wasn't uncommon then.

When Auntie died, Lowell and Will were both sad. We all were. My Grandma Locke died not long after Pauline was born. Now we'd lost the last of our matriarchs, and our hub. I didn't understand Lowell's family except that there weren't any men—the grandfathers and uncles were all dead, like Lowell's father, of heart attacks, before the age of forty. My kids had no grandfathers or uncles. Bob Begg, Dot's father, left his kids with Auntie when he was widowed in 1918, and then he remarried and moved away, which made perfect sense to them somehow. Lowell's mother never talked about it, but in the pictures of her, even the happy pictures taken at Christmas, she's got the saddest eyes of any little girl. Auntie raised not only her but also Lowell, who spoke of her as his real mother and how he always was a disappointment to Dot. No matter what he did, it was never enough. Your cousin Walter, she'd tell him, and then list all the homes and cars he'd bought. A real estate salesman in Scottsdale, Arizona, he wore a tie and suit to work. If my husband was uneasy and awkward at times with our son, it was because he was uneasy with himself.

Auntie left money in her will to be used for Will's speech lessons. Lowell's mother inherited the house, and agreed to help us buy more powerful new hearing aids for Will, one for each ear. His first hearing aid was used. And he needed them in both ears, the doctors said. In those days, hearing aids cost more money than most working people could afford, more than a used car. After I'd talked with the nurse and the principal, it was clear Will needed every advantage if we were going to keep him in a regular school. He didn't talk much as it was and when he did, people outside the family couldn't understand him. They'd ask me what his accent was.

"Deaf," I'd say. "His accent is Deaf." As if Deaf was a place like Idaho or Utah, where everybody spoke that way.

It sure stopped those stupid questions, like: How hard of hearing is he? But I knew he wasn't normal and worse, Will knew. Even when he was seven, he knew.

One day he told me, after someone said something rude, "It's okay, Mom. You can see what's wrong with me." He pointed to his chest. "With other people, it's hidden."

I looked at him, with the white cloth sack slung around his neck containing his hearing aid. At the time, I thought what he said was too wise for a seven-year-old, but his friends Jackie and Kenny were kids no one was nice to—you could see what was wrong with them. Jackie was simple and Kenny was the opposite, precocious as hell, and wily, calling me Clare one day, until I corrected him. He'd missed out on some part of childhood. Some kids are damned from the start. Will, at seven, knew who got left behind.

Lowell wasn't good with the babies, but when the kids got older, he took them for drives and built a wading pool out of material he scavenged from job sites. He taught them how to play croquet and put up a swing set. When we went camping with Mom's family, he organized everything, the tent and all the food, and gave the kids jobs to do. Will followed him around the yard or garage, handing him tools, watching quietly, and when his dad was away, I saw him trying out the tools. Lowell didn't like the kids playing in the garage alone, but I let him. I didn't want to squelch that curiosity. I didn't want him to grow up as awkward as his father.

When I told Lowell, he smiled and said, "Maybe it's time he came to work with me, I could use a helper." Lowell's work was always a place he felt sure of himself.

I'd see Will in the yard, lying on his tummy, watching his pet garter snake, eye-to-eye, as it slid under his arm and nested in the grass. He was my water baby, I liked to tell the kids—born blue and nearly drowned, spitting up water, he was drawn to it. How, while fishing with Mom, he'd walked right off the pier at Chestemere Lake. He'd drop out of sight and wouldn't make a sound, she said. Mom hauled him in by his shirt collar and he was grinning.

Another time, when we took the kids to the fresh water ponds at the gravel pit—there was no pool in our neighbourhood yet—I was watching the twins on the sand. Lowell had the kids out on inner tubes, and Will slipped off the tube, without a word, down into the deep pond. When I screamed, Lowell dived and found him swimming along the bottom, like he thought he was a fish. He had no fear.

After Emily was born, I heard from one of Will's teachers how she'd congratulated him on his new baby sister. He'd told her, "It's okay, we have enough, thanks."

I never connected the rage, the silences. He seemed so self-contained, maybe too much so, I realize now, but storming inside. But, of all my kids, I thought I'd not have to worry about Will getting into trouble.

"Auntie left money for new hearing aids and speech therapy," Dot said.

Trout didn't respond.

"I'll help where I can," Dot said. And that was all. *Said and done*, he listened to the ringing echo of his grandmother's voice after he hung up. "Ther-apy," she'd said. A crisp and final word, like medicine.

After school on Friday, Trout rode the bus past the oil refinery with its cracking towers and the distillery wafting malt, where Kenny's father worked, through the stench of chicken guts at the poultry plant and the sweet cowshit stench of the stockyards and punky rendering off the meat-packers. Aroma Avenue, Kenny called it, a name he got from a book about a boy with a pet skunk named Aroma. His grandmother waited in her hat and white gloves under the Bank of Montreal clock. She was the most glamorous person downtown, in her hats, always with the purse and gloves. She never smoked on the street and insisted a gentleman walked a lady on the outside, so that's what Trout did. Mind your manners, she reminded him.

Sometimes he felt as if his auntie wasn't even gone. Trolley buses rained sparks from the overhead power lines as they scooted through downtown. People hustled by and he still expected her to step down from the Number 8 South Calgary bus as she always had. But she wasn't coming back. That's that, rang in his contraption.

At the Medical Arts building, the contraption man

mixed up a potion that smelled of banana bubble gum and packed it into a big needle like those used to baste turkeys. He pumped Trout's ears full and the potion expanded, making the inside of his head feel stuffed. When the impressions of his ears cured, the contraption man gently tugged them and put the castings in an envelope.

"Minneapolis, Minnesota," he said, "where all the new ones came from." The new hearing aids would be fastened to his glasses and Trout would now have one for each ear. "Binaural," the contraption man held up two fingers.

They wouldn't be as noticeable, his grandmother said, and he would hear so much more. Trout wanted to hear everything. The gophers and the magpies from whose open mouths no sound came; the senseless cackling of Joe the parrot; and the conversations that seemed to whisper all around him. He wished, more than anything, to be in on the joke and to laugh too. When they were done, Dot took him into the basement of the Medical Arts Building. Trout wanted to look at the ear trumpet, but his grandmother didn't stand for Dallying. Don't Scuff Your Feet, she'd say. You're Dragging Your Heels. A sound he couldn't hear, and which therefore didn't matter.

The speech lady's office was bright as a kindergarten in blue and yellow, with alphabet letters scotch-taped on the wall over a blackboard. There were tape recorders and an upright piano like his grandmother's. After she left, the speech lady introduced herself. Shannon's hair was like sheets of new copper and short like his mom's. She gave him a glossy scribbler and a brand new pen with which to write his speech exercises. Sitting on a small chair opposite him, she placed his hands on her cheeks and they began to practice sounds. Trout mimicked her; the sounds passed along his fingertips and he began to feel the vowels and consonants that he had studied in school. Before, they were parts of words he lip-read; now he could touch them.

Trout found it hard to concentrate. Shannon's eyes were green as new poplar leaves. He could smell the lotion from her hands. As she shaped the words her breath warmed his face, and he dared not look down at her breasts, two large bumps under the white smock that covered her dress. She made him repeat each exercise until he got it right. She was so pretty and smelled so good. He struggled to focus. He would do anything to please her.

The last lesson before his grandmother returned was the wh sound: Shannon put a feather on the table and softly puckered her glossy lips and puffed her cheeks to show him. Then she blew the feather across the table. "Wh-oosh," she said, like a kiss, and he imitated, blowing it back to her. Like a real teacher she gave him homework on the board. He was to practice, she enunciated to him, stressing the soft c and the s, "I think mice are rather nice," and "She sells sea shells by the sea shore." Trout tried, his head a dumb wooden bell and his tongue a clapper that clacked dryly. He wanted her to like him, so he read painfully from the neatly printed text in his exercise book.

After speech lessons, he walked home with his grandmother through the 8th Avenue underpass. As he raised his hands to his nose, he could still smell the sweet lotion from the speech lady's hands. When they got to the red brick house, with its sandstone casements, twin turrets, spruce trees and windowed front porch, he knew. It was Dot's house now.

And when he went in, for the first time since his auntie died, he saw that the living room was changed. Gone were the ferns, the diaphanous old curtains, as his mother called them, her tongue light and breathy as if it lifted the curtains like a breeze. New drapes covered the windows and all the furniture was moved. Gone was the piano. In its place was a television on a tall wooden stand, but the room seemed empty. Dot showed him into her old bedroom. She had moved into Auntie's room. When Dot went off to Safeway, Trout searched his auntie's old room. The Colt revolver was missing and all the money from the back of the linen cupboard. But the crystal dish of scotch mints was still there in the living room as was his auntie's silver letter opener. His grandmother liked Nice Things. Trout cracked a mint in his teeth.

When his grandmother returned, she made fried chicken. It was flat and greasy. They sat in the kitchen instead of the dining room. Without his auntie, the house felt lonely. Then Trout realized—Joe the parrot was missing. His cage was gone. After dinner, when he watched television with his grandmother, even during Sea King, his favourite show, he couldn't stop thinking about Joe. He couldn't imagine what she had done with the parrot, but Trout would have adopted him. Although, his mother had said that only his auntie could handle him. Joe was a biter. Nasty old bugger, his father warned. And Dot wouldn't stand for the old parrot biting, he knew.

That night, he stayed awake a long time, surrounded by the scent his grandmother left behind, as he slept in her old room and she slept in his auntie's. Lavender talcum and lilac perfume mingled in the air with the old smell of wood varnish and wax. He hadn't washed his hands before supper, though he'd run the tap so his grandmother would hear. The scent of the speech lady's lotion lingered. He couldn't believe her hair, so electric when his hands brushed against it as he read the speech lessons through her cheeks. In the hush of the room, he could feel the slight movements of the people upstairs, the new tenants his grandmother had brought in. She needed the money, his dad said. Auntie hadn't left much, but she'd left enough for speech lessons.

He reached into his pyjamas under the soft folds of the duvet that comforted him like a body. His hands, sweet with the speech lady's lotion, slipped up and down. He dreamed of her with his eyes wide open, startled by this new drive that pulled him after it, as he lay there in the child's pyjamas his grandmother had bought him, covered with upside-down cowboys and flannel Indians. At home, he slept in his underwear now. Betrayed by his body, he surged out of control. How could something that felt so good be a sin? He drifted to sleep smelling lilacs and lavender. Daydreams slipped into night dreams, dark and awful. He and Auntie trapped, never being able to get out of Death. Death, the real Devil. The dreams chased him into day and then back into night. Strangely, he didn't miss his great-grandmother Bean. The already dead were not lost because they were already gone. A clod of hurt stuck in his heart like wet earth, forgotten for a while when he touched the face of the speech lady.

Trout avoided Kenny all that week, and the following one. Kenny made his best Kenny faces and walked Trout home although it was the long way. But Trout was silent. Betrayed by Kenny, he didn't go out to the prairies at lunch hour anymore. Kenny had tricked him into exposing himself and there was no way they could ever go back now. Something greater than themselves had been unleashed. And it was all Kenny's fault.

Trout was tired but he could not sleep. When he did finally drift off, he spun into space, rising high above the clouds like John Glenn in his space capsule, until the logic of daytime intruded on his sleep and reminded him he couldn't fly. He plummeted back to earth through the floors in his grandmother's house, into the basement, among the steamer trunks, dodging bayonets. Sometimes he knew the dream was coming and he clawed the earth, trying to hang on before he spun upwards while everyone else he knew remained behind, and the houses and school and the palomino prairie below him fell away. He dared not meet his auntie in those dreams. Even the logic of dreams wouldn't change what was final and irreversible. He could not bear it.

The next morning his father waited at the kitchen

table. His grandmother fried bacon and eggs and brewed coffee in her sleek new electric percolator that matched the chrome toaster.

"How are we, Sunshine?" His father faced the doorway holding a cup of coffee, his elbow on the table, and his cigarette burning in the ashtray.

As they ate breakfast on the back verandah overlooking the empty hen house, the barn, and the green apple trees, the porch smelled of sharp new paint and the wicker chairs of fresh varnish. He was to help his father clean out the barn and the basement. When they went downstairs, he could see his grandmother had at been at work. The old cellar was bare with all the boxes and trunks stacked by the door. Some of them would go to the Glenbow Foundation, she said. His auntie left other things to the museum. But Dot was a cleaner. He wondered what she'd done with Joe. She hadn't volunteered anything. And he knew not to ask. What's done, is done. As he and his father carried the last of the boxes to the alley, his grandmother set one aside for him. In it he could see books, some old seashells, a ratty set of binoculars and old-fashioned postcards that all looked as if they were taken in a haze. His dad got the good stuff: bayonets, a dummy grenade. An infantry helmet to hang over the bar in his new rumpus room, and a rolled–up bear skin. Bean had shot the bear one fall, Auntie'd told him, when it wandered onto the ranch. Its yellowed fangs were bared but its glass eyes seemed sad and old.

Trout's dad gestured to the bottles of whisky and the five-gallon wine jugs, when Dot went upstairs.

"Old Hiram was either one helluva of a drinker, or he bootlegged out of the bakery," his dad laughed. "Auntie crowned him with a cast iron frying pan one night. Came home drunk. Once too often, she said." His dad seldom talked about his family.

"She was quite a woman," he said, as they took the whisky bottles to the Pontiac. He blew the dust off a jug and tasted the wine.

"Just to be sure," he said. "Whah, it's turned," he gagged and poured the wine into the gravel.

"That's disgusting, Dad," Trout laughed.

His father wiped his mouth with his work hankie. "Forty-year-old vinegar."

They threw out the dry-rotted harnesses. Everything in the empty barn smelled of dust and leather. His father showed him the saddle that belonged to Bean.

"Side-saddle." He put it on a sawhorse and showed Trout how the women rode on the side, one leg crooked up, the other lower, their shoulders facing forward.

"She wore skirts," his father said. "She sure wasn't a cowgirl, like Annie Oakley." Trout said nothing about the pictures he'd found.

The saddle was going to the Glenbow too. And there were old wooden-handled tools, and a toolbox that his grandmother insisted his dad take. "You can use them," she said, and Trout put them in the back of the Pontiac. Even his dad didn't argue with her. Trout wanted that side saddle, but Dot had decided it was going to the Glenbow, and that was that, he knew.

"Mom means well. Doesn't always come out that way. Most of 'em are junk," his father shrugged. "Some were my dad's and his dad's." When they got home, he put the toolbox under his workbench in the garage. "When you're ready."

In the weeks afterward, when his father was away at work, Trout visited the jumble of mechanic's and blacksmith's tools, ancient tire irons, tongs and hammers, spirit levels and wooden-handled pipe wrenches. Hefting the blacksmith's tongs, he slipped a piece of scrap iron into the woodstove, to warm it, like the movie blacksmiths did, and he brought the hammer down on an imaginary horseshoe fashioned on the anvil in his father's garage.

That night, back in his parent's house, everything seemed brash and cheap, different from the old and familiar things in Auntie's house. The ceiling in his room seemed close now, like a coffin lid, and he could no longer bear it. He thought again of Joe and wondered what Dot might have done with his auntie's parrot. Dot fed the squirrels and brought soup bones for the neighbour's dogs. Maybe she had Joe put to sleep. Since his auntie's death, Joe was all that was left of that other time, the turn of century: Bean, Uncle Hiram and his great-grandfather, Bob Begg. Dot was from a newer time. And even Kenny had a grandfather, and an uncle, a goalie for the Toronto Maple Leafs who sent him autographed sticks, even though Kenny hated hockey. Trout wanted every scrap he could get. Maybe he could miss what he'd never had, even more deeply, unspoiled by memory.

But tonight, he did not cry and he didn't go to his

mother. He stared at the acoustic tile flecked with sparkles and hundreds of holes descended on him like meteors. Frightened, he succumbed this time to rage, possessed by a frothing inner sea boiling in him. Wave after confused wave of grief, lust and anger washed over him. He raged in this deep Devonian place he did not recognize, in the sea and within him.

Clare

I named our only son after William Butler Yeats, though Yeats was Irish and we were Scots. Everyone thought Will was named after his dead grandfather, or one of my uncles. I didn't mind the nickname my Uncle Jack gave him—always at family gatherings, if you shouted William or Bill, at least three people answered. I named all my kids after poets—my eldest daughter after Pauline Johnson, the twins, Christina and Elizabeth, after Christina Rossetti and Elizabeth Barrett Browning, and the last, my Emily, after Emily Dickinson. I took their middle names from Lowell's family or mine, but their first names were the names of poets. It was my little secret.

The four of them and Emily, now in diapers, were the poetry in my life, random and rambunctious at times. I'd written some when I was younger. Mostly love poems, grand sweeping odes to imaginary lovers, long before I ever had any boy friends. I never did write a poem for my husband. Early in our marriage, I'd get out my book of love poems and read them silently while Emily napped and the others played in the yard. I spoke the lines. No, actually I worried them under my breath, the rhythms soothing me, real as rosary beads and useful as my grandmother's old country recipes: "I love thee with the passion put to use/In my old griefs, with my childhood's faith./I love thee with a love I seemed to lose." I'd always loved the *Sonnets from the Portuguese* that I'd memorized in school. "How do I love thee? Let me count the ways."

My passion for poetry got put to practical use as I wrung the children's diapers and made great vats of food, as much for Lowell as for my kids. I had a rectangular turkey roaster, a huge aluminium jobbie with a deep matching lid nearly as wide as my oven. I'd make cabbage rolls in the bottom, and bread pudding in the top, my grandmother's old recipe, feeding us all from one pan and one oven. Sometimes, I'd make butter tarts or raisin pies with rich crusts and oozing centres that dripped down the kid's chins or later, their favourite, Chicken Aloha—chicken with pineapple and Minute Rice.

Poetry sustained me. My life was busy with cooking and washing, and getting the kids to school. Lowell said nothing when he found the book with the inscription from Roly Faro in the laundry basket. I didn't know whether or not he'd even opened it. But the time I found for poetry were brief moments stolen for me. Around the time Auntie died, Lowell started to pull away, or I imagined that he did. And Will too had withdrawn from me. At first I didn't worry. I knew I had to let him go. He had his new hearing aids now, and his speech lessons. He seemed to be doing well enough in school, though his teachers couldn't explain how one day he'd have the highest marks in the class and the next day the lowest. Later I found out he'd been tested for all sorts of things—not once did the school call me. Unless Will told me, I didn't know, and after a while he stopped telling me anything.

And I had the others to worry about. Will had started spending all his time with his friend Kenny out on the prairies. Pauline played with her friends too. Like her father, she was a social one. I'd tried to get Will involved with the twins, reading to them, and later Emily, the Doctor Seuss books, *The Cat in the Hat, Sam I Am,* and *Papa Small* and Beatrix Potter's *The Fierce Bad Rabbit.* I'd hear him in their room, "Sam I am, I do not like green eggs and ham," then their laughter and they'd all shout if he left out any parts, chiming along in unison, or screaming at the scary parts. All of them in their flannel pyjamas. I wanted to hold them all, keep that time—my girls with their white fluffs of hair, and their big brother— safely in the cup of my hand. My children were my poetry now.

Lowell was good with the girls, especially with Pauline. She was her daddy's girl. I think he was disappointed we hadn't had more sons. I was running out of names of women poets, as it was. It would have been so easy to name my children if they had been boys. Robert Browning or Robert Burns, I'd always wanted a Robbie. We wanted more kids, but the last two were miscarriages and one was stillborn, a girl too. Will and his father were, on the surface, as far apart as you could get. He'd always go to his father to ask for something, but Lowell would always have a job to go to. In those days, it wasn't an excuse, the men went to work and the sons in time joined them. I encouraged Lowell to take Will on as a helper.

In the old country, it was the fields or the mines, the fishing boats or the army. The young boys went off with the men when they were ready. Some, like my Uncle Jack, never finished grade school. Mom said it had always been that way, in the stories told to her by her grandmother and her grandmother's mother. You were lucky if they came back in one piece, she'd say. I listened to the radio all day long. We all did then. Listening for the names, when a wall collapsed on a construction site downtown, or there was a fire at the refinery, or when Doreen Lewicky's husband was one of the men killed when the explosives plant went up. Our husbands had jobs where men died. We cried for them and for ourselves too, thanking god it wasn't one of ours—this time. That was the way we lived then. I didn't hold it against Lowell—work was everything. We felt lucky to have what we did.

But after a while, Will stopped trying to connect with his father. And that, I think, was when it started. After Auntie's death, Lowell seemed to react the same way too, staying later at work, taking more overtime. In that way they were alike, retreating to their separate pain. But Will, although he had his father's small quick hands, was a thinker, not a doer like his sisters. He was thinking and listening, and he was a reader like me. I always wanted him to find his own way. I was glad he went with his father on those jobs. It was as close as they ever got. For he had a passion more mine than his father's—a passion women weren't supposed to show and men don't trust themselves with. My husband didn't know how to deal with it in me much of the time, let alone in Will. But I think I did everything I could to help them.

Trout stepped out of the contraption man's office with his new binaural hearing aids. In each ear, a clear plastic ear mould connected to a sleek aluminium-and-brown hearing aid packed with transistors and diodes was attached to the temples of his glasses. The best of modern technology, the contraption man claimed. Standing in the hallway of the Medical Arts Building, with his grandmother, he could hear the tat-a-tat-tat, then a final bass thump of the carriage return, coming from the offices behind the stencilled glass doors. Trout recognized the industrious rhythm of typewriters, from hearing them in his grandmother's office in the parish hall. Typewriters clacked and telephones jangled, mixed with the office smells of cigarettes, carbon paper, India rubber bands and Gestetner ink, new and exotic as one sense flirted with another.

During his speech lesson, he could almost hear the *sh* and the *wh* sounds now, but he could still not hear *th* in south, although Shannon practiced with him. It sounded like *souh*, and north sounded like *norh*, like he was about to clear his throat. Over and over he'd tried in front of the mirror at home, carefully making *th*, imagining her tongue and glossy lipstick in front of him. Although he still could not hear what he was saying, he trusted her that the greatly exaggerated sounds were right. Silly to say something he couldn't hear. *Thilly*, echoed in his new hearing aids. And in Shannon's office, he still couldn't hear the sounds clearly, even with his new hearing aids. Despite the enthusiasm of his grandmother, the contraption man, and Shannon, all of whom told him how much the new hearing aids would do for him. He told no one, not wanting to disappoint them. True, he was glad to no longer have the hard single button in his left ear, or the cloth sack around his neck, but even as he sat in front of Shannon, trying to mimic the sounds she made, he couldn't hear her.

She was sharp now, making him repeat each exercise. "No." Her tongue thrust between her teeth, "Like this." The sound eluded him and he had no idea what came out of his mouth. Hearing people spoke like snakes. His nostrils flared at her perfume. He wanted her to like him.

But she seemed relieved when the lesson was over and his grandmother returned. She had never been impatient with him before. As they went to the waiting room, a man about her age in a sports jacket, twirling a set of car keys, came into the office. Shannon smiled at him through the doorway. "Almost ready, honey," she said and hung up her smock. Trout was crushed.

On the street, rush hour roared and engulfed him. He watched Shannon's boyfriend climb into the low seat of a green MGB convertible. Trout sighed while his grandmother repeatedly stabbed the button at the pedestrian crossing. Diesel engines rapped in idle and as the light turned, roared to deafening. It had been a long time since Trout had seen bubbles come from the mouths of the people around him as surely as they had in his aquarium. The sounds were not clear and his grandmother's voice faded to nothing when she turned away. Alas, a hearing aid was not an ear.

"The light's green." His grandmother picked up the pace, as they walked under the railway overpass to her house. "Don't daydream." Boxcars rumbled and slammed overhead like bombs detonating in the Sunday war documentaries.

"There's your father." The green Pontiac was parked in front of Dot's house, and his father sat on the front steps, smoking. After she said good bye, Trout could hear the electric purr of her vacuum through the open screen door. His father grinned. "One of her boyfriends coming over."

As they drove home, Trout thought of the handsome man waiting for Shannon. Embarrassed about his speech and his contraption, Trout didn't talk to the girls at school. Earlier that week, Carol Warnecke had waved him over. Blonde and short, she and her tall girl friend, Debbie Caron, stood laughing by the carousel in the playground. The prettiest girls in the school, they had never paid attention to him or Kenny, but he was thirteen now. Things had changed. His mouth went dry as he walked towards them.

"We were wondering." Carol Warnecke looked at him. "Where'd you learn to talk like that?" He went to turn away, but the taller girl stood in front of him.

"Yeah, we were wondering," her friend said. "You don't even know what I'm saying, do you?"

The short girl hooked her forefingers in the corners of her mouth and pulled. Her face contorted like the rubber man on the Midway at the Stampede grounds, "Bill-way—whaw's Ken-nay?"

"He your wife or something?" Debbie Caron smirked. Carol Warnecke giggled, her sweater tight with young breasts.

"Yeah, Billy and Kenny sitting in a tree. K-i-s-s-i-n-g. First comes love. Then comes marriage. Then comes Kenny with a baby carriage."

Her words trailed as the two of them spun the carousel so fast that no one else could get on. Just as quickly, they jumped off, their attention elsewhere. Then they were gone and the carousel rattled empty long after they'd left. The words he couldn't hear coming out of his mouth, mixed with the fear of the ones he'd heard from theirs, had paralysed him. Each new hearing aid seemed to take him further into their world, where he couldn't fight back. He was a freak who spoke in shards, and it was their language, more than his. Debbie Caron was right. He didn't know what they were saying. But he didn't want to be fearful anymore, or hurt.

As he washed his face before supper, he looked at the new hearing aids, with the heavy plastic and metal frames, the temples thick as his forefinger. The big plastic ear moulds dangled from the temples, with the tubing running to the insides of his ears. They were not invisible. They seemed like the ear trumpet in the contraption man's office, freakish as an iron lung. He hoped these too someday would be in the display case of the contraption man's office, replaced by an ear, or at least the heart of an ear.

But his chest swelled, and Trout felt stupid about liking the speech lady and about not saying anything to the girls. He was a freak and a fool. After the girls

118

taunted him, he'd smashed one of his shells, a fragile spider whelk, its pink and ivory tines shattered on the floor of his room. His mother found the pieces in the garbage. "Dropped it," he lied. Her mouth tensed, but she said nothing. She knew. He'd wanted to strike out at himself, to feel something as he broke it, part of him broken, like bones. He raged at everything, and he couldn't stop. He hadn't been ashamed of Kenny, until now. And he was ashamed of the shame, coiling inward as infinitely as the conch.

After supper that night, he hiked down to the river. He could hear its rush from the bottom of the cliff, the textured current rising and plummeting in his ears. It was clearer now. The sound of water. The river ripped the air as it gorged towards the Carseland dam. He liked that. Its cool wetness soothed him. When the wind rose, its fingers brushed over the microphones of his hearing aids. For this, he was glad. He scrambled up the soft clay toward the sandstone shelf. Kenny hiked towards him and waved. Trout did not wave back.

"You gonna hate me forever?" Kenny asked, when he got to the top. Trout was sickened at the sight of him, as if he was the cause of all this hurt, this confusion. Each day the child world closed further behind him and there was nothing but the coming of darkness in front of him. Trout dropped his knapsack and swung and punched Kenny in the face. But the smaller boy kept his hands by his sides. Kenny's cheek purpled from the sucker punch. He dropped his pack and raised his fists.

"Give it your best shot," he dared.

As Trout swung again, Kenny pushed him down on the dry grass, and jumped him, pinning his arms.

"Not hitting you back," Kenny was crying. "But you're not beating the shit out of me like my dad." Trout had never heard him say that before. He'd wondered about the bruises on Kenny's legs when they changed for gym.

He could smell the cigarette smoke on Kenny's breath and blood trickled from his nose. He tried to get up, but Kenny lost his balance and the two of them slid on the clay and tumbled down the slope. Out of control they held each other's jackets, afraid to let go. With the lip of the river below them, they dug in and kicked as they rolled, stopping just short of the cutbank and the run-off that could have swept them both away.

Trout felt his face and pawed the ground beside him. He'd lost his glasses and his new hearing aids on the hill. They cost hundreds of dollars. Kenny took off up the slope. Trout sat dazed, near-sighted and deafened, on the riverbank, inches from the rising river. Kenny came back and held the new hearing aids in the palms of his hands as if he were carrying a small animal. They were dirty, but had landed unbroken on the grass. Trout said nothing, but cleaned his glasses and plugged the ear moulds into his ears.

"You're bleeding," he said, pushing his handkerchief towards Kenny. "It's gross."

Kenny lit a cigarette after they climbed back up to the shelf and watched the river into which they'd nearly fallen.

"Here, asshole." He shoved a white bakery box at

Trout, as he reached into his pack for two bottles of Coke. "Knew you'd be here."

There were four cream buns from the Dutch bakery. They said nothing as they ate and wiped their faces with the backs of their grimy hands. Later they washed in the river, their faces and hands numb from the icy water. Kenny set fire to the bakery box and floated it on the water and Trout watched it burn like a Viking burial ship until the undertow took it down. When they walked back across the prairies, the gophers stood upright on their mounds and squinted, but Trout could not hear them. He shook his head as if to clear the water from his ears and yawned to clear his ears, but nothing helped. There were no miracles. Kenny smoked another cigarette on the long walk home over the blonde prairie.

"Give me one," Trout said.

"You sure?"

Trout drew hard and gagged. Kenny laughed and Trout pounded him on the shoulder and laughed too.

"Asshole," he mouthed.

"Asshole," Kenny mouthed back.

Kenny kick-boxed, and then tripped when Trout caught his foot and lifted it up past his shoulder, dumping him on the grass. He grinned as he sat up. Trout helped him to his feet and they both went home, partners again in nearly everything.

Clare

About the time I found out I was pregnant again, Lowell got laid off. There wasn't much building going on and he'd already lost nearly a month in January. In those days, construction shut down in the winter. But he'd heard about a gas plant going up in Pincher Creek, two hours south of here. He'd have to live in a trailer camp and could only come home twice a month. We'd manage—it was what we had to do. I didn't tell Lowell I'd missed two periods. I thought he'd be furious. It was a surprise because we didn't make love as often any more, with the kids around and both of us always tired. I was barely twenty-eight, with five kids—and another on the way.

I didn't mind at first, when he took the job. I had time to myself in the afternoon, if the kids napped, and again at night after they went to bed. I'd take Emily into bed with me, while the twins slept downstairs. Our house was small. After the twins were born, Lowell split the rumpus room in half to make a bedroom for them. But the kitchen was tiny, and at Christmas and Thanksgiving we set up a card table for the younger kids in the living room, where everyone ate with branches from the Christmas tree poking in their backs.

The night Lowell left, Will didn't come home for supper. I'd taken the girls to church that morning. They all had nice clothes and hats—I made sure of that: Buster Brown shoes with buckles and porkpie hats with velveteen ribbons tied under the chin and fuzzy pom poms on top. Pauline still went with me to church, though her dad and brother didn't. Lowell was napping on the couch in his dressing gown. He was still asleep when we got back two hours later. I didn't believe in forcing church on anyone. If there wasn't any joy in it, making them go wouldn't help. Will went out on the prairies before we left that June morning. I told him to take a jacket, as a bank of clouds was coming in from the mountains. We were all to have an early supper together before Lowell left for Pincher Creek.

When Will hadn't come home by suppertime, Lowell said nothing, but we were both worried. We started without him. His plate sat empty at the table and finally, I warmed his supper in the oven. I'd made a pot roast, with carrots and potatoes stewing beside it, a treat for him and his father. A horn sounded. Lowell's ride had shown up. He'd be leaving the car, but I couldn't drive— not many women did, then. I wanted to go out looking for Will. There had been a flash storm, one of those snowstorms Calgary gets in June, but it blew over fast. Will was sometimes late coming back from the river. Lowell told me not to worry. "Boys," he shrugged, as he kissed me goodbye. Pauline hugged him before he picked up his duffle bag and his toolboxes.

"Bring us a present, Dad," the twins chimed.

Lowell laughed. "I'll bring you some gas."

Emily clung to my neck. I felt nauseous. I'd tried to hide the morning sickness, but the smell of the pot roast and the heat in the house caused me to heave. Lowell looked at me.

"You alright? You know, Will's done this before."

Lowell's ride honked again and I pushed him out the door. "You better go."

We all stood at the picture window, with the twins waving long after the car was gone. Two red taillights disappeared, and for a moment I wondered if I was watching my marriage drive off. I felt as if something were being taken away. Nothing is what we expect, Grandma Locke had warned me. The girls and I watched as the streetlamps slowly came on.

When the phone rang, I jumped. "I'll get it, Pauline. Take Emily." It was Ivy Dawes, Kenny's mother.

"No, he's not home. I'm worried too. Call me if you hear anything." I hung up the phone. I wanted to take our car and look for him. Emily started to cry and the twins joined in. Pauline took Emily and tucked her in while I got the twins ready for bed. But I couldn't drive. I felt trapped, looking at the car parked in the back yard.

An hour later, Ivy Dawes called back. I asked Pauline to watch the girls and called Mom. I threw on my coat and ran down to the Dawes' house as fast as I dared, my stomach distended and biting back the nausea in my throat. Then I saw the police car.

Trout

On Sunday morning, Kenny Dawes tapped on the basement window, as he always did, before he came to the door. Every outing was a mission against the adult world, as if he and Trout were infiltrating it rather than steadily advancing into it themselves. Afterwards, they would scurry back to their basement bunkers.

"Bye, Mom," Trout yelled as he grabbed his knapsack and sandwiches. His mother was already dressed for church and handed him his jacket. "It's your dad's last night," she frowned. "Don't be late."

The air was chilled and the mountains still snow-capped that morning. Trout and Kenny headed across the prairie, glad to be free after being cooped-up all winter, and pulled by a childhood habit that seemed somewhat silly now. For Trout, the prairies and the river would be tinged always after the death of his auntie. He and Kenny walked now with a greater distance between them, seldom lapsing anymore into their silent lip-speaking as they once did. On the top of the hill, lines of orange-tagged survey stakes marked the cul-de-sacs of a new subdivision. White clouds bunched in the west.

"Snow." Trout nodded.

"Fucking cold enough." Kenny mashed his hands together to warm them. Neither of them had brought gloves. It was June, after all. Down on the Ogden flats, among the houses, it was warm, but out on the prairie, they could see the weather coming in from the mountains. As the wind rose, flocks of Franklin gulls milled in the face of the storm and screeched out a racket even Trout could hear. His new hearing aids hissed and cut out at the high cry of the gulls against the constant buckling of the wind over the microphones.

Clouds boomed over their heads, fast and large as railway cars. Scary and exciting, the wind scored their cheeks. Kenny turned and cupped his hands around the lighter he'd boosted from the drugstore. He'd palmed it, he'd bragged, pocketing it like a pro, not obvious like the kids who got caught. He'd pointed with his left hand to the cigarettes behind the counter and handed the clerk the forged note, supposedly from his mother, then slipped the lighter into his sleeve as the clerk turned away. No one ever checked the elbows of his coat, he laughed.

"Want one?"

Trout shook his head.

"Cured you?"

"Maybe later. We better head back." Both of them were red-cheeked, their ears freezing, as they headed towards the houses overlooking the flats. Kenny snapped survey stakes, tossing them into the long grass.

"Bastards. This is ours," he shouted. "Ours." Smoke puffed from the cigarette clenched, tough-guy style, in his jaw. Together they yanked stakes and flung them at each other. Hail pitted their faces as they crossed the park.

"Woo, whiteout," Kenny roared, giddy with the rush of wind. Snow swirled around them now and

Trout made windshield wipers of his fingers on his glasses. Water clotted the microphones of his hearing aids and they shorted out again. He couldn't see the edge of the park now.

"Let's go." Kenny pointed to a small brown building where everyone tied on their skates in the winter. The boards were still up. Ovals of banked soil marked the dried-up skating rink and the ice was gone. Kenny jiggled the door. "Locked."

They went around to a window on the side of the cinder block building. It was covered with heavy mesh. "We're stuck." Kenny's lips were blue and he shivered.

"Screws are outside," Trout said.

"What?" Kenny's soaked hair started to freeze.

"Here."

Trout pulled out his pocketknife. In a minute, he had the screws out and the mesh against the building. He slipped the blade along the latch of the window, and carefully worked it loose. He went in headfirst, dropped on the concrete floor in a tumbling roll and opened the door for Kenny.

Trout ran his hands under hot water in the washroom. His fingers felt as though they were stuck full of pins, as they thawed.

"Chips?" Kenny offered a bag from behind the concession counter. "C'mon, have one bag." As they both ate their sandwiches, Kenny opened a cream soda. Trout helped himself to a Coke. Light-headed from the cold and sugar rush, they chortled and snorted. Then there was a bang outside.

"Shit. What was that?"

"Cops." Trout looked at his friend. Both of them flattened behind the counter. After a few minutes, they climbed onto the counter and peered out the window.

"Some cop alright," Kenny ducked back down behind the counter. "Fucking screen fell down."

"I'm warm," Trout said, his heart pounding through his coat. "We should go." High with adrenaline, he wiped the bottle and replaced it in the rack beside the cooler and tucked the chip bag in the barrel under all the other trash, while Kenny locked the back door and the window. "Evidence," they'd both agreed.

"We're good." Kenny said outside, as Trout tightened the screws in the window, snapped his knife shut and slipped it back into his pocket. He said nothing, surprised at how easy it was. Thou Shalt Not Burgle, he thought. Dot, in a smart outfit, purse on her arm, looking down at him from the pulpit.

It was too soon to go home and too wet to go back to the river. Kenny led as they cut across the snow-covered park towards the row of stores one street over from the Canadian Pacific Railroad tracks that passed above the town on a steep grade. The storm had forced the streetlamps on, and as they walked on in semi-darkness down the gravel of the back alley that backed onto the C.P.R. line, Kenny tried each door. At the back door of the hardware store, he stopped. It was dead-bolted, but Kenny pointed. A small window above the steel door had the same latch as the one on the skating shack, and it was not covered with mesh. Trout shook his head.

"No way."

"Bet you can't."

Trout stared at the window: brand new canvas knapsacks and canteens, gopher traps, razor-head arrows, Daisy pump-action B.B. guns, and C.C.M. bicycles with streamers pouring out the handlebars. Display cases full of bone-handled knives and walnut stocked rifles. Fishing rods and tackle. Leather ball gloves. Loot. There was a wooden pallet and crates behind the grocery store.

"Okay, we go in and we look." Trout stared at Kenny. "We look."

They leaned the pallet against the door and stacked crates, tilted and loosely balanced. Kenny steadied them as Trout stepped onto his shoulders to the window. His knife jimmied the lock and as he squeezed through the window, the sweet and sour spikes of hardware smell seared his nose: fertilizer, weed killer, polyethylene, turpentine, and newly tanned leather. The darkness of the closed store momentarily blanketed his eyes. His heart sped as he looked for a clear place to jump, but the floor was covered with lawnmowers. He dropped hands first onto a wheelbarrow, knocked it over and landed on a bundle of garden rakes, gashing his arm through his coat. He tore a brown strip of wrapping paper from a big roll near the cash register and matted it on his arm as he unlocked the back door.

"What took you so long?"

Trout held up his arm.

"Don't bleed on anything," Kenny warned. "Crime scene."

With nobody there, the dark store was eerie. They

had all this treasure to themselves. Trout handled the yo-yos in front of the wide-open cash register. The change and cash drawers were empty, he was relieved to see, as he saw Kenny check them and palm a pocketknife and reach for a yo-yo.

"Take one. Old man Warner won't miss it. We only take one of everything," Kenny rifled through the boxes in front of the cash register and then through the sporting goods, stuffing his pocket with leaders and bobbers. High on daring, he ran up and down the aisles, trying on a football helmet, and raising an axe at Trout like a Viking warrior.

Trout reached behind the counter into the display of Hohner harmonicas, beside a case of pocket watches and clocks. His hand hovered. He reached for the smallest one, a vest pocket harmonica, the case said. He filled a flashlight with batteries and shone the light on Kenny, who had a pump-action .22 out of the gun case and a box of shells in his hands.

"Let's get out of here." Trout turned to the door. "Kenny, put it back." He knew why Kenny wanted the gun. He'd seen the strap at Kenny's house, made out of baseboard rubber like that used in hospitals. It was wide and thick as a cricket bat. His father called it the Black Doctor, Kenny said.

"Put it back." As Trout beamed the flashlight on the back door, he saw metal contacts and followed the wire running along the ceiling.

"Store's got a silent alarm."

For the first time Kenny looked afraid. They had been in the store for about five minutes since the alarm must have gone off. Old man Warner or the cops were on their way. As they closed the back door, Kenny still carried the gun and a box of shells.

"We're caught, we're gonna get it the same anyway." Kenny shoved the gun under his coat. They ran across the alley, up the grade to the railway tracks. Kenny hid the gun and shells under a pile of railway ties. Trout still had the flashlight in his hand. He threw it like a grenade into the bushes along the tracks.

They lay heaving and winded on their knees in the wet grass, and watched as a van pulled up behind the hardware store. Old Man Warner.

Warner checked the back door and the window before he went inside, leaving the door open. He had a baseball bat in his hand. A few minutes later a police car pulled into the alley, with lights flashing.

Trout looked at the trail of footsteps they'd made crossing the snow and up the bank in front of them. The storm was lifting and the sun's sharp light stung his eyes. It was a matter of time. There was no way back without going past the cops. He spasmed as his teeth chattered. His knees were muddy and the blood that soaked through his sleeve had turned cold. He felt the mouth organ in his pocket. He gave it to Kenny who emptied everything from his pockets under a transformer box.

"We're gonna need a story."

Trout said nothing, but got up and crossed the tracks towards the police car, sliding down the grade on the slick snowy grass. For that moment only, he was glad Auntie was dead. He was now one of her stories. Like firebugs or burglars. And what to tell his grandmother and his mother. Worst of all, his father.

He walked toward the police car, and Kenny ran after him, for once not leading, but following.

Kenny was right, they needed a story. A good one.

Clare

I ran towards the police car parked in front of Ivy Dawes's house, and I let myself in the front door. I could see the uniformed backs of two policemen with their gunbelts. My son and his friend Kenny were sitting on the couch in Ivy Dawes's living room. Will's head was in his hands. Kenny stared straight ahead. His father, Ken Dawes, and big Donny Kovack, the police constable who lived in our neighbourhood, stood over them. Donny was the town's lone policeman before we became part of the city. The younger cop, one of the new city police, seemed familiar too.

Don Kovack turned to me. "Mrs. Dunlop, the boys here broke into Ed Warner's store." I stared at Ivy. My stomach fluttered and I was nauseous in the small, close room, heavy with cigarette smoke.

"We're waiting to hear if anything was taken. They're a little quiet," he said. "Anything you boys want to tell me?" He looked at both of them.

"Let's take 'em downtown, Don." His partner bristled. "Let juvenile sort it out." I watched the young cop's jowls. "You're off to Bowden now, boys," he said. He was just to trying to scare them. Bowden was the reformatory for adults in a town north of here and they didn't take kids. But I didn't say anything. Then I realized why the younger cop seemed familiar. He was the one who'd pulled Lowell over, and made us both get out of the car. He didn't recognize me, I thought.

The phone rang. Ivy Dawes handed it to Don Kovack.

"I see, that's a whole different picture. Call you back, Ed." The policeman hung up the phone.

"Ed's missing a rifle. Box of bullets too. Want to tell me about that? This is serious, boys. Somebody covering for somebody here?"

Will looked down at his feet. He wouldn't meet my eyes when I came in. Kenny Dawes turned his head. His father leaned over him. "You little bugger," he muttered.

"Let's book 'em." The younger cop seemed happier now. But Will had learned from his father that the worst thing is a squealer, a rat. Lowell hadn't ratted out his pals in the gang. That was why he gotten hard time. I knew my son. I couldn't see him stealing a gun.

"I want the gun, boys." Don Kovack told them. "Or we go downtown. Right now."

"Wasting our time," the younger cop smirked. "Hey, Don?"

"Maybe you're right. Nobody's talking, let's go."

The younger cop took Kenny's arm. Both boys started sniffling.

"I did it," Kenny sobbed. "I'll show you."

His father glared, the cords in his neck visible. Kenny cowered when the younger cop touched his arm.

"Better go get that gun before some other kid does." Don Kovack looked at his partner. "I'll call Ed."

"I'm coming with you," Kenny's father said, pulling on his coat, glowering at his son.

Don Kovack sat down beside Will. He was a third-generation cop. We knew him from the community dances. He played trombone in the Legion band, and his family all went to mass together.

"Got some Kleenex?" he looked at Ivy Dawes. Will took one and I did too.

"Coffee, Don?

"No thanks."

"Clare?"

I nodded at her. My son's eyes were red. His coat was filthy and the knees of his pants torn and wet. He favoured his arm and his sleeve was bloody.

"Your arm okay?" I asked. He shivered.

"Can I have a look at that cut?" Don Kovack asked. Will pulled up his coat sleeve to show a dark gash. "Ivy, you got iodine and a washcloth?"

"I'll get it," I offered, glad to do something, anything. My neck ached from the tension and my stomach churned.

"In the medicine cabinet, Clare," Ivy called from the kitchen.

"We're not going to be doing this again, are we? Look at me, son. You broke the law." Don Kovack had five sons and four daughters of his own. "Next time will be a lot worse." He wiped the cut clean. Will flinched at the iodine.

"Some of these guys will do anything to protect their stuff. Ed Warner's got a family just like your dad. You understand?" Will nodded and wiped his nose with the Kleenex.

"I know. I'm sorry." His words stuck in his throat. I

bandaged his arm and he started to shake. Ivy brought him a blanket. The phone rang again.

"It's your partner, Don." She offered me a cigarette.

Don Kovack still looked out for the local boys as he had when he was in charge. Often he'd turn the younger ones over his knee or make the older ones pay for damages. Nobody minded that then, but everything changed when the city took over.

He replaced the receiver. "Got the gun."

The adults looked at each other in relief.

"They're on their way back."

Kenny's father came in first. "Warner won't press charges, if we pay for the damage." He shook his head at Ivy and turned to Don Kovack. "Your partner wants to take 'em both downtown, give 'em a taste. I gave my kid a good licking." He shook his finger at my son. "You got a good one comin' when your old man gets home."

Ivy didn't say anything. And she wouldn't. We all knew on our street about Ken Dawes's temper and how he'd yell at Ivy even in front of the neighbours. I wondered what else he'd do behind closed doors.

Don Kovack asked me, "Can you pay for the damage?" We had no choice. I wondered what Lowell would say. The baby was coming. It was all I could do to keep from running to the toilet.

"Yes." My stomach heaved again.

"I'll talk to my partner. Be right back." Don Kovack went out to the squad car. When he returned, Kenny came with him. He had a welt on the side of his head. I looked at Ivy Dawes, but she smiled as if everything were fine. It was a foolish smile though, a sweet weak mask. I knew she was scared. I wondered what Ken Dawes would do after we left. He was a wiry little man who looked as if he would snap in half like a pencil. I wonder what he'd be like if Lowell ever got a hold of him.

"Have to talk to my sergeant. Won't make any promises, boys. Should've told me about the gun right away." Both boys looked terrified. He turned to Will. "For now, we'll send you home with Mom." My son nodded blankly.

"Someone will be in touch about the damages, Mrs. Dunlop. You can go now."

The younger cop sat out in the squad car smoking and writing on a clipboard. He motioned me over, after I sent Will on ahead.

"Mrs. Dunlop, one more thing." As I leaned in the window, hot air radiated from the heater, as the police radio squalled and cigarette smoke stung my damp eyes.

"Mrs. Lowell Dunlop?" He didn't look up from his notes. I wanted to smash his smug round face with its rosy jowls. I remembered the cold cranky morning in early November of 1951, seven months before my son was born. It was near Remembrance Day because all the vets, my uncles, and those coming home from Korea, and the court officers, wore their poppies. My son was already three months in me when the judge looked at my husband, Lowell, lectured him, and called him, Babyface. The detectives sitting behind the Crown smirked. All of them, Lowell, the judge, the detectives huddled together, even the lawyers, acting parts from movies that had played not long before at the Palace Theatre.

"You, young man, at the age of twenty, are at a crossroads. You've had two chances already. You need to make up your mind whether you will have a life of crime, or whether you will reform. I'm going to give you some time to think about that. Two years, less a day. Hard labour." The judge banged his gavel. They led Lowell away and I stood at the back of the courtroom unable to touch him, my head in my hands, ashamed, my thin dress no longer hiding my condition. Both papers covered the trial. One of them ran red headlines and a front-page story that ended: Dunlop's pregnant young wife stood weeping in the back of the courtroom.

I've forgotten many things about that long-ago time, and I was pregnant in the back of that courtroom that day, but I was not crying. I was seventeen years old in the fall of 1951 and I was thinking of this child stirring in me. Not about Lowell—that had been decided for two years. I wondered what we would do, this child I was carrying and me.

"Like father, like son, Mrs. Dunlop?" the young cop jeered, as my head snapped back from the window.

I walked home to my children, counting out my steps, and determined he'd not see me cry.

Trout

Trout folded his jacket into the cardboard suitcase his mother gave him and looked around his room one last time. He woke before the sun rose that day as he usually did, but he didn't go back to sleep. His blood sparkled with excitement. The sun in the oval mirror of his dresser filled the room with light. As he stood in his cold stockinged feet on the checkerboard tiles his father had laid, his room seemed small, not a sea anymore but a cave. He reached for the conch shell in the windowsill. If his auntie could carry it all the way from New Brunswick, he would take it a little further. His room had been stripped of all its shells, for it would now be his sisters'. Outside, the turquoise sky warmed the breeze blowing through the low window that opened onto the lawn. Everything was alive and green in the last week of June.

He placed the conch amongst the books in his knapsack. His auntie's copy of *Who Has Seen the Wind* was wrapped in tissue paper to protect it. His mother had given him a fountain pen, a hardcover journal with lined pages, and a book of love poetry with worn leather corners and translucent pages that felt like air in his hands. It seemed an odd gift. The inscription read: "For Clare, my love. Roly." She told him it was a friend she went to school with. At first he believed her, but he knew there was more. That kind of love seemed, for him, such a mysterious impossibility then.

At his mother's insistence he read some of the poems in the days before he left, although the poets' meaning was lost on him. But their rhythms carried him when the words could not. And she had said, before closing the door to his room, "Will, listen to the reverie!" But, he was confused and the reverie of the poems hadn't appeared yet in his young life. Unless reverie was mysterious and blissful: his grandmother's singing in the cathedral, or his late auntie's stories, or down by the river with his conch. Reverie seemed a lonely and long ago thing at first, that belonged to the past.

But he wondered too if how his mother talked might be a type of reverie. How she'd leave him with a thought or a poem, dropped like a riddle that tumbled out of her own moments of rapture. Like the day when, in a breezy and celestial mood, she had said of Kenny, "He is of the tribe who knows Joseph." He had no idea what that meant, but if a tribe was lost, surely it was Kenny's. But he wasn't sure if this reverie of which his mother spoke could be trusted.

As abruptly, his mother plunged back into the dark moods, which wrapped her like a fog and for days silenced her. Trout would come home to the curtains drawn, the radio silent and her bedroom door shut. Pauline met him at the door on those days when time stopped, "I'm making supper and you're getting the girls washed." Her eyes commanded him, say nothing. And he didn't, slipping into the duty of husband to Pauline as they tiptoed through the house, knowing not to disturb their mother, fearful already of the rage it prompted.

And then, without explanation, their mother

emerged—hours, sometimes days, later—threw open the curtains and windows, cranked the radio and took over from Pauline without mention of her disappearance. They learned to dance with her, taking their cues from her. They no longer tiptoed. The house was alive once more.

After the first time, he had stopped asking when he got home to find the blinds drawn and the radio silent. Pauline simply nodded towards the closed bedroom door, "Everything's fine."

He'd raised his eyebrows.

"Fine, fine, just fine," she stressed, before she turned back to the supper she was making. That became the code between them when things were anything but—the truth in its tone. Everything's fine, when clearly it wasn't.

In one of those moods, in the weeks after his auntie died, his mother had left her book on his dresser open to a poem by a Welshman he'd never heard of: "Do Not Go Gentle into That Good Night". The rhythms of that poem welled over him as he read and reread it alone in his bedroom. At first he had not the faintest idea what it was about. "Rage, rage, against the dying of the light," he repeated, and gradually he did rage against the dying of the light, instead of the living. This was his mother's wisdom. He knew she'd known rage, as had his father.

His own small rage, captured in the poem he read over and over, subsided in the lonely weeks of June in the traces of a forgotten language the rhythms hinted at. Instinctual and primitive as the flash of a dragonfly's wing reflected on water, it signalled beyond words, snapped the old reptile brain out of its long sleep. This time it came not from the puckered mouths of his tropical fish, the miniature barracuda or the Asian fighting fish that swam through the underwater bridge in his aquarium, but from the mouths of poets. And it was, as his father said, ten years older than dirt. Older than this strange new language of Shannon's he was learning, spoken in the hiss of snakes. Tide of the ancient sea, before words, and hands and feet, before reason, the language of fishes.

Those rhythms disturbed him and soothed him. When his mother gave him the book, in the sad weeks of June, she said, "This will help." He hadn't wanted her words then, but he was glad now, and also glad that he was leaving. The riptide of her moods was too much and he knew Pauline would go too, eventually. He could already read the determination in his sister's eyes.

Their mother was prone to days punctuated with laughter and then to unpredictable silences interrupted by short but seemingly profound instructions. She worried him now. The day she gave him the book of love poetry, she had come to his room, and had said: "You'll need these." She laid down the book, the fountain pen, a box of ink cartridges and a hard-covered blue journal, each with a snap of her wrist, as if laying out cards in a hand of solitaire.

"Poetry's the heart's reckoning with reason," she said. Then she closed the door and was gone. If the book were treasure to her, then so it would be to him, like his auntie's book and the conch. All of them, silent witnesses to love.

He'd twice emptied his suitcase in a panic. Two bags only, she said. He counted his socks, sweaters and pants once more. He was going away for a long time. It could get cold there even in summer, she'd warned. He reached into his bottom drawer for the copy of *The Pilgrim's Progress*. The shabby cover reminded him now of that awful time, earlier this year, after his auntie's death.

For Trout the New Year always began with the Victoria Day weekend and his own birthday. The real beginning of spring, when the icy edge finally came off the wind, although it could still snow. He and his father posed for his mother's Kodak Brownie in the yard in July one year, both of them in t-shirts, with snowballs in their hands. It was planting season, and his mother showed him how to crease a line with the hoe, dropping wrinkled peas or nearly invisible carrot seeds into rows in the black loam. The garden and her hands upon the cat soothed her restlessness, the act of touching earth or fur calmed her.

"No planting 'til the Victoria Day weekend," she advised, "when the danger of frost has mostly passed," and thus she initiated him into the rituals of her family. The great-aunts and uncles shared their bedding plants now, along with the secrets the great Scottish gardeners brought from the Highlands, Kingussie and the River Spey, where they'd grown their food in short seasons. Gradually, his mother, busy with the girls, had let him take care of the lawn, trees, and flowers she had planted when he was a baby. He would miss the garden. The peonies sticky with ants, the green blades of bearded irises he and Pauline duelled with, and the tall rods of scruffy hollyhocks with their Kleenex pom poms.

His thirteenth year began badly. First, the death of his auntie, and then the business with Kenny and the police, as his mother called it, although she didn't know half of it. After the burglary at the hardware store, Trout had written his father immediately to apologize for what he'd done. His dad had come right home the following Friday from Pincher Creek. Trout knew his father's temper. If his mother's was a long and devastating silence, his father's was noisy, but mercifully quick and done with: doors slammed, tires squealed. Unlike Kenny's father.

Kenny hadn't come back to school and was sent to the Don Bosco Home for Boys. Maybe not such a bad thing, his mother said. Maybe, maybe not. The beating Kenny's dad had given him when he skipped school was just a warning, Trout knew.

That Friday, when Trout saw the car pull up outside, he went to his room. His father had come downstairs and taken the creased and dirty letter from his shirt pocket, and sat on the bed beside him.

"This," his father stammered, "is the right thing." He seemed choked up. His father shook the letter. His father had small hands, with grime permanently etched on them, and fine fingers like Trout's. "I've worked out a payment plan for the damage to the hardware store. We're lucky that's all." His father lowered his head.

"I don't know what we'll tell your grandmother."

His father seemed closer than he'd ever been. "She thinks the world of you, Sunshine."

Trout worried about Dot too, as if he too wasn't clean anymore, his hands no different than his father's. Maybe that wasn't such a bad thing, maybe. She gave his father lotions and cleaners, but his hands never came clean no matter how hard he scrubbed. "I'm sorry, Dad." Trout spoke to his knees, not daring to look in his father's eyes.

His father didn't hit him, although Trout had been expecting it and had even wished for it, thinking it might help ease his guilt.

"It's not the end of the world, Sunshine," his father said, before he went upstairs. "It just seems like it. Auntie's death has been hard on all of us. Even your grandmother, in her own way. Auntie wasn't much of a church-goer, but she paid someone to drive her down to visit me in prison. None of the others came. Not even my own mother." His father shrugged. "Auntie brought the inmates bags of candy each time. She always gave everybody candy. That damn candy—the guards took it," he laughed. *You're gonna come home one day*, Auntie told me. *You got a wife who loves you and a son who needs you*. Didn't know how I could possibly do it. She gave me this." His father opened his wallet to a smudged snapshot of a baby with a toy drum. "It's you," his father said, handing him a picture he'd never seen before.

"I'll tell Dot I'm proud of you." It was the only time his father had ever talked about jail. "Because I am."

Trout sat down on the bed, and looked at the pictures that he'd found in the front of *The Pilgrim's Progress.* His Grandma Dot was a baby then, in one picture which was taken with her mother, brother and sister, at the ranch house. Her mom, Bean, died before she was thirteen, the age Trout was now.

Unlike the picture of her as a happy baby, the later pictures of Dot showed a very different little girl. Dot stood in front of the house she still lived in, wearing a floppy red bow and holding a giant striped candy cane as long as a baseball bat, which she'd acquired from Auntie's candy store. Dottie's sad eyes stared at Trout from the photo.

The last picture Trout had found, of Dot watching her mother's body carried to the hearse, explained so much, he thought. His grandmother's eyes haunted him. He was glad to be leaving that behind too. He slipped the pictures into *Who Has Seen the Wind,* to protect them, and returned Pilgrim to his drawer.

His mother rapped a broom handle on the floor above him to get his attention.

"What are you doing?" she called from the stairs. "Honey, let's go." He slung the knapsack over his shoulder and took up the suitcase.

A bag lunch waited on the counter. His sisters played in the yard, and came in to say goodbye. None of them had ever been apart from each other more than a few days. He kissed Emily, and hugged the twins, ducking down, his eyes level with theirs, but Pauline stood back. They were shy with each other now, afraid of what they'd become. Their bodies had broken out, his in the spastic cracking of his voice and hers in blemishes across her face. She closed the bathroom door now, even to the twins. *Pauline's a woman*, their mother said cryptically, months before she got a bra. Two years younger than Trout, she stood an inch taller than him already, and they both towered over their sisters. Her hair had darkened, like their mother's. Her eyes, too, were quick and bright. The other girls her age, and some of the boys, thought she was attractive. And she had their mother's complexion.

"Ew, zits, Mom," she pointed accusingly to a blemish on her cheek at breakfast, as if their mother was the Zit fairy who'd put them there in the night. The adult world was one of reversal, where children became their parents.

Pauline handed Trout his lunch, put her arms around the twins and, in her grown-up voice, said, "Good luck, Trout. Write us a letter when you get there, big brother. Right, girls?"

Emily and the twins all nodded. Trout might be the oldest, but Pauline was the boss.

When his mother left the room, Pauline leaned into him and said, "It'll be fine." His eyes questioned her, but she hushed him and kissed his cheek before he could speak. "I'll take care of Mom, don't you worry."

But he was worried, even as his mother gave him his Greyhound ticket from her purse and they left the house. Everything had changed.

Real summer began in the last days of June, and the neighbourhood was full of new bikes with rainbow streamers spilling from the handlebars and clothes-pinned playing cards rapping like motors against shiny spokes. Even he could hear the pent-up screams let loose, but not the smack of ball gloves at the park. Kenny told him of the high quick slap of a perfect catch that didn't sting. Trout's father had got him a glove, which was hanging on the coat hook in his room. Trout wouldn't need it where he was going.

He ached for what he was leaving behind as he and his mother rode the city bus downtown, past Scotsman's Hill, over the Stampede grounds where he and his father watched the fireworks for free at the midway every July.

Downtown, his mother had a coffee and smoked at the counter of the Greyhound coffeeshop while they waited for his bus to be announced. She seemed flushed and asked the waitress for a glass of water. Trout toyed with the straw in his Coke, and watched his mother, not paying attention to her small talk, but nodding nonetheless. Sitting with her legs tucked under the chrome stool, she brushed her hands through her dark hair and pulled it over to one shoulder, so he could see her face and lips clearly. Her hazel eyes were alert and alive, zooming in on his, laughing, then zipping away somewhere in the beyond where he could not see, as they pounced on an idea and flashed back in an instant, animated and erratic.

Two men at a window table eyed her. He could read their lips across the room and as one of them smirked, he squirmed. He was proud his mother was still young and pretty. A looker. He felt protective of her, but had no idea what to do.

The PA squawked gibberish and for a moment he was lost.

"The Edmonton coach is loading, honey," his

mother translated. She stood with him on the platform and saw his luggage loaded.

Trout was already taller than her and when she
kissed his cheek, he felt the nudge of her belly through
her loose summer dress. He reddened. He'd seen her
pregnant enough times to know. He looked away, but
she took his face and put her finger to his lips.

"Not a word." She fussed with his hair. "Not even
to Jack and Shelagh. I'm superstitious."

She was fragile now. He felt the tremor in her
voice and the uncertainty in her eyes.

"Not a word," he said. Then she let him go.

Clare

I told Will to write to his father and own up to what he'd done. If Lowell had come home and then had found out what had happened, he wouldn't have had time to think. As it turned out, he made good money in Pincher Creek. The gas plant was cold, windy work, but there was nothing to do down there except work overtime and play cards, Lowell said. The damage to the hardware store wasn't much, but we couldn't very well go there anymore, though it was the only store of its kind in our area. And worst of all, everyone knew.

Even I was surprised that Lowell didn't punish Will. But whatever had happened to him in prison, he never laid a hand on our children. He left the punishment to me. The Dawes boy was sent to a juvenile home and now had a record. We still had no idea what had happened that day. Neither of the boys would talk.

Lowell said, "The shame is punishment enough. He's ashamed, isn't he?"

I thought he was, but nothing surprised me anymore. We'd talked over the situation with my mom. She said she'd ask her brothers for advice. They were all wild ones until they went overseas, signing up even though they were underage. All of them were tall by the time they were fifteen, and they lied about their age to get off the farm. Finally, we decided Will would have to go away—for the summer at least.

When that Greyhound pulled out onto 7th, Will

reached out the window and waved at me. I'd splurged on a chocolate bar, pop and *Classics Illustrated* comic books for him though I was afraid he wouldn't like them anymore. And I hugged him before he got on the bus, but he was at that age—Pauline was too—where they think they're not kids any longer. Neither of them talked to me much anymore, but when they did, they were full of longing to get away. All my own dreams came back when we talked. Then suddenly, they'd catch themselves and when I tried to bring them back, they'd dismiss me, as if I was the enemy.

"Moth-er," Pauline would say—not Mom anymore. And I was alone at the table until the next time they orbited back to me, unpredictable and irritable.

I couldn't hold them—though I so wanted to sometimes. You get used to letting your babies go, but you're still the one who's in control. Then one day, just like that—they let go, for good. You're left standing there like a fool, with empty arms. But the truth is, while I missed Will already, I was also relieved, knowing he'd be loved and safe.

I needed a walk and an hour to myself after my son's bus left, so I cut over to Eau Claire and took a footpath along the river. Pauline could manage the girls till I got back. I crossed the 10th Street Bridge to our old neighbourhood in Sunnyside, past the house Mom and Dad rented before he went overseas. The caragana hedges had opened and the big poplars shaded the river. The fire engines were out in front of the firehall. One of the firemen smiled at me as he polished the fender of the ladder truck.

It had been years since I'd visited our old neighbourhood. Mom and I would walk down to the Saturday matinee at the Grand, where Mom's cousin worked in the coffee shop. She'd bring us fries and gravy, never letting us pay. Later, I was an usher at the Grand. I would meet Mom and walk her home across the 10th Street Bridge. We had that house for a few years after Dad left, until the owner sold it and we had to move. My elementary school was over on Kensington and the river was a block away. The poplars were like big green umbrellas over us and everyone had a garden with a rhubarb patch and a little greenhouse in those days.

When I went into the Lido Café on 10th, the owner recognized me and waved as I walked over to the payphone. I was starting to show. When I came back, my milkshake was poured and waiting at the counter with the aluminium container beside it. I wouldn't need lunch. Lowell'd got mad when I told him I was pregnant. Before, he'd always been happy about having a new baby, but this time he just stared like it was my fault.

"We're just getting ahead," he said. He looked exhausted, and I started to cry. Eventually, he came around, and we planned a new addition on the back of the house. He said we'd probably have to sell the car, get something smaller. It was the newest car we ever had. I told him we'd get by and it wasn't necessary to sell the car, with the money he was making, but I was touched he'd sacrifice for the kids.

I remember taking the kids to the zoo on the bus one Saturday, when the twins were little. We were like homesteaders with our baby carriages, picnic baskets and blankets. Everybody carried something. Lowell was at work, and I was trying to do fun things with the kids, but they were a handful.

Pauline and her brother were ahead of me on the bridge to St. George's Island. I stopped halfway across. I swear to God I could have pushed the twins off the bridge. They'd been sick all winter, and then Pauline came down with the mumps, and then with the measles. Will had had his tonsils out. The two of them were always fighting and sometimes the twins got into it and then Emily started crying. It never let up. And I was never alone, not for a minute.

I didn't tell anybody about that feeling until years later, when my friend Marnie and I sat up one night. She worked with the women's group in the church. When I told her that story, she said she'd felt the same way after her daughter was born and other women had told her they'd felt that way too.

I might have thrown my kids over the rail that day, but Pauline stopped me. Otherwise, I'd have been in the papers like that woman in Victoria who threw her daughter from a bridge and said it was an accident. I know how it happened. It was no accident.

But Pauline ran back to get me. "Mom, hey Mom," she said. She helped me push the twins' buggy across the bridge. "Look, Mom." She pointed to Dinny the Dinosaur, the green concrete dinosaur near the front gate of the zoo. That little head on that great big body, not really menacing. Goofy and grinning, just like a baby. I started to laugh. We had our pictures taken beside the big dinosaur, with the twins sitting on the tail. We're all smiling. You'd think I was happy, but I was just so damn grateful.

"How many kids?" Sam Lee asked me, bringing me a fresh ashtray. "Five," I said, pouring the rest of the milkshake into my glass.

"Now maybe six," he laughed at his joke. "Lily, come." His wife came out wiping her hands on a cook's apron, smiling and bowing slightly as she shook my hand. We'd always come to the Lido for a treat when Mom got paid

"How's your mom?" she asked.

"Fine." I took her hand. "Still with the Singers."

When I left the Lido, Sam Lee wouldn't let me pay, and his wife hugged me. I should have been happy, but tears started as I walked towards the bus. So much of my life had centered on the Lido Café. I'd met Lowell there.

A man getting into a car across the street called to me and waved. It was Roly Faro. When he saw me smile, Roly ran across the street. Roly was my boyfriend from high school.

"Clare? What are you doing down here?" I knew he knew I was pregnant. I tried to be nonchalant. He looked surprised.

"Roly Faro, never thought I'd run into you here."

"My mother is still on Memorial Drive."

"My mom told me. You're a teacher. Good for you, Roly."

"In University Heights. Got four of my own and I'm teaching everyone else's. You?"

"Five and another one on the way." I didn't say where we lived.

"You need a ride somewhere?"

"No. I'm meeting Mom downtown," I lied. "But thanks." We both stood there awkwardly. My Romeo, and me, his once upon-a-time Juliet, pregnant, in a housedress. I pulled my purse to my chest.

"You're sure? Well, I should go. Nice seeing you, Clare."

"Nice to see you too, Roly." He looked away for a minute.

"It's none of my business," he stared at me. "You're still with him?" I nodded, suddenly feeling ashamed that he saw right through me and my thin summer dress. I sure didn't need this now. "Still" with Lowell.

"He broke my jaw, Clare." Roly shook his head. "Remember that," he said, over his shoulder as he walked away.

I was stung. I started to cry.

Although my feet ached and the weight of the baby slowed me, I couldn't get on a bus now, with my red eyes and streaked make-up. I had to walk and I headed across the bridge to catch the bus back to Ogden from downtown. But what really hurt was I knew I'd been wrong about Roly. "Still," he'd said.

If you're lucky, the passion that chooses you is the one you've chosen. I wasn't so lucky. The passion for Lowell had chosen me. Oh, I thought I'd chosen it, as it had me in such a terrible grip. Roly Faro loved me then and I'd taken him so lightly. All those damned books ruined me. All I could think now was how things ought to be, how they could have been, not how they were. I caught the bus driver staring in the rear-view mirror. I covered my face with my hands.

The sun in all the windows, a perfect bloody day, and I'm crying again.

Lowell worked all through that summer that we sent Will away. He took no time off and worked overtime every chance he got. He came home only for a long weekend in July. We took the girls to the Calgary Stampede. Emily and the twins loved the horses and cows and pigs in the barns. Pauline and her dad rode the Wild Mouse rollercoaster twice and he took her to the freak show although I didn't want him to. But she was growing up fast and I saw myself in her sometimes. I'd discovered a pack of cigarettes in her school bag. I didn't want her to turn out the way I had. I'd started at the same age.

The morning sickness gave way to calm, and the baby moved inside me sometimes. The Calgary summer was hot during the day, but at night, with all the windows open, our small house cooled down.

We got only a letter and a postcard all that summer from Will. I have them somewhere. It was Mom's idea to send Will to Jack. He was her oldest brother, nearing retirement, and he and his second wife didn't have any kids of their own. Jack had four from his first marriage, all of them grown. There'd been five, but one had killed himself. Mom's was a close family and all the aunts and uncles tried to visit Jack and Shelagh, despite the isolation, at least once a year. Sometimes their kids stayed for a week or two. It would be good for him, Mom said. I hoped so. Jack was my favourite uncle. He'd taken to Lowell right away and he'd be good for Will. The Dawes boy was bad news. I didn't trust Kenny anymore with Will. But when we sent him away to live with my Uncle Jack and Aunt Shelagh, we didn't know how it would work out.

I kept myself busy with the girls that summer. Mostly it was just the twins and Emily taking the bus with me downtown, once or twice to Bowness Park on a picnic. Emily was old enough to walk. Pauline was moody, the way they are at that age. If she felt like it, she'd help me take her sisters down to the zoo or Prince's Island for a picnic, opposite where the old Eau Claire Lumber Company was. My grandfather worked there before he homesteaded near Olds where the big agricultural college is now. He and my grandmother built the farmhouse with his lumber money. I thought about Roly Faro. His mother's house was on Memorial Drive just opposite the island, one of those two storey ones with a balcony overlooking the river. As we walked around Prince's Island after the twins went swimming I could see its bright blue porch and the eggshell window frames.

Roly and I had been in school plays together. I was usually the director as well as playing one of the parts. We did several plays, but the one I remember was *Romeo and Juliet*. I'd known Roly since kindergarten and to get to school, I walked past his house everyday. He was also the first boy who ever kissed me—in Grade One, right on the front steps of the school in front of the teacher. She laughed when I said, "We're kissing cousins."

I never really thought of him as a boyfriend—he

was just always around. In high school we were in the drama club together, and we'd go to his house to practice after school. His mother was a dietician at the hospital and his father was a professional traveller, a salesman. Sometimes, I'd stay for supper. Roly's mother brought supper home with her and she poured wine with dinner like we were grown-up. She was the only educated woman I knew other than my teachers.

We rehearsed and rehearsed, but nothing prepared me for everything that happened on opening night. I'd go out onto the balcony of his house, imagining it overlooking Capulet's Garden. We were so earnest and young.

"O Romeo, Romeo! wherefore art thou? Deny thy father and refuse thy name; Or if thou wilt not, be but sworn my love, And I'll no longer be a Capulet."

We'd cut through his mother's bedroom to get to that balcony. I loved her bed with its fluffy duvet, and the vanity with the silver toiletry set, the brushes and combs. Sitting on the stool, I'd brush my hair with his mother's silver brush before going to my Romeo on the balcony. I was always careful to clean my long hair from the brush before setting it back just so.

One day after rehearsal, Roly led me by the hand to his parents' bedroom. His mother had cut flowers everywhere in the house and the bedroom had a canopy bed with a big high mattress that made me think of the Princess and the Pea. I couldn't read that story to my kids without thinking of that bed. We'd both undressed, turning away shyly, although I could see him in the vanity mirror, his body soft and hairless. We'd kissed for a long time. His lips passed along my neck and floated over my eyelids, my earlobes. His tongue flitted down my neck and between my breasts. Then he said, "I take thee at thy word: Call me but love, and I'll be new baptiz'd." How could I resist?

As he took a safe from his pocket and unwrapped it, it shot down into the bed somewhere between the big feather comforter and the sheets. Frantic, we tore apart the bed covers and sheets. Finally we found the safe in the folds of my dress and he climbed back into bed, laughing. He was tender at first.

"If thou think'st I'm won too quickly, I'll frown," I teased him, then he furiously gripped my shoulders and at the moment of pleasure for both of us, the mattress dropped to the floor—the slats had fallen out. Roly had to go the Eau Claire Lumber Company to get new ones before his mother got home. Poor Roly. I never forgot the look on his face as the two of us went through the bed frame to the floor. Everything with Roly was like that. He was a clown and contrary—what was sad to me made him smile and what was, to me, a happy time, pained him terribly.

When the play finally opened to a large crowd, including Roly's parents and my mom, he hammed his Romeo and turned it into a comedy. All I remember is the rows of laughing faces. When I swooned, "O Romeo, Romeo! wherefore art thou?" Roly glanced at the audience, pulled out a pair of sunglasses, and, in an Edward G. Robinson voice replied, "Over here, doll." He ad-libbed all through the play and I played it straight, like Gracie Allen, but I was in tears afterwards. This was to be my showcase and Roly had turned it into a joke.

I thought of what Lowell did to Roly. I could well imagine Lowell breaking Roly's jaw. I'm sure I hadn't told Lowell the story of the play, not knowing how he'd take it. Roly and Lowell were as far apart as two men could get, on the surface. Except for the passion, that is. But Lowell seldom made me laugh, and he never said my name when he talked to me, as Roly had. I liked both those things about Roly. Running into him again had reminded me of what I missed. Maybe it was the baby coming and my own moods that made me confused, but one day I told Mom about seeing Roly. She was dismissive.

"That was then, this is now. Oh, you're a dreamer, Clare."

She was right—she always was. I was a brooder too, and I wondered what would become of us. Lowell and me. My daughter, the wild one, and our son.

"But Mom, I dream grandly," I said, rolling a Gaelic *r* like her mother did. "Isn't that love too?"

She gave me an exasperated look, and then bought each of the girls Love Hearts at the candy counter before she went back to work. She took Lowell's side sometimes. *Clare, if you were a little more practical,* she'd tell me, when I was younger. *Then what,* I'd ask her. Since Dad left, she's dated plain men. Men who didn't dance or play cards, who drank weak rye and ginger ale.

I'd always liked Mom's oldest brother, Jack, because I knew he was a brooder and a dreamer too—not just a doer, I reminded her. *Let me count the ways.*

And maybe that was Lowell and me. The doer and the dreamer. I wanted my kids to be both. To be one without the other was to be lost. I trusted Jack and Shelagh with Will, although it seemed to some people that I was punishing him by sending him up there.

Trout

Trout cupped the wind out the Greyhound's open window in the palm of his hand. In the front of the bus sat a rambunctious group of girls going to camp at Sylvan Lake. The driver joked with them as he shifted gears on the long climb out of the city through the quicksand flats of Nose Creek, a green slash below the palomino shoulders of Nose Hill.

At the back of the bus sat the smokers: a native man who rolled his own and shared his seat with a duffle bag; and a dark-haired girl, a beatnik, in a black leather jacket and turtleneck. A young family, farm-hands in work clothes, sat with their three boys and a girl. The eldest son took the aisle seat opposite Trout, and regularly smacked his sister, who tried to duck his blows. Their parents seemed too tired to care. Out on the highway, Trout closed the window as the bus speeded towards Red Deer, where his mother had told him he'd have to change buses, and catch the local to Rocky Mountain House.

Up on the ridge, Highway 2 North straightened and young crops of mustard and wheat covered the fields, which were a yellow blur through the windows as the silver dayliner streaked past to Edmonton. One of Kenny's uncles was a conductor on the dayliner. Trout hadn't heard from Kenny since he'd gone to the Don Bosco Home for Boys, but Trout was glad Kenny had spoken up in front of the police. His mother said that if Kenny behaved, he'd be back home next year. Trout couldn't ever see Kenny behaving.

It was his first trip anywhere by himself, and he leafed quickly through the *Classics Illustrated* comics—one on *The Trojan Horse* and another on the *Fall of Rome*—but the rush of the scenery, and the wide flat land they rolled into, and the open sky, mesmerized him. He didn't miss Kenny now, or his parents, but already he missed the twins and Emily. And there'd be a new baby to come home to. Pauline, smart-alecky and bossy, was hard to miss anymore. The speed of the bus, the new scenery, and the adventure of travelling were almost more than Trout could bear, although he had no idea into what he was going. He'd met his great-uncle and great-aunt once on a camping trip, years ago. They'd had a station wagon full of St. Bernards. They were both dressed in plaid bush jackets and his uncle also wore a plaid hat. Someone was to meet him in Rocky, his mother had said, and they would take him on to his uncle's place.

Trout hadn't heard from his grandmother Dot since his father had told her about the incident with the police. Trout knew she was angry. There were times she didn't speak to him or his father for weeks. Then she'd phone or show up. Unlike his mother's mother, Ruby, who called every day, and chatted with him or his sisters before his mom got on the line. Trout's father said not to worry, when Dot was with one of her boyfriends, she disappeared for a while, which only made him feel worse.

"Mom's Mom," his dad shrugged. Trout tried not to think about her, or about Kenny in the home for boys, focusing instead on heading towards some place new, where no one knew him. After the break-in, he'd been taunted at school, but most of the kids seemed afraid of him now.

He thought about all the books he'd read, like *Tom Swift*, and the *Hardy Boys*. He too was going on an adventure. Kenny would be jealous if he knew. Trout was going to the land of bears and cougars, Indians and explorers, forest fires and snow slides.

Just before 11 a.m., the bus pulled into the Red Deer terminal. Trout ate his lunch at a bench on the platform, and guarded his suitcase and knapsack with his legs. A noisy group of girls waited to board the local that stopped in all the little towns, including Rocky Mountain House, Condor, and Eckville, before going on to Edmonton. He'd marked the route in red coloured pencil on the Alberta Motor Association map his dad gave him.

When the Greyhound local boarded for Rocky Mountain House, the native man got on after Trout and the girls, and went to the back with his bag. This bus was nearly empty, but as they headed towards Sylvan Lake, people flagged the driver down. He stopped to let them board the bus, and then again to let them out in the next town, or further up the road. Trout sat up front beside the driver now, and faced out the front window. Even his dad had never been to Rocky—he'd called this the milk run when he saw it on the map.

As the driver stomped the air brakes and opened the front door at the level crossings, then geared back up to speed, Trout looked cautiously each way and craned his neck, just to be sure that the road was clear.

At Sylvan Lake, the girls got off the bus and the driver unloaded their luggage outside the hotel across from the beach. A wide strip of sand lined with cottonwood trees ran along the highway and Trout watched the swimmers dive from the end of the pier into the green waves.

Back out on Highway 11, the bus climbed steadily. The land was forested now, with patches of standing water and muskeg full of spruce whose trunks were grey down to the white waterlines. As the driver turned off to Condor, a truck hauling logs that hung almost down to the road, with a red flag spiked on the longest log, passed them on its way to Rocky Mountain House. The bus stopped in front of a store with a Greyhound schedule posted in the window. An older lady climbed the narrow steps with a cane.

"This seat taken?" she said, rather loudly. She didn't have any luggage, only a large purse. Trout shook his head and moved his knapsack.

"You're just like me, like to see where you're going," she said sharply, and smiled at him. "Where are you going today?"

"Rocky Mountain House."

"I'm visiting my daughter in Rocky. You got family there too?" Trout nodded shyly. She looked right in his ears at his hearing aids. Trout pretended to look the other way and turned red.

"Don't wear mine. Can't stand the noise. How are yours?"

"Fine," he lied. He wished she would just shut her yap, as his dad said sometimes. He was sure the whole bus could hear.

"Well, good for you. Drives my husband crazy. *Mil, turn the radio down, you're scaring the dogs*, he says. But he snores and I sleep like a baby. There's a silver lining in every cloud, don't you think?"

The bus driver grinned.

Trout liked old woman. She was like his grandmother Dot, a little dotty and a nosey parker.

"Someone meeting you in Rocky? You need a ride? My daughter could drive you."

"I'm going on past Nordegg."

"Really, that's a ways out. My brother was a miner there in the forties. Used to be a railway line. During the war they kept the Germans in a camp near there. It's a ghost town." She nodded her head knowingly. "They keep men from the prison there now." She didn't listen much, like his grandmother, but Trout understood. If she was talking, then at least she knew what was going on. There were advantages to being a talker.

She talked and he nodded until they were just outside Rocky Mountain House, when the native man came up to the driver. The big bus crunched to a stop on the gravel shoulder. After the man shouldered his duffle bag and started down a gravel road with no houses on it, Mildred looked at Trout, as if she expected him to say something, but he pretended to be fascinated by something out the window. She tilted her head at the native man and gave a little sniff. It was the same look his grandmother had when she thought people were rough, but Trout didn't say anything. One of his mom's uncles had married a native woman in Edmonton. Auntie Tina was a full-blood-ed Cree and sometimes when the aunts and uncles all went camping, she came too. She hated fishing though, and never wore buckskin. Trout was disappointed, but he thought Tina was beautiful. She wore expensive perfume and was a secretary for the government in Edmonton.

"Here's Rocky," Mildred piped up, before the green and white government highway sign announced it. The bus went by the forestry compound on the outskirts of town. A helicopter waited on a pad alongside red and yellow barrels of aviation fuel.

As the bus turned off the main street into an alley behind a store, Trout saw the trucks angle-parked on the gravel and mud. Smoke rose from the sawmill burner, which looked like a giant teepee behind the piles of logs by the river. The rough dry smell of gravel dust, burning bark from the sawmill and the raw muddy musk of the Saskatchewan River filled his eyes and nose as he stepped down from the bus.

In the small Greyhound station, Trout waited in the chair by the door and read the bus schedule:

Twice Weekly Service To
Calgary, Red Deer and Edmonton.
11:00 a.m. Southbound.
15:00 p.m. Northbound.

Trout watched through the station window as Mildred and her daughter drove away, and the Greyhound pulled back up the alley towards the highway. Trout was alone in the bus station now. He knew no

167

one here, and he worried that his ride hadn't shown up, when a lanky man with a weathered face opened the outside door of the station.

"And you might be Jack's nephew?" He took Trout's suitcase and knapsack and walked out into the parking lot. "Let's put these in here," he said, lifting Trout's things onto the front seat of a green Alberta Forest Service pickup with a winch on the front bumper.

"I'm Frank Jones, by the way. Jack says you're called Trout." He put his hand on Trout's shoulder and steered him down the street. "That's a good name to have around here." He looked more like a cowboy than a forest ranger, with his Western boots and big tanned hands. He seemed about Trout dad's age.

"You hungry?"

Trout never said no to that question.

The coffee shop window faced the street, with rows of muddy trucks and jeeps angle-parked out front. The air was hazy with cigarette smoke and everyone wore cowboy hats or lumberman's caps, even the natives with their braids over their shoulders. A few wore the peaked caps of the forest service or the Mounties. Trout ordered a cheeseburger and Coke.

"We got a drive ahead of us. We'll pick up some supplies for your Aunt Shelagh and go by the forestry office. How's the burger?" Under the forest service cap, Frank Jones was bald and his arms were dark with the tan of someone who worked outdoors.

Frank stopped the truck at the Hudson's Bay store. Unlike the department store in downtown Calgary, this one was full of bush clothing, snowshoes and guns. Next, Frank stopped at the forestry compound and gassed up the truck. Trout helped load bundles of fire hazard signs, which displayed the forest service mascot, Bertie the Beaver, holding a shovel like Smokey the Bear. The helicopter waited on the pad nearby and Trout wandered over to look while Frank chatted with someone in the office.

"Let's go. We'll try calling your aunt once we get past Nordegg. Radio's out of range till then."

Trout stared at the helicopter.

"Ever flown in one?" Frank asked, as they pulled onto the David Thompson Highway past the old fur-trading fort. No one Trout knew had ever been in a helicopter. He shook his head.

"Well, maybe your Uncle Jack can get you a ride, when the 'copter comes to service the lookout. They're not supposed to. Just don't let me hear about it, I'm his boss." Trout looked at him. Frank laughed.

"As much as anybody is Jack Locke's boss." Frank tipped his head. "He sure knows when to call a spade a shovel." Trout grinned back.

Once they crossed the Saskatchewan River, muddy and swollen high up its banks, the air turned colder and dense patches of scrub bush gave way to boreal forest. In the west, Trout could see the snow-packed mountaintops range through the windshield of the truck.

"Upper Saskatchewan Ranger Station's ninety miles that way. Where we're going." Frank pointed left. "Howse Pass's over there. Take us about an hour and a half. We'll stop in Nordegg to meet Beth, and I'll take you over the Bighorn." Trout craned to hear the soft-spoken man over the whine of the tires and the pounding of gravel in the wheelwells.

The two-way radio crackled, then a woman's voice came on and Frank turned the volume up.

"X74359 to Clearwater Car Five. Do you read me?"

"Clearwater Five, copy." Frank grabbed the mike hanging above the big Motorola radio on the transmission hump. "We're on our way. Should be there within the hour. Over."

"Copy. I'll relay Shelagh, you got him."

"Copy. See you soon."

"X74359 over and out."

"Clearwater Five out." Frank hung the mike on the dash. "My wife, Beth."

Another voice called X74359.

"That's Red Wilson at the Cline River lookout in the backyard of the Upper Saskatchewan. You'll get to know all these guys by their call signs. He'll be able to see us coming once we cross the Bighorn."

Trout drank it all in and memorized everything Frank Jones told him. He patted his conch shell in his knapsack between his knees. He wanted it on the seat beside him so it too could listen.

As they headed west into the Clearwater Forest, the pavement ended at Ram River crossing. Gravel and boulders bucked under the truck, and banged in the fenders now, but Frank Jones didn't slow down. Adventure was now as close as the truck Trout was riding in and as large as the front ranges of the Rocky Mountains that loomed in the near distance. Trout pretended he was driving, and holding the mike one-handed on the wheel, and downshifting into the turns as they sped towards Nordegg. As Frank Jones's legs pumped the clutch, Trout pressed his own feet on the floorboards.

The ghost town of Nordegg nuzzled the base of a mountain. Frank said there were schools and a hospital, churches and stores, all with nobody in them. Ghost town: Trout imagined classrooms of ghost children and ghost clerks bagging ghost groceries, and churches full of ghost choirs, an invisible town full of Caspers in headless tee-shirts and shorts, housedresses and suits moving without arms or legs in them. Trout looked at the locked gate and guardhouse as they passed.

The Clearwater Ranger Station consisted of a group of houses, all painted Forest Service white and green. There was a barn, and a large garage with green forestry trucks parked out side. A dozen horses grazed in a corral behind the barn, and a fuel dump of red and yellow oil drums marked the end of the airstrip. As Trout and Frank unloaded the fire hazard signs, a deeply-tanned blonde woman in jeans and a girl about thirteen, blonde too, but paler than her mother, came out to see them.

"We'll need these. Fire season's coming. Beth, Heather, meet Trout." Frank clapped his hand on the boy's shoulder. "My wife. My daughter. You need to use the men's room? No? Then we better get you back on the road."

Beth shook his hand while Trout and Heather looked each other over. She was pretty and her hair was wispy in the wind.

"Your name's not really Trout?"

"It's a nickname my uncle gave me." Trout blushed. "Name's really Will."

"You can come for a visit some time. Right now, Shelagh will have supper waiting. I'll radio her." Beth nodded. "Nice to meet you."

"See you again there, Will," Heather called out, before the truck turned on the gravel.

On his map, Trout watched the David Thompson highway drop from a solid dark line outside Rocky to a dotted line past Nordegg and then to a hairline without bridges, marked with only campgrounds and waterfalls, past the Bighorn Reserve. There was no road, only a seasonal logging trail, and the small box indicating a ranger station and on the mountain opposite it, a fire lookout tower. As they passed the locked gate to Nordegg again on their way out, Frank turned to Trout.

"Get your Uncle Jack to take you in there some day. In 1941 the mine blew, killed twenty-nine men. My dad's brother was almost one of them. Another guy took his shift so he could go to a wedding."

Frank looked out the window.

"Still goods on the shelves in the stores. Brazeau Collieries shut down in the fifties and people just walked away. Funeral parlour still had coffins on display. Nobody there now but the prisoners from the jail."

Outside Nordegg, they passed the Bighorn Indian Reserve and not long after, as construction barricades narrowed the road, Frank swung the truck around them and geared down. Recent rain had left the road rutted and soft. Up ahead, yellow earthscrapers dropped loads and graders levelled the road as bulldozers lumbered up the cutbanks and pushed gravel along the grade. Frank picked his way among them and waved to the flagman.

After the construction zone, the forest closed in again. The road narrowed to a one-lane dirt track and the truck slowed to ford a creek, then jumped the bank on the other side before picking up speed again. The ride was hushed now, with soft earth under the tires. Out of range of Rocky, the radio fell silent. Passing the log shelters of a campground, Frank slowed down again.

"You see 'em?"

In the outside mirror, Trout watched a mother bear and her cub amble away from some trashcans.

"She knows it's camping season." Frank sped up again. "Camp's empty. Have to keep an eye on her, though. People shouldn't feed 'em." He grimaced.

Coming from the dry prairies, Trout couldn't believe all the water everywhere, in ponds and the backwashes of the river. A beaver dam blocked a tributary of the Bighorn River and trees without trunks rose magically out of the watery land. Even the dry patches were damp and green, as though they'd been flooded recently. Out along the river flats before the main channel, Trout could see the muskeg spotted with scrub bush and thin aspens. A small herd of deer darted away at the sound of the truck. Frank cranked the wheel, pulled off the road and waited. Moments later, a logging truck roared by on its way to the Edwards Lumber Company in Rocky.

As the truck rolled out of the forest and onto a wide plain, Trout could see the open sky rimmed by mountains, some with snow well down the slopes.

"Kootenay Plains," Frank announced. "We're here. Where the Kootenay came over the mountains to trade with the Plains Cree." An orange windsock lifted lightly from a pole at the end of a dry grassy landing strip. A steel span bridge marked the final curve and a sign said: Cline River. If the forest they'd come out of had been green and damp, Kootenay Plains was a desert, pale and dusty.

"Moses Flats. Your uncle named it after one of the Stoney chiefs who had a camp here. Jack was our first ranger here. Opened up this district for us in the fifties. Named nearly half of everything around here. Says it helps him remember where he is," Frank chuckled. It was hotter and drier out on the flats, with the late day sun beating down on the dusty road.

Along the dry upper bank of the Saskatchewan River, there was a barn, and a pasture fenced in barbed wire. Surrounded by a varnished log fence, the Upper Saskatchewan Ranger station had a garden plot and a greenhouse in front. Laid in orderly rows facing into the middle like the fort at the Stampede, the outbuildings backed onto the river and the lookout mountain behind it. With half dozen horses in the nearby pasture, it looked like the cavalry post of an army, Trout thought. In the sideyard, a bunkhouse and radio hut stood beside a tall antenna and a generator. A large garage and propane tank also stood across from the ranger's house, with a flag pole and the logo of the forest service, AFS, spelled out in flowers on a well-kept green lawn.

The front doors of the buildings all opened into the yard. Wood smoke wafted from the chimney of the main house. Frank swung the truck into the yard and backed up to the garage. Trout saw the pens, with a dog sled under a tarp. A row of sleepy dogs slowly rose to greet them, as if puzzled by the visitors. The deep slow woofs of the St. Bernards emerged first, as they shook the mesh fence with their big mitts. Then the short whelps of the Samoyeds started from a thin white mother and her mate, with a recent litter of bent-eared puppies who followed her myopically and bumped over each other. They clustered like cottonballs around her legs as they leapt for her nipples.

"Give me a hand with these signs. I'll get the firehoses," Frank said, as he shut off the truck. The door to the house opened and a dark-haired woman with sinewy arms came striding towards them.

"Quiet!" she shrieked at the dogs, and most of them reluctantly came down off the fence. "Down, Junior. Down, boy!" A broad-shouldered St. Bernard in a pen by himself let out one more slow woof, before hanging his big head, as she faced him down.

"Got your mail, Shelagh. Where do you want the supplies?"

"Thanks, Frank. I'll take the mail. We can leave the supplies for Jack in the garage. So you're Jack's nephew." She held out her hand and squinted at Trout through the bottom of her glasses. His great-aunt was tiny, but her grip was as strong as his father's.

175

His mother said Aunt Shelagh had been a nurse in London during the war, and was a war bride. His aunt said garaw-age, not grage. Her face and arms were freckled and there were strands of white in her hair. Together, the three of them quickly unloaded the truck. His aunt helped Frank haul in the heavy canvas firehoses.

"Stay for supper, Frank?"

"I should get back. Tell Jack I'll radio him about the trail crew. There're the signs he wanted, and the hoses. Oh, we saw a sow and her cub in Saddle Creek Campground. No campers yet."

"He knows about her, but I'll tell him you mentioned it, Frank."

After Frank Jones's truck roared back over the loose boards of the Cline River Bridge, leaving a long wall of dust hanging in its wake, Shelagh showed Trout his cinderblock-lined room in the basement of the ranger station. The floors were concrete. A battery radio and flashlight, dozens of canned goods, tinned hams and corned beef, and a first aid kit lay on the shelves. A bunkbed and small table filled the rest of the small room. On the bed, his aunt laid two towels and a face cloth.

"Come and get washed for supper after you unpack. Jack's on his way." His aunt went upstairs, and Trout could smell roast beef cooking. He folded his jacket and looked at the bed. He'd take the top bunk. He laid the conch, his new fountain pen and the journal his mother had given him neatly on the desk like he'd seen in pictures of famous people's houses.

On the wall was a poster with instructions on what to do during an air raid. It showed a mushroom cloud, and debris raining down on a cartoon family hiding in their house under a staircase. Trout's new room was a fall-out shelter.

Outside the shelter, the rest of the basement looked like the backroom of Waterfield's General Store, with shelves and shelves of large jars, cans, packages of instant milk and whole boxes of chocolate bars.

"Wash up in there," his aunt said, when he came upstairs. She pointed with an oven mitt and slammed pans of roast beef and Yorkshire pudding onto the woodstove.

In the office next to the kitchen, Trout could hear the steady crackle of radio static. Guns and maps were mounted on the wall. On his way back from the bathroom he looked in the living room at the walls lined with animal skins: cougar, wolverine, bear, and, on the floor, some he didn't recognize. A large glass case held dozens of books, some with gilt lettering and hard covers. Another wall was covered with family and dog pictures and a china cabinet held trophies and bright show ribbons for the dogs.

"Here's your uncle," Shelagh called from the kitchen. Trout stepped into the back just in time to see a man on horseback in forest-service khakis and a policeman's peaked cap come into the yard at a trot. A Winchester rifle was in the saddle scabbard. He was followed by a horse with packboxes roped to the packsaddle, and a tent roll on top. Behind him the mountains loomed, some higher than the clouds, and most had snowcaps, except for the near peak with the fire lookout, whose windows glinted in the late sun. The dogs barked again, but this time they bounced on the fence at the sight of Jack and the horses.

"Hey, Trout," said the gruff man, as he dismounted and held out a strong scrawny hand. His Uncle Jack had named him, he knew, a long time ago. He was humbled as he reached for his uncle's hand.

"Quiet," Jack snarled at the dogs, slapping the rein on his pant leg, but he was grinning. On horseback, he'd seemed huge. Standing on the ground beside his horse, he was small and bent, his hair grey, his face baked and wrinkled like the mud flats in the river. He beamed at his young nephew. In each of his ears Trout saw the plastic tubing of ear moulds, and the huge temples of hearing aids in the stems of his uncle's eyeglasses. They were just like Trout's own, only black. No one had ever mentioned to him that Jack too, wore hearing aids. But it didn't matter, for now.

"Open the gate for me, will ya." His uncle swung the packbox down into the garage before throwing the saddles and saddleblankets onto the corral fence. Trout lifted the log gate, and they turned the horses into the pasture.

"We'll get those after supper. You hungry?" Trout nodded, awe-struck. His uncle handed him the radio-telephone.

"Welcome to the Upper Saskatchewan." Jack put his arm around Trout. The holster of his revolver bumped Trout's arm. They walked towards the house, watched by the dogs, and by the mountains around them.

Clare

I was lonely all that summer, even as the baby grew in me and I became aware of its small movements as it turned like a swimmer. I wondered how I could be so lonely while carrying someone inside me. But my husband was away, and now my son was too. Pauline spent several nights a week at her girlfriend's—I didn't stop her. Emily would come into bed with me; we'd nap in the afternoon, my neck sticky with her sweet kisses as she curled against my back. The twins played in the playhouse Lowell built them out of a chicken coop he'd got somewhere. Their voices echoed in the background of my sleep; I knew I'd have to run to the door if they left the yard. But I needed the rest as the baby grew inside me.

On cooler days, I'd bake and the twins "helped"—flour all over the counters and floors. They were happy being with me. Many of the women in our neighbourhood went out to work now that their kids were older, except for a few, like me, with little ones at home. I'd see those women dressed up, smoking at the bus stop, going to work in the stores downtown—few of us drove in those days, even if we'd had cars. I was older than the other mothers in the neighbourhood. I'd read late at night, borrowing from the Bookmobile parked across from the I.G.A once a week. It was a summer without sleep or conversation, when I'd wake at midnight with the baby bumping in me. Some nights I'd watch the sun start to come up just after five. Mom told me that when she was a girl and the fish were running, her grandfather stayed out all night on the boat, off Orkney. It was so far north that the sun went down at eleven and rose again at three. That summer was like that.

But I couldn't forget Roly. Lowell's phone calls were curt; he called from a payphone outside the trailers at the gas plant, and there was always someone in line behind him. Or sometimes he'd call me from a bar and I could hear the crowd in the background. I wondered sometimes if he was lonely—I know I was. He promised to be home for the Labour Day weekend. One night, I looked up Roly's number—there were only two Faros in the phonebook. He lived in Bowness. The other number was his mother's. I don't know whatever possessed me, but I dialled his number. His wife answered.

"Hello, hello? Who is this?" she said. I hung up. She sounded assured and confident, like his mother, an educated woman.

After Roly's stunt in *Romeo and Juliet*, I'd stopped seeing him. People thought we had planned it as a gag. I knew his mother knew the truth. She left angrily, without a word, and Roly told me she'd been furious when he got home.

Now, after all these years, I thought he'd been right. We all overacted and our drama and English teacher, Mrs. Siegel, directed us in a sappy production. Her huge loose body shook as she acted out the parts, her low-cut dresses showing too much as she leaned over the stage. Sometimes in class the older boys threw pencil erasers at her cleavage trying to score a basket. Her husband was a puff of a man with a waxed moustache who waited for her after school on Friday. She was an unlikely director for *Romeo and Juliet*, we all thought.

One day, after I had argued with her over a poem, she told me, "Clare, you are not to speak out again in class."

Roly shot me a look that day and I think that the gag was his revenge on her. I had mine the day she came into class and announced, "It seems as though we have a prize winner here." She looked at me and said, "Clare Dunlop has gotten the highest marks in the province on the departmental examinations for language and literature. Congratulations, Clare." She put her hands together. "Class?"

The class applauded, all except for the older boys who tossed erasers, rolled their eyes and hooted. She took me aside after class. "Don't throw it all away, Clare."

And after the play, I thought I had thrown it all away thanks to Roly. I ran home when he tried to talk to me. I ignored him, but it wasn't about the play, it was about trust, I'd thought then. But I kept that book of poetry Roly gave me after we'd made love in his mother's bed. It was an expensive gift and I knew his mother must have given him the money. It had a leather cover and parchment pages. It was to be the beginning of something, not the end of it. For years, I hid the book from Lowell. Thank God he hadn't read the inscription when he found it in the laundry basket—ther's no telling what he might have done. He was so fiercely jealous, though he had no reason to be.

None of my girls were readers, although Emily eventually took after her brother. After Auntie died, he cherished the book she'd given him, as I had as a girl. Books were my trips to the forbidden world. Someday I'd explain the inscription to my son, but I knew my secret was safe with him, for now. I knew his father would have torn it to shreds—not in front of me, of course. It would have just disappeared. But my son was a keeper of secrets; even then, he saw everything. I was glad he wasn't here now to watch me. He'd started to ask questions I couldn't answer, not truthfully, anyway. But I wanted him to know about me and Roly. I wanted to tell someone.

I was glad Roly's wife answered the phone that day. If he had picked it up, I don't know what I would have said. When I saw him that day in Kensington, there was an awkwardness between us at first, and no words. Then a rush of them as the embarrassment, that first shyness slipped away, giving way to relief. And later, the laughter. And the fierceness that came with knowing that not a thing had changed, even though everything had changed. Knowing that if I let myself, I could pick up where we'd left off, throwing everything else aside. I knew exactly where this could go, and mustn't.

Towards the end of July, I got a letter postmarked Rocky Mountain House from my Aunt Shelagh. She and Jack enjoyed Will's company—he was a good boy, she said. There was nothing to tempt him there, I thought. I felt guilty about sending him away, but I didn't know what to do with him any more. He'd lose his temper with me. Pauline and he were always fighting. I caught her baiting him, trying to make him fight.

"Deafie," she called him, when I wasn't looking, and I'd slapped her and put her in her room, but that made things worse. "Everybody stares at him, Mom, and he whistles through his nose when he breathes. He's so weird. He farts out loud. It's so gross." Both of them were mad at me. I wondered what else she'd heard from the kids at school.

Shelagh said she wanted to ask me first, but she and Jack would like to have Will stay with them for a year. She'd taught her step-kids, from Jack's first marriage, through correspondence lessons, and three of them had gone on to university. No one talked about the youngest.

We all knew the story. He'd let a prize colt get out when Jack and Shelagh went to town. They came home to find a gun missing and the barn door wide open. The son lay by the drowned colt, the rifle beside his head. The note he'd left on the kitchen table said he was afraid of his father's wrath. I wondered about Jack's temper. When I called Mom, she said he'd changed—that was a long time ago, she said, and I believed her. The death of his son changed him. It all happened before my son was even born.

I wrote Shelagh the next day and told her to invite Will to stay. I'd never been up to the ranger station, but Mom and all the uncles had. There was so much there that they could do for Will. I had the baby to think about and the girls—Pauline especially.

The next time Lowell called, I told him about Shelagh's offer. He was silent, like he thought we'd failed Will. I knew his mother believed that Will's troubles, like everything else, were my fault.

Dot hadn't called since June, sending a card with a gift certificate from Birks for the twins' birthday. They were scared of her, the way she just showed up and swooped through the house. And that's what she did the Saturday Pauline turned twelve.

She arrived with one of her boyfriends, Mr. Jones—I think his name was Arnold—who puffed on a cigar while he waited for her in his convertible with the top down. With her white gloves and her white-brimmed summer hat, she looked like something out of a Doris Day movie. The neighbours all gawked from their yards.

She was attractive, I have to admit, but she usually never stayed even if I offered her a cup of coffee and a sandwich. She'd sweep through with her white gloves, which matched the white polka dots on her blue dress, and she'd check the coffee table for dust, saying nothing, just looking at her white cotton-clad fingertips. I was baking a birthday cake—my hair was in my eyes and the twins were in the yard, staring at the convertible.

"Call him Grandpa Jones," Dot had told the girls, but they just blushed at this man who came three times a year as her chauffeur. I asked him in anyway. You could tell he wanted me to.

She'd gotten Pauline a cashmere sweater. No one in Ogden wore one any more than they wore pearls to the Legion. *She means well*, Lowell always said. Mr. Jones was nice to the girls though—he told us he had three of his own. He and Lowell's mother sat in the living room waiting for coffee, while Pauline opened her grandmother's gift in front of the glass case Dot had given my son for his seashells. She bossed everybody like the Queen Mother herself, filling our house with all her damn junk. My husband and son both happily took whatever love she offered.

I knew she wanted something that day. She cornered me in the kitchen, offering to help with the coffee, which I'd already poured in mugs. "Where are those nice cups I gave you? No, no, use those," she sniffed.

I wanted to say, yes your Highness. I wished Lowell was here, but he'd just laugh and let her blow through, leaving a trail of hurt in her wake. I grabbed the cups and saucers from the china cabinet. Our house was too small for it, but she'd insisted we take one that had belonged to her mother. It cast a dark shadow over the blonde coffee table and chrome ashtrays we'd bought to match the shiny black-panther lamp with the fiery tongue and matching red shade that my sister gave me. Ricky Ricardo furniture, Emily calls it now.

But when she asked me for her grandson's address, I scalded my wrist filling the fancy cups. If it hadn't been for her boyfriend and the girls, I would have hurled the pot of coffee at her. Instead I gave her the address. They drove away, her silk scarf flying as the convertible sped down our gravel street, the two of them waving. One of my neighbours said, "What a nice young grandmother!"

"You don't know the half of it," I muttered, and waved goodbye.

After the girls ate the birthday cake I'd made, we cleared the chairs from the kitchen, closed the drapes and put Jan and Dean on Pauline's new record player. I'd bought Mack the Knife because I knew Lowell liked it and Bobby Darin was a favourite of mine too. I danced with the girls. Pauline was going out, but I asked her to dance with me.

"Mom. Nobody dances with their mother."

"I used to. Humour me, I've had an awful day." After the music started, she put her head on my shoulder. "I won't ask again, honey. I know you're too old for this."

"It's alright. Don't be mad at her, Mom. Grandma's Grandma." And then she was out the door. She had her father's patience at the damnedest times. When I didn't need it. She wore that cashmere sweater when Lowell took her to visit his mother, though I don't think she was ever the girl Dot wanted her to be.

That night I thought about Roly's mother. Her clothes were as nice as Dot's, but she wore the clothes—they didn't wear her. It was just a costume change to her. She'd had a university education, unlike Lowell's mother. And she had a father.

My mom and I talked about everything, but we never talked about my father. Mom tried to *get on with it*—one of her favourite expressions back then.

I couldn't.

I'd wanted Roly's parents to adopt me and I think now that they would have. It occurred to me more than once that I wanted to break Roly's heart. I was damned if anyone was going to do to me what my dad had done to Mom.

Dad had just gone out one night. Mom waited up, finally falling asleep with the radio on, probably that damned country station she listened to—C.W.B.Y.— Voice of the Cowboy in Country Music Country. She woke up the next morning with an empty pillow next to her and knew she was now on her own, with a daughter to raise.

It was scandalous then, not like now. We were so ashamed. I've thought about that and about how, if I'd been old enough, I'd have tracked him down, marched right down to his boss's office. By the time I thought of it, I was twelve, and he'd already joined the Calgary Highlanders and gone overseas.

After the war, he came back, alright, but not to us. He had a whole new family, Mom said. He started over again like nothing had happened. There didn't appear to be any reason why he left. It was just one of those things men did because they could. I learned to hate him at first because that was what Mom seemed to want, but it didn't stop me from thinking about him and what I might have been if I'd had a dad.

I worried myself to sleep, running my fingers over the soft moon of flesh rising out of my body. I could feel my heartbeat and the murmur from my belly. Emily crawled into bed with me. The three of us in that big bed. I knew then that the baby was a boy, maybe only because I wanted him to be. I thought then that somehow I'd failed Will, and I wanted to give Lowell a healthy son, even if I could give him nothing else. This time would be different.

Trout

For nearly three weeks his fountain pen and journal lay unused on his table in the fall-out shelter that served as his bedroom. Each night Trout tumbled, tired out from work and from the thin mountain air, into his bunk. He woke early to the light in the curtainless windows of the basement, and to the movements of his aunt and uncle above him.

When he came upstairs, the St. Bernards' tails swung happily, fanning out like large brooms. His uncle ordered the dogs to lie under the kitchen table. A pair of wooden baby gates stretched across the dining room doors to keep the dogs out because their tails could sweep a table clear.

After breakfast, his uncle added milk to his bowl and placed it on the floor for one of the dogs. Shelagh poured some in hers, and Trout did the same. Blondie and Dagwood lapped up the milk, bowls held between massive paws, their ropy drool slobbering onto the kitchen floor. To his aunt and uncle this ritual seemed not the least bit out of the ordinary.

Blondie, dog-wife of Dagwood, was pregnant and due to give birth soon. Trout's aunt and uncle fussed over her and made a bed of old towels and blankets for her in the basement, beside the furnace.

Shelagh showed Trout how to split wood from the tall pile of salvaged burn wood, scarred and blackened from forest fires, just outside the ranger station's gate. She brought the double-bitted axe down swiftly, and split each log, often with only two blows, while Trout slivered kindling with a small axe. Together they loaded the wheelbarrow. Shelagh strained under the heavy load, but her arms were as strong as his father's despite her small frame. A chute in the basement wall led to a woodbin and it was now Trout's job to refill the box beside the woodstove in the kitchen. Eventually, it was understood, he would split the wood and bring it to the house himself.

After the woodbox was full, his great-aunt showed Trout how to refill the reused tin lard pails with water for the dogs, and dole them huge portions of dry food in galvanized wash basins, carefully measured with a tobacco can. She mixed in bread scraps and powdered milk for the pregnant bitch, and he made sure each dog got its share.

The grinning Samoyed puppies circled him, and their tiny strong teeth fastened onto his pant legs as he scooped dog dirt—his aunt's name for dog poop. Whenever he bent down, the pups hung from his shirtsleeves, searching for nipples. For such little pups, their teeth were surprisingly sharp and he gingerly tugged them free as their mother watched him with her lip curling in a growl.

After chores Trout helped his uncle in the corral or the garage, loading the truck before setting out on patrol for the day. Together they went off, carrying the lunches Shelagh made—usually, thick slices of home-made bread with meat for his uncle, peanut butter and jam for Trout, all neatly wrapped in waxed paper and stacked in a clean flour sack tied with a large knot. Drinking from a steel thermos full of scalding sugared tea, he and his uncle sat in the truck listening to the banter on the two-way radio.

Most days they mended bridges over the creeks, or put up signs or cleared deadfall. Jack worked the chainsaw, and always sharpened it before he replaced it in its homemade scabbard, while Trout hauled boards or brush. Other days they built log gates on the fire roads to keep tourists off the dry hazardous slopes.

Trout learned the language of his uncle, who spoke gruffly, and who kept the two-way radio turned on loud. Jack cocked his good ear and squinted with his left eye, as if it helped him to hear. He leaned into the radio or conversation to hear, and Trout began to do the same. He memorized the names of the hazards of this dangerous place he had come to: deadfall, snags and widowmakers. He learned to distinguish between the different types of trees, that looked all the same to him at first, and how to roll the needles between his fingers: spruce was three-sided. Pine was round. He learned the names of tools and how to care for them: come-alongs and winches, for bridge work and fence building; adzes and mattocks, for trail blazing and firefighting. Packpumps carried by a man on his back, and canvas hoses, stacked, waiting for fire. The forge and its bellows, an anvil, blacksmith hammers, and stacks of horseshoes beside the Western saddles and ropes, packboxes and the wooden X frames of pack saddles, bridles and halters, curry combs, saddleblankets and small dog-sized yokes and harnesses for the sleds alongside snowshoes and skis.

Seven kinds of hammers he learned, saws, screw-drivers and chisels, pliers traced in red on pegboard and beside them, cutters and wire stretchers, above the rolls of wire and kegs of nails. Jack told him each name once, and he was expected to know it and to re-place each tool on the pegboard where it belonged.

"If we don't have it, we make it," Jack said. Trout spent his time in the garage, studying as though it were a library. He wanted so badly to please his uncle who promised, once he learned, to take him on horse patrol. For now, Trout would have to prove himself.

Towards the end of his third week on the Upper Saskatchewan, when Trout's arms and back were strong enough, his aunt let him split wood and they found another wheelbarrow, which he half-filled. By the end of the month, he split all the day's wood and loaded it himself, new calluses knobby on his hands.

After chores, he wandered past the pasture and barn, exploring the dry bed left when the river re-treated after the June runoff. Flooding had left pud-dles teeming with floating clots of bloodsuckers and leggy waterstriders that scooted across the surface of the water. Tadpoles zigged along the edges and startled frogs jumped as he stepped from one spongy grass island to another on the dry tufts that rose from the riverbed. A misstep meant sinking into the boot-sucking quicksand and mud that reeked of decaying vegetation and swamp gas.

Trout found a larger island. There, he gathered driftwood logs and, with his splitting axe, notched them as he'd seen Jack do, then chinked the gaps with river mud and dried grass. Slowly he built a small cabin on his island in the river, big enough for two squatting. He made a log ladder, lashed with used bindertwine, to climb up to the entryway in the roof made of shakes. He built it with scraps, and without nails, for he knew already, nothing was wasted here on the Upper Saskatchewan. Even food scraps were given to the dogs, and the rest dug into the compost heap. He made a cover for the roof doorway of branches and leftover shakes from a pile near the barn, pulling it over him when it rained, like a hermit crab in a host's shell. His cabin was warm and safe, even when the big packhorses thundered by when Jack turned them out to pasture.

Always, though, he was on an invisible tether back to the ranger station. The riverbed was dry now, but if it rained, the river swelled up to the dog runs on its old bank. And the woods that surrounded the ranger station would easily cover his trail back. Deer and bears, Shelagh warned, would charge if frightened, although for now it appeared the bears kept to the campgrounds.

His aunt devised a system for calling him for lunch, using Jack's old police whistle, but it failed miserably. Safe in his cabin, Trout didn't respond because the whistle's frequency was too high to be heard through his hearing aids. His aunt came looking for him just minutes after he'd returned from the Stoney settlement, which he was not supposed to visit.

Another time, she found him in the pen outside behind the doghouses. When she got back in the house she called Red Wilson, the fire lookout, to thank him. The tower was directly across the river and while the dog pens and Trout's small cabin were invisible from the ranger station, the lookout saw everything he and everyone else in the Upper Saskatchewan River valley did. But this Red Wilson wasn't a squealer about everything, for Shelagh mentioned nothing about Will going to the Stoney cabins.

Comforted by the thought that Red Wilson, like God, saw everything, Trout realized he'd better face away from the lookout next time he peed behind the dog pens. He always looked over his shoulder now, when he wandered past the end of the fence.

He'd been told never to go beyond the confines of the fences, but one day he slipped away to the next pasture. His heart pounded, for he'd walked a long way. Jack was on horse patrol and Shelagh was busy with her garden. Eventually, he came upon small domed frames of aspen clustered in an open field along the fence.

At first he thought them part of the pasture until he saw that there were several frames, like skeletons of something, all carefully bent into shape and low enough for him to duck into. He pushed further into the area well beyond the fence and found cabins, windowless, with their doors hanging off the hinges, grey and weathered, smelling of decay and dust. In front of one of the cabins' porches lay a chipped white kettle, on its side, and a fry pan beside it, as if it had been dropped in a hurry. It was a place of sorrow, Trout felt, but he had no idea why. Later that summer, when he and his uncle stretched the wires on the fence around the old settlement, Jack told him how the Stoneys had abandoned the place.

"Forestry got the orders to force them back on the reserve. Shoot their horses if we had to." His uncle was grim. Trout knew already, Jack was Forestry here, the only ranger within fifty miles.

His uncle told him that the bent frames were covered with skins or branches for sweatlodges.

"I've been in 'em," Jack said. "You fill 'em with heated stones. How the Stoneys got their name. Cooked their food with stones. "Trout looked at his uncle. There was more to Jack than the uniform.

"They burn sweetgrass to purify the soul." There were sweat circles under his arms from stretching fence wire, and he grunted with exertion as he talked.

"I'm not religious," his uncle said. "But there's something to it."

Jack drove along the fence checking for breaks. At the end of Moses Flats, they reached an aspen grove beyond the airstrip where a new peeled log fence surrounded a dusty patch of tall grass. Weathered planks stuck out of the ground among a few wooden crosses with stones outlining the graves. The log fence was freshly stained, like the ones around the ranger station, and the notches were his uncle's work. Some of the crosses were small,

"Babies," his uncle shook his head. "This is a sacred place."

That night at supper Shelagh turned to Jack. "I think your nephew has something to show you," she said.

Trout blushed. He was in trouble. Shelagh hadn't said anything about his cabin. But somehow she knew.

After supper, the three of them ducked under the fence and followed the horse path to his cabin. Trout felt his neck collared in shame. He hadn't asked if he could build the cabin. When they reached it, his uncle walked around it, inspecting the ladder and the roof, and squatted to look at the mud and grass chinking.

"Built ya a wee cabin, did ya?"

"It's all scrap," Trout stammered in defence.

"No, no, you did well," Jack said, nodding to his nephew and smiling at Shelagh.

"It's a sturdy one," she assured him.

More than anything Trout wanted to be one of them here on Kootenay Plains. He did not want to fail his uncle.

Back in the house, Jack opened his desk and showed Trout a worn booklet written in Cree. He read parts aloud in the high singing language, translating into English a passage that Trout recognized as the 23rd psalm, *The Lord is My Shepherd*.

"I found it in one of the cabins, Trout. Belonged to Father McDougall from the Morley reserve. The Stoneys left it behind when they broke camp. They asked me to keep it for them."

Trout had studied how the missionaries wandered among the tribes of the mountains and plains, and knew the booklet was old. He held it gently, looking at the long-ago words of Father McDougall's, written in a strange script he couldn't read.

Jack poured a tumbler of rye while Trout and Shelagh drank tea. She fussed with the kettle and cut into a pan of chocolate cake with white mint icing.

"The mint's from our garden," she said proudly,

setting a piece of cake down in front of him. "Have more. There's lots."

He was included in the *our*—he heard that in his aunt's voice.

When Trout said good night, his uncle was still at the table reading, the bottle of rye by his side, while his aunt wrote letters.

"God damn it, Shelagh," he heard as he went to bed, and then something he couldn't make out. Jack's boots pounded across the kitchen into the living room. Trout listened at the bottom of the stairs. The boots thumped down the backstairs and the screen door slammed on its hinges.

Trout saw his uncle's boots marching past the open window of his basement room, and then he heard the sound of bagpipes. He stood on a chair and watched.

Jack paced the yard and pumped the plaid bag with his elbow, while the dogs stood in a mute line at the front of their pens. Their tails wagged half-expectantly as Jack's fingers drummed the chanter. The tassels on the ivory-tipped pipes skirled when he turned hard on his heel, and as daylight faded behind him, the sounds of the bagpipes rose. His uncle, who rarely spoke of the old country, played a spirited "Scotland the Brave," and several marches that Trout recognized as tunes his mother hummed. For the first time, Trout missed her, but the woods were neither quiet nor lonely.

After supper, Jack told Trout that not only did Red Wilson scope the river valley with his powerful binoculars several times a day, but he also heard all the sounds that floated up from the valley floor to the lookout: the bagpipes, the pounding of the Stoney drummers, and the cries of their dancers. He heard these sounds even over the rush of wind through the Howse Pass that brought the warm weather from the coast.

As Trout lifted the conch to his ear, wind and bagpipes echoed, bent and swirled, in its pearl folds. Later, the light at the top of the stairs went off, and then the kitchen light. Soon the house was silent, and he sat in the dark listening. The faint light from the yard creased his desk, and he held the conch to his ear and started to write. With these new words, he filled three pages until he fell asleep, his head on his arm.

When the cold air woke him, he closed the window, lay down in his bed, and fell instantly asleep. The woods and mountains were full of spirits now, and his dreams danced with the ghosts of Stoney babies.

Every two weeks the mail arrived, carried in by the Nordegg rangers or the trail boss, and taken out by whoever else happened to be going to Rocky. The pony express, Shelagh called it.

One afternoon, Trout received a parcel in the mail with a note: "For the squirrels. Love, your Grandmother."

At his mother's request, he had written to his father's mother, telling her about life on the ranger stations: about the dogs, the packhorses, and the squirrels that tormented the dogs by running along the fence just out of their reach.

Trout didn't tell her about the pack rat that had

bitten him after he'd cornered it under Junior's dog-house one day. Or the bloody flap of skin that hung off his thumb afterward. Or how Archie Baptiste, the Metis trail boss, flattened the pack rat with a shovel and buried it in the bush. Archie told Trout that if he got rabies, he'd need an injection with a big needle in the stomach.

"Don't tease the poor boy," Shelagh said. "That old packrat has been there since we moved the doghous-es. He's not got rabies."

The can of nuts his grandmother sent him was salted. Shelagh said it could kill the squirrels, so he shared them with his aunt and uncle as they sat at the kitchen table reading mail. There was a letter from his mother saying she missed him, but she hoped he'd enjoy his year in the mountains with his Aunt Shelagh and Uncle Jack.

Trout missed his mother and his sisters, and even Pauline sometimes. And he missed his grandmoth-ers. He wrote to tell them about the birth of the pup-pies, and that he'd accepted Aunt Shelagh's invitation to stay at the Upper Saskatchewan for a year.

He told them how his aunt had stayed up all night when Blondie gave birth, and had taken the pups from under the big dog so she wouldn't roll on them. Each was about the size and colour of a hot dog bun, and Shelagh had stroked the head of the mother, telling her over and over, "Good girl, such a good momma." She'd finally sent Trout to bed, but the light in the furnace room was still on when he got up the next morning. His aunt was pale and tired, but she was happy.

"Four puppies, out of a litter of ten," she said, with as much affection as if they were her own. Trout wondered why she wasn't sad about the other six.

After breakfast Jack took a feedbag that held the six dead puppies out behind the barn. Together he and Trout dug a small grave. He didn't put that in his letter either.

Jack had promised that they'd all go into town one day, and would visit Frank Jones and his family on the way back, but July turned dry after the last rain in June.

Each morning after chores, Shelagh took the readings from the weather station in the garden, and relayed them through Nordegg to Rocky. For twenty days straight, the rain gauge registered zero. The wind through the mountainous chute to the west blew hot and dry and seared the floor of the valley and Trout sought the shallow shade of the aspens in the dog pens. The Samoyeds and Saints, cold-weather dogs, hung their heads between their paws in the doghouses dug into the gravel bank. Blondie hid her puppies in the cool dark, all of them too hot to move. The small ponds around Trout's cabin dried up and lumbering horseflies and wasps hung on the still August air like pencil marks. When the wind didn't blow, the valley was silent, and the river became a distant whisper, inaudible to Trout. Tourists stopped coming. Only the log trucks broke the strange quiet, adding another white layer of glacial flour to the Indian paintbrush and black-eyed Susans along the road.

"Gets any drier, have to shut down the logging,"

Jack said one day as they watched a log truck slow for the Cline River bridge.

His uncle gradually raised the red line on the wooden thermometer on the sign in front of the station. It now showed: Fire Hazard: Extreme. No Camp Fires.

Town would have to wait, Jack said. Instead, they drove around to the campsites and nailed up fire warning signs. The pickup easily forded creeks that normally reached its doorwells, but now barely splashed the tires. Dust coated everything in the house as the log trucks continued to roll past the yard and his uncle had hoses irrigating the parched garden.

His aunt snapped at Trout one night when, dizzy with heat, he'd dropped one of her china saucers. Then Jack yelled at her and Trout burst into tears.

"Oh, for gosh sakes, don't cry dear boy. It's only a dish," Shelagh chided, as she swept up the pieces. "I can get another one." He knew they came from England, and they were her mother's.

"Shelagh, for Christ sakes!" His uncle's jaw clenched as he stomped to the garden to pick raspberries for dessert.

"Here, go shell these for me." Shelagh handed Trout a colander of early peas.

Trout shelled peas in the shade of the back porch while his aunt readied the roast in the oven. His uncle, who'd grown up poor in the old country, insisted on a roast every Sunday.

"Fried with onions," Jack said, and told Trout how, as a boy, he'd often eaten porridge for dinner. "It wasn't bad."

Trout didn't believe this. Anymore than he believed that haggis, a sheep's stomach filled with porridge and served with boiled turnips, was edible, let alone a treat, as Jack insisted. Trout knew his uncle kidded him sometimes.

But the kitchen his aunt worked in was over a hundred and twenty degrees. As he came in the house, he wondered if he'd made a mistake agreeing to stay. Shelagh watched over the garden through the kitchen window as she washed and peeled potatoes.

"Take these to the compost." She handed him the peelings. Suddenly she dropped the pot of potatoes in the sink.

"Oh God, no." She pushed past him into the office where he watched her slap a clip in the 303, ratchet the bolt, and shove a shell into the chamber before running out the back door. Through the kitchen window he saw her stop at the end of the garden and raise the gun to her shoulder. He ran outside and saw the look on his uncle's face as she fingered the trigger. She'd finally snapped in the heat. Shelagh was crazy.

"Jack," she screamed. Her husband stared at her, his mouth open, saying nothing.

On the end of the row of berry bushes a small cub sat on its haunches. Its mother was on the other side. Both swiped berries into their mouths, their brown backs to Jack, who was at the far end of the row filling a small pail, oblivious to the danger. Trout had already learned that to be caught between a mother and her cub could cost him his life. And surprising the sow would ensure it.

Shelagh fired once into the air. Jack froze. She

pulled back the bolt, reloaded and fired again. At the first shot nothing happened, but after the second shot, the smaller bear went over the garden fence and across the road, nearly getting stuck on the top log. It was followed by its mother, leaving broken raspberry canes and tufts of fur on the fence.

"Jesus, Shelagh," his uncle said, as they sat down to supper, "I thought you were gonna shoot me." Shelagh set his roast down in front of him. Her brow was red and sweaty.

"Thought about it." Her lips were set, but there was a smile in her eyes as she looked at Trout. "Decided against it."

"Best roast of beef I ever had, Shelagh," his uncle grinned.

"Hungry as a bear are we?" Shelagh peered over her glasses at him.

"Like Jack the Bear," Trout added. His uncle laughed and poured Shelagh a shot of rye. After supper, he opened all the windows, letting in the cool night breeze. He put on a record, and danced with his wife in the living room under the glowering glass eyes of the bear and the lynx and polished fangs of the cougar. Shelagh showed Trout a polka step.

"No reason you can't learn to dance." She counted out the time for him—one-two, one-two, one-two-three—before she sent him down to bed early. Not long after, all the lights went out upstairs.

Later that week, after twenty days without rain, they sat in the cool of the yard after supper, watching black clouds roll down the valley. Then lightning flashed to the north, followed by a rumble that echoed against the mountains. Large drops pelted the yard and disappeared in puffs of dust. Several more flashes streaked across the sky, each brighter and louder, as thunderclouds passed overhead. Jack looked at Shelagh. A few minutes later, the two-way crackled through the speaker box Jack had rigged in the yard.

"X78278, this is X78294. Do you read me?" All three of them ran inside. Jack grabbed the radio mike in the kitchen.

"X78278. Loud and clear, Red. Go ahead."

"Copy, got a hit above Pinto Lake. Standby X78278 for a location."

"Standing by, X78294." He handed the mike to Shelagh.

The radio crackled again and Trout stood beside his uncle as Shelagh called out the locations.

His uncle checked the vectors on the fire map in the office. "Just below the treeline. Dammit. There's no water up there." The more serious things became, the calmer Jack got.

Shelagh called from the radio in the kitchen. "Copter's on the way from Rocky."

"Call Archie at Two o'clock Creek,"

"Righto. Jack, they're not answering, must be away from the radio,"

"Keep trying. Let's go, Trout. You bring the walkie talkie." Trout ran with his uncle to the garage. Jack pulled long-handled shovels and firefighting gear from the shelves. Together they loaded the truck and pulled up behind the ranger station.

Shelagh met the truck with a grub box and an

armload of empty canvas water bags. "Archie's on his way. Copter will be here in thirty minutes."

"If this one gets out of control, the valley's gonna go." His uncle pulled on his coveralls as Trout and his aunt filled the canvas bags from the hose. The bags had already started to sweat in the back of the truck.

"Here's Archie, Jack." His uncle kissed his aunt on the cheek, something Trout had never seen him do before. The trail crew's stake truck roared into the yard, with three men in the cab and two more standing in the back. Jack waved them down.

"Follow me. Copter's on the way. He'll put it down across the road. If we can get in there before dark, I think we can contain the fire. But we'll have to walk up to it."

Archie peered down from the cab, "I know that ridge. There's no way he can land up there." The other men looked worried. "Let's go, Jack," Archie said, turning the big truck around the yard.

Trout and his aunt watched the helicopter lift four times from the field in front of the ranger station. Each flight took two men and their gear, as the pilot lifted off nose down and swung over the Cline River before disappearing into the horizon west over Pinto Lake. Jack and Archie went out on the first flight and soon all the men and gear were gone. Trout stared, disappointed at being left behind. He knew not to ask, but he would have given anything to be on the fireline that night.

Inside, he and his aunt sat by the two-way with a pair of binoculars on the kitchen table until the sun went down. The helicopter went over to Nordegg to refuel and park for the night. The other firetower on Old Baldy above Nordegg called in strikes as the storm moved down the Upper Saskatchewan valley. Often they could only hear one side of the call as the transmission cut out. Then Trout heard the call sign of his uncle's radio-telephone, and Red Wilson radioed back the vectors of the fire to Nordegg to relay to headquarters in Rocky.

"No water here, Red. Just scree and spit."

"I'm standing by, if you need me, Jack. Over and out." Someone else cut in.

"X74359 calling X78278."

"X78278, go ahead Beth."

"We got two strikes down here, Shelagh. One above Goldeye Lake, another at Teepee Creek. Scrambled all our crews. Rocky's on standby. Over."

"Copy. Looks like the storm's past us now and heading down the valley, Beth. X78278 over and out."

"Gonna be a long night, Shelagh, 'til the boys come home. X74359 out."

That night, his aunt let him stay up. She made mugs of tea, cut thick slices of homemade bread, and spooned jam right out of the jar, something she didn't normally do. The radio grew silent as the storm passed Nordegg. Shelagh took out a crib board. As they played, she talked about the bombing of London during the war.

"All the houses had blackout curtains. All of London was dark until the searchlights went on. Air-raid sirens would go off, night after night. At the first sirens, Mum and I'd go down to the tube. Then the anti-aircraft guns started firing, as the Luftwaffe bombers flew over. And we waited for the bombs.

"This was Goering's firestorm—his blitzkrieg. Night after night, those bombers came, wave after wave of them. Afterwards, when the all-clear siren sounded, I'd pick my way through the rubble to the hospital. I knew I'd be needed. There were weeks when I lived there. Hitler vowed he'd bring England to her knees. Of course, he didn't, but he tried."

Trout loved the way she said *England*, as if each letter was touched on lightly, like piano keys, each of them important and musical. And defiant. His mother called Shelagh's accent plummy, and that was how he heard it now, ripe and sweet.

Trout wondered how she could be so jaunty, when he himself could barely concentrate on his cards.

"Don't lose your place. This isn't bad, you know. The V-1's, now they were bad. You could hear the drone and the ground thumped when they hit. But the V-2's were terrible. They were rocket-propelled. They'd suddenly cut out and you couldn't hear them until it was too late.

"The hospital where I worked was hit and I was sent to the countryside near the Canadian regiments. That's how I met your Uncle Jack. In France, he'd hit a landmine on his motorcycle. He was a lucky one. The sidecar took most of the blast, but he lost all of his hearing in one ear and most of it in the other."

Trout thought that was tragic. He'd never had hearing to lose, but his uncle was different—he'd learned to play the bagpipes as a boy.

"He'd say to me, *Shelagh, I can't hear you*. And he'd stand closer. I knew what he was doing; he didn't have his hearing aid then. He'd tell me stories about Canada and being an Indian agent—that's what he did before the war. And when he got over to France, he found his brothers, all in uniform, all underage, and him a military policeman. All tall fellows they, your great-uncles Robbie and Charlie and Mac. Jack's the shortest of the bunch.

"One day, I walked eight miles to get a recipe for bread from the camp cook at Beaver Mines, where I came to be with him after we were married. That was after the war. It was the first bread I ever baked. Never forgot that recipe."

She picked up a slice of bread and tore it apart, stuffing bits into her mouth, then she got up from the table.

"Getting tired, are we? Well then, put it away." His aunt swept up the cards and stacked them. "Let's turn out the lights."

Trout put their dishes in the sink. Shelagh took off her glasses, picked up the binoculars, and scanned the ridge above Pinto Lake. "There's a flicker. See it?" she handed him the binoculars.

Trout couldn't see anything, but he smelled smoke in the cold mountain air. He handed the binoculars back to Shelagh.

"I smell smoke," he said, scared.

She laughed. "That's the stove's backdraft, silly boy. Forest fires don't smell nearly that clean. Oh gosh, no. And it would have to be a much bigger fire than this one for you to smell it."

When she turned on the light, she took the barrettes from her hair, and it dropped past her shoulders. Without her glasses, her eyes were blue and bright as iris petals when she looked at him.

"You're worried, aren't you?" He could hear the worry in her voice too. She hugged him and said, "Jack will be alright. Toddle off now." She tuned the big Grundig to the BBC overseas service, and settled down to a game of solitaire.

Tired but unable to sleep, Trout sat at his table with the conch shell in front of him, and scribbled in his journal:

V-bombs. Blackout. Tube. Beaver Mines.

Blitzkrieg. Firestorm. Miracle.

He looked at the conch and thought of his auntie, who'd given it to him, and tears trickled down his nose. Maybe his miracle was this: whenever he was lost, he always found love.

But he didn't want to lose anymore. The last words he'd had with God were curses, out on the prairies, that day of his auntie's funeral.

Trout prayed now, for his uncle, to the only God he knew, the tangible and real God of fire vectors: Red Wilson, the lookout man who waited on standby at the top of Mount Cline. A God not great, nor in heaven, but close enough.

In a voice he could not hear, and in a language he was learning, Trout spoke his prayers. And on the windowsill, the conch listened.

Clare

Lowell hadn't said much on the phone from Pincher Creek, when I told him that Will was staying with my uncle for a year, but when he came home for the Labour Day weekend, he was furious with me.

"He's our boy." Lowell threw his fork down on the dinner plate and pushed it away. I knew then he was jealous of my Uncle Jack. "That's a helluva ways up there. We can't even visit him."

I had to sit down. The baby was heavy now and I didn't have the patience for this. "Shelagh says they like him and he's no trouble. I can't manage him anymore, and you're down in Pincher Creek."

"Then I won't go back."

"We can't afford that, Lowell."

"They'll be thinking we can't raise our own boy."

"We need their help. Look at all we've taken from your mother." Lowell was silent. "This is how my family helps—your mother's different, you said that yourself. Let them do this for him."

"A year?"

"A year."

After supper, we took a drive out behind the school and followed the dirt road past the new houses down to Beaver Dam. There wasn't a beaver dam there any more—it was just a name now.

The twins, who loved to run, set up an impromptu baseball game. Lowell pitched to them while Emily stayed close to me and she and I watched the Canada geese crowd the pond formed by the dam.

New houses were going up around the school and people were talking about fixing up the little island and the dam that the older kids used for drinking parties. I had watched as women like myself, only younger, moved into the neighbourhood. Some of them drove—one or two even had their own cars.

I wasn't a young mother anymore, though I was plump with the baby and if one more person said how radiant I looked, I'd have to deck them. My breasts were so full of milk. *One thing about the Locke women*, my grandmother used to say, *we're fertile.*

Lowell could have found my pregnant body sensuous—I thought Roly might have—but that wasn't my husband, or our time. My daughters are so different from the way I was then. They expect, and get, so much more from their men.

Lowell seemed frightened for me when I was pregnant—like I was a delicate egg that would break—but he was good with the babies. Pauline scared him now, especially when we went shopping for school clothes.

"Dad, go wait for us at Kresge's," she'd say to him.

"What's wrong?"

"Women's things," I said.

"Oh," he said, his face crimson.

When we met him at the lunch counter, he'd bought some Beatle wigs on a whim. They were just polyester hair, but each of the girls got one, even Emily, who wore hers as we drove back from downtown.

Even before the Beatles played on the Ed Sullivan show, Lowell and Pauline knew who they were. Lowell got Pauline a transistor radio when they first came out, a cheap Japanese model, not much larger than Will's first hearing aid. I thought it funny how she was tuning out, first with the little forty-five rpm player Lowell got her for her birthday, and later the big flip-down one with the stereo speakers.

Lowell was always drumming a beat on the steering wheel when we drove. Pauline sat up front with him and they played the teen station, while the twins sat in the back, on either side of me, and Emily sat in my lap. Lowell was still a young dad, but I felt so old that year.

We'd had my mom and her new boyfriend over for Labour Day. Mom was dating the Captain at the fire hall in Sunnyside. His wife had left him, Mom told me. Ian MacGrenaghan was a good-looking man, with wavy red hair and a belly laugh. Mom and he held hands once or twice when they were over at our house, while my girls tried not to stare.

Ian played ball with the twins and asked Emily about her cat, calling it her kitty with a Glaswegian burr. Lowell was a good grill cook and he made steaks for the adults and burgers and hot dogs for the kids. Mom came in the house when I went inside to make the salad.

"Well?" Mom asked. By the look on her face, I knew this was serious.

"Great, Mom. And he's not Scottish!"

She laughed.

"He got kids?"

"Boys, two grown, one in high school."

"He fish?" I laughed this time. Mom blushed and I

hugged her. "Don't throw this one back." I wanted a grandfather for my children.

Lowell was going back to Pincher Creek early the next morning. We both lay in bed, facing away from each other, but I knew he was awake. His breathing was short and tense.

"Is there someone else? You seemed so distant on the phone."

He took a long time to answer. Too long, I thought.

"No."

"Sure?"

"Sure I'm sure. I think about it. Some of the guys go with the local girls."

"You know if you're with someone else, you can't come home to me, Lowell."

"I'm in a trailer at a gas plant. I work twelve hours a day, seven days a week. When I call you I'm exhausted." He turned to face my back. "What about you?"

"What about me?"

"You're here; there're men."

"I'm a blimp with four girls at home."

"You seemed so abrupt on the phone."

"I was lonely."

"So was I, Clare."

I could feel his breath on my neck. "Let's not fight," I said. I felt his hands around my waist. "Do you miss me?"

"Always."

I took his hand and traced the outline of his fingers

with mine. They were small, almost feminine, with narrow tips, calloused and cut. Except for the cuts, they could be the hands of a poet or painter. Will's were the same, and like his father he spoke with his hands and listened with his eyes.

I kissed the white band of soft skin on the inside of Lowell's wrist and we made love that night the only way we could, with him behind me and the baby in front of me. I wasn't lonely then. I had so much to be thankful for.

When I woke the next morning Lowell was gone, and the girls were up, getting their own breakfast.

I decided to call the baby Stephen, after my father. Will was named for Yeats and William was also Lowell's middle name, as well as his father's name. I knew Mom wouldn't like me naming the baby for my father. She wanted me to like Ian MacGrenaghan, and I came to love him, maybe more than I ever could my own father. But there was only one Stephen Magnus Taylor, my father. If he couldn't be in our lives, I'd give his name a life.

The girls were excited about the new baby, and I shared its growth with them—not wanting my pregnancy to be a dirty, dark mystery as it had been in Mom's time. The twins liked to stroke my belly and put their ears against it and talk to the baby.

One day I got a call from the school to tell me that Pauline was being sent home. She arrived with her new paisley blouse torn and a bruise on her face. At first, she wouldn't tell me what happened.

The school secretary said that there had been a fight

213

with one of the Lynnwood Heights girls at recess and both girls had been sent home. She said they'd fought all-out, tearing off each other's blouses, pulling hair and tugging pants down. I always thought women fight to humiliate, men to dominate.

When Pauline got home, I threw her muddy clothes in the wash and ran a bath. She could be tight-lipped and proud like her father. I put on a pot of tea and sat down at the dining room table. When she came out of the bathroom, wrapped in a towel, she reached for one of my cigarettes. I didn't stop her. I knew she was smoking and I didn't want her to sneak around, as I had with my mother.

It turned out that a girl in her class—the hardware store owner's daughter, who lived in one of those big new houses up on the hill—taunted Pauline about her brother and Kenny Dawes breaking into the store.

"And I know about your Dad," she'd sneered. "He's a crook." By then, Pauline said, a crowd had gathered.

"And your brother's a deaf mute," the girl continued. "Losers!"

"That did it," Pauline told me, trying not to cry. She was tougher, in many ways, than Will, and stronger than I'd ever been. I wanted to call up the school and have them move the girls to separate classes, but I knew that would only make things worse.

"What'd Dad do, Mom?"

I hadn't planned on telling the kids yet. Lowell wanted just to forget that time in his life, and although I was there through his whole trial, I didn't even know everything that had happened—none of them talked, especially not Lowell.

"He wasn't a crook, that's for sure, honey. And your brother's not mute." For the first time, I was talking to my daughter, not as an adult, but as if we both wanted her to be. She sensed that, and took another cigarette.

"Your dad was eighteen and he was in a gang." I told her about the Lido Café—she'd been there when we visited my Mom—and the Zoot suits, the big fedoras, the long watch chains, the movie-gangster swagger, all working-class kids, too young to enlist in the war.

"Kind of like the Mods and Rockers?" Pauline had taken on the Carnaby Street look and the house was filled with the sounds of the Beatles.

"A little," I said, annoyed by the way she romanticized the gangs, but then I had done that too, when I was her age. "They'd pick fights with the boys back from overseas. Those guys came back having killed and seen more than anyone should ever see. There was always drinking and fighting. Now we know it's caused by stress."

"Like a rumble?"

I nodded. "There were rumbles, alright. It got so bad, the police chief wanted all the soldiers to sign in at the police station, so he'd know where they were. Nobody admitted there was a problem then."

One of Lowell's friends from the Legion, who'd been a fighter pilot in the R.C.A.F., had threatened his wife, then put a shotgun to his head and pulled the trigger. His wife said that before the war he had been the gentlest man. When our kids were young, he'd sometimes show up at our back door, his face outlined in the screen like a ghost, incoherent and rambling, asking for Lowell. He'd spend hours talking, but he couldn't cry until he got drunk and Lowell said he never got over the firebombing, and guilt over those young German pilots he'd shot down.

"We were boys, so were they," he told Lowell. "I could see their faces."

"What's this got to do with Dad?"

"Your dad and the gang, seven or eight of them, crashed a party at the Army and Navy club. Over a girl. One of the vets had taken a girlfriend, or so they said, from one of your dad's friends."

"I can't believe they did that." Pauline stared at me.

"Part of it was they were drunk and all worked up. They believed their own stories and thought they were tough guys. Yes, in hindsight, it was stupid. The papers called your dad the ringleader, but that didn't make sense to me. There was one other man who was older and he was a soldier. And then there was the judge's son, he and your dad had gone to Lord Strathcona together." I lit a cigarette and added more water to the tea.

"Private school?" she snorted.

"When he was younger, your Grandma Dot—your auntie actually—had money. Here, help me roll some more." I pulled the roller and can of tobacco over to me.

"The girl got engaged to one of the soldiers and the gang went to break it up. You take all those guys, and love and wounded pride, and when you stir them all up, there's going to be trouble. A huge fight broke out. The girl's fiancée lost an eye; two or three people got broken ribs and arms. These were guys who'd fought hand-to-hand in the war. The gang didn't stand a chance, but according to the papers they held their own—all considering. It was pretty foolish—they were just punks acting big."

"Who did it?" Pauline, then as now, never got sidetracked. She would have made a good cop, Lowell used to joke.

"You mean the eye. Nobody knows. They couldn't prove anything—it was a brawl. Your dad had a record, for fighting, and so did the soldier, so they both got hard time—hard labour."

"What about this judge's son?"

"He was in the gang too. He's a lawyer here now. I think he was the real leader. A sharp talker, your dad always said, but they all clammed up at the trial. The judge, this guy's father, was trying a case involving the friends of his son, if you can believe it—but the son was quietly tried by another judge. Anyway, everybody wanted blood because it was veterans. One of the papers even had bright red headlines when the gang got sentenced. You'd think they were Chicago gangsters and it was a mob hit, not small town punks and a brawl. The cops and lawyers all played the part to the hilt, swaggering and strutting. Everybody got carried away. Your dad and the soldier in the gang got two years less a day and the others got a year. The veterans got off scot-free, although they broke a few bones too and if the police hadn't gotten there in time, it would have been worse."

"What happened to the judge's son?"

"He was acquitted."

"How come?"

"I honestly don't know, Pauline. Your dad's put it behind him. We should too. He might have been a punk—that's the worst you could say—but he was never a crook."

Pauline shook her head. I couldn't tell what she thought.

"If he decides to tell you himself, let him, okay? This is between you and me, okay, honey?" My daughter said nothing and looked away. I never told anyone about Lowell breaking Roly Faro's jaw.

"What am I going to do about the kids at school?"

"Do you want me to call that girl's parents? I will." It bugged me how they brought my son and daughter into this.

"No." Pauline shook her head and rolled her eyes. "No."

"Then walk away from her."

"Walk away?"

"Your Grandpa Locke used to say that to me when I was in the same situation. I wish you'd known him. He was in the First World War and his brother died at the Somme. *Sure, it takes courage to fight. But it takes twice the courage to walk away and find a high road,* he'd say."

I could see through the dining room window that the kids were starting to drift down the hill from the school.

"Mom, can I get a mini-skirt?" I watched Pauline flip the cigarette papers into the roller and spin them out.

"We'll see. Let's make supper, okay? Your choice. Why don't you bring your record player up and put something on. I like those Beatles."

"The Beatles, Mom. How 'bout Chicken Supreme?"

The sounds of "We Can Work it Out," filled the dining room, and my daughter hummed along as she set the table for dinner. Like the song said, I wanted to see it her way instead of just my way.

I felt the helplessness my mother must have felt when I was driven by passions that seemed childish to her. So sure I couldn't possibly be wrong. Nothing she said to me then, would stop me doing what I wanted to. I hoped Jack could show my son a better way than Lowell's.

Trout

The kitchen windowpanes rattled as the helicopter carrying the firefighters flew in low and dropped them in the field across from the ranger station. Trout bounded down the stairs and out the door to greet them, trying to hide his excitement. He and his aunt had been up since dawn and Shelagh had breakfast ready for the men: bacon, sausages, fried potatoes and tomatoes, eggs and pancakes, homemade bread and muffins, sweating jugs of orange juice and powdered milk, all waited on the dining room table.

The pile of coveralls outside the back door reeked of smoke, and the exhausted men sat at the table black as coal miners, with their tired eyelids white above their soot-covered faces. They shovelled food into their mouths, too busy to speak and no one spoke until the eating was done. Trout and his aunt brought plate after plate to feed them.

Once they had their fill, the men began telling how they'd fought the fire.

"First one I ever put out with my feet." Archie Baptiste laughed.

"Whole bloody night," Jack smiled. "Stamping our feet." He passed a can of Export A and papers amongst the men.

"Those sparks drifted downwind. Thank god they went out," added Archie.

"We'd have had a crown fire all down the valley," said Jack. The ash of his cigarette flared as he drew on it and the others nodded knowingly.

After the crew left, carrying their coveralls over their arms, Jack fell asleep with a cup of coffee in his hand.

"Jack, go to bed." Shelagh woke him and Trout did the dishes while his aunt gathered his uncle's sooty clothes and started the laundry downstairs.

That morning Trout began a ritual he followed until fire season ended. He sprinted down the stairs and out the back door, and waved to Red Wilson, the lookout man, who he imagined always watched over the valley.

Later that week, Red Wilson radioed to say he could hear the Stoney drummers six miles away on Kootenay Plains.

When Jack drove Trout to the Sun Dance, he was amazed to see dozens of cars parked around the perimeter of the plains with license plates from B.C., Saskatchewan, Alberta, Idaho, Montana, and one from Washington—a Rambler station wagon flying an American flag from its radio antenna.

Jack told Trout about the different tribes: the Kootenay, Shuswap and Carrier from B.C., the Sarcee and Blackfoot from the south of the province, the northern Cree and the Plains Cree from Saskatchewan, the Nez Perce from Idaho, the Sioux from Montana, and the Spokane from Washington State.

"These are a powerful people. I've learned much from them." Jack looked at Trout with one eyebrow arched high, as if he were reckoning through the scope of his rifle. Trout nodded blankly.

"They were warriors. And they're gonna rise again, someday. They teach you in school about the great chiefs? Big Bear? Poundmaker? You know, he was part Stoney."

Trout shook his head. "We learned about Crowfoot."

"You're gonna meet their relatives today."

Spread amongst the cars were teepees, trailers and tents, and in the centre of the huge camp was the Medicine Lodge built for the Sun Dance. His uncle told him about how the Sun Dance had been revived.

"A year ago Chief Moses came to me and said his people would like to have the Sun Dance here. It's been fifty years since there's been a Sun Dance on Kootenay Plains." His uncle talked as he circled the truck around the camp and inspected the fire pits. "I gave him permission." He stopped and turned off the engine. "Don't think my boss will be too happy." Trout wondered what he meant.

Jack told him how the Sun Dance had been outlawed near the turn of the century and the Mounties had closed it down. He described the ceremony: how the young men had sharp sticks thrust deep under the skin of their chests, tied to a long piece of rawhide tethered to the centre pole of the lodge. The rawhide was strung so tight each young man rose on the balls of his feet, and danced around the lodge pole until he was cut down by an elder, or until the stick ripped from his chest. Then, he became a brave, toughened and fearless and ready for battle.

Nowadays, they just wrapped the rawhide around themselves, Jack said, sounding a little disappointed that bravery was only ceremonial now.

The white man was not allowed in the lodge, he explained. He and Trout would have to watch from a respectful distance. But when they got out of the truck, one of the Stoney chiefs welcomed Jack, shaking his hand in greeting and invited him and Trout to watch the dance.

"Nice to meet you, Trout." Silas Moses was a short dignified man in a pale buckskin shirt. He wore his white hair in braids, and his smile, ringed with oval laugh lines, made his weathered face look warm and grandfatherly. More lines creased his brow and circled his eyes, which were powerful despite his slow walk and bent back.

Trout did not feel strange to be there anymore. Jack nodded as an older man in a brightly coloured blouse ringed with beads and fur, and wearing a fur hat with buffalo horns and feather tassels, walked over with his hand extended. His eyes hesitated as they took in the boy.

"My half-brother has told me about you." He grasped Jack's hand with both of his as if he might wrestle him to the ground. His chin was flecked with white stubs of hair and his shoulders were straight and broad.

"George McLean—that's the name the missionary gave him," Silas said, as he introduced them.

"Of course, Tatanga Mani, Walking Buffalo," Jack beamed as the older man looked at his brother, Silas. "The Medicine Man from Morley. It's an honour." Walking Buffalo's nose was broad and triangular with deep parallel lines on each side of it and his large lips now formed a slight wary smile.

"Walking Buffalo, this is my nephew, William Dunlop. We call him Trout." Jack put his hand on his nephew's shoulder. Trout held out his hand and Walking Buffalo took it.

"Trout?" he nodded and bowed his head slightly. "Two names. Like me." He smiled and turned back to Jack, who'd worn his dress uniform with his regiment's tie clip, but not his Sam Brown belt with the holster that day. A native woman came over with a camera and focused on the two elders. Walking Buffalo stopped her.

"Just a minute." He bent over her camera and shook his head. The woman's smile fell as the medicine man took her camera.

"You got the wrong shutter speed." He adjusted the camera and handed it back to her. "Too fast for the overcast. Now take a picture." Walking Buffalo stood beside Silas Moses and waved at the camera.

He turned back to Jack. "We are glad to have the Sun Dance here, again. Let me introduce you to the other chiefs, Paul Smallboy from Hobbema and Joe Cloud of the Kootenay."

Silas Moses interrupted.

"Your nephew can watch the dance with my family." Silas walked Trout over to the Medicine Lodge.

"This's my son, Charlie." Trout extended his hand to Charlie Moses, who looked more like a cowboy in his Stetson and western shirt. He was about Trout's dad's age and his grip enveloped the boy's hand.

"Charlie, this is Jack's nephew. His name is Trout. Where's Carrie?"

Silas motioned to a teenaged girl sitting nearby on the grass and introduced her as his granddaughter.

Trout sat with her and the younger Moses children just outside the Lodge, which was like a teepee, only much bigger, with a huge lodgepole pine stripped of branches in the centre, and walls made of small poles covered with pine boughs.

Silas's granddaughter, Carrie, was older than Trout and pretty, with dark hair and white teeth. She sat cross-legged on a blanket, wearing a ceremonial buckskin skirt and beaded shirt. Trout kept looking at her during the dance, but each time she smiled at him, he turned away and pretended not to notice. She was what his mother called a big girl, but he could not keep his eyes from her and every time he looked, she noticed and he blushed. She had an oval face, like her grandfather and jolly lines around her mouth and eyes that rippled outwards when she laughed. His mother always said laughter is the voice singing, and he thought hers sang of plums.

Inside the Medicine Lodge, the drummers started. Four of them kneeled and pounded together, and as they chanted, the small hairs stood up on the back of Trout's neck. The ancient sound travelled through him, as the large circular drum reverberated and boomed, first through his feet, up from the earth, and then around him in the air and through his skin. Piercing cries came from the singers' throats and he could feel the hairs on his head and arms spark as he listened with his whole body. He needed no hearing aid here on Kootenay Plain.

Trout watched in awe through the doorway as the

dancers moved in a dusty circle around the lodge, in a ceremonial shuffle. No sticks were driven into their chests, for the dance was now symbolic, as Jack had said, but to Trout it was splendid.

Trout and his uncle stayed at the Sun Dance all day and into the evening. They ate frybread and a kind of meat stew that Carrie brought him.

Later, she invited Trout to sit with her and her mother when they went to visit at various teepees. Trout flushed and stammered before getting up to follow Carrie. Small puffs of dust rose from her moccasins. Trout felt clumsy in his running shoes, but he followed the soft folds of Carrie's figure, and her brown calves.

When Jack came to get him at sundown, Trout didn't want to leave.

Together they went into Chief Smallboy's teepee. A small smoky fire glowed in the centre of a stone circle dug into the dusty plain. Trout sat with his uncle, but Silas motioned him to sit between him and his half-brother, Walking Buffalo.

"You will want to hear," the old chief said gently. "My brother is a great speaker. He has been to Buckingham Palace and met the Queen."

As his eyes became accustomed to the darkness, Trout could see some of the dancers had joined the circle around the fire, while others stood near the doorway. On the other side of the fire circle sat Chief Smallboy and, beside him, the young chief Joe Cloud. Carrie stood behind Trout. His neck flushed, but he didn't turn around to look at her.

Silas produced a small soapstone pipe and tobacco

pouch. Walking Buffalo ignited sweetgrass and fanned it across the air while Silas tamped tobacco and passed the pipe to his half-brother.

"This is a pipe of friendship," Walking Buffalo said, as he lit the pipe. "We were a lawless people. But we were on pretty good terms with the Great Spirit, creator and ruler of all."

He looked at Jack. "The white man assumed we were savages. He didn't understand our prayers. We saw the Great Spirit's work in everything. The sun, the trees, and the moon, the wind and the mountains. We approached Him through these things."

He passed the pipe. His gaze stopped at Carrie and Trout.

"Did you know that the trees talk? Well, they do. And they talk to each other. They'll talk to you, if you listen. Trouble is, white people don't listen. They never learned to listen to us. So, I don't suppose they'll listen to trees. But I have learned a lot from trees. Sometimes about the weather, about animals, sometimes about the Great Spirit."

Walking Buffalo turned to the other chiefs and the pipe went around the circle. Smoke rose towards the open top of the teepee.

"We're here today as friends. And friends must listen to each other. For many hundred years, maybe more, our people came to these plains to hunt. Our people and Chief Cloud's people came to trade furs with the white man from the fort. Once, we were enemies."

The other two chiefs nodded and took the pipe as

it went around the circle. Jack took it too, and puffed on it before passing it back to Walking Buffalo.

"Once there was a massacre here on the Kootenay Plains. Our people came over the Dolomite River down the Siffleur to the Plains to hunt and they met a strange people." He looked at Chief Cloud whose glasses reflected the low burning fire.

Chief Cloud spoke. "So it goes. My ancestors told a story too. They met a strange people with guns and all the Kootenay were killed except for one, a pregnant woman. My grandmother she used to say, 'Got baby in belly, could not run'. The girl was captured by the people with guns."

Silas listened and then he looked around the circle. "In our story, the Kootenay people took fright and ran over the mountains."

"They left behind a woman who was pregnant," Walking Buffalo said.

"I have heard of that girl." Chief Smallboy looked at Walking Buffalo and Chief Cloud. "One of our dancers here, his grandfather was the baby in the belly of the girl." He began to chuckle.

Joseph Cloud smiled at that and he too began to chuckle. The drums of the Sun Dance had started again. "George McLean, you gonna pass the pipe again. Then I think we should go watch that dancer."

As Trout and his uncle drove home that night, they could hear the drummers behind them. Jack stopped the truck just before the Cline River Bridge. He shut off the engine and got out, and Trout followed him. "Listen. Can you hear that?"

Trout nodded. In one hearing aid, the river rushed

over the stones to the North Saskatchewan, but in the other, the drums pulsed through the cold mountain air.

Trout shivered, as much from the sound of the drums as from the excitement of the day. Around him, the sharp plates of the ancient seabed rose into the sky. The evening stars appeared, and in the west, the tops of jagged ridges glowed with the remnants of sun. The wind rose and rustled through the forest, rushed over the river and the distant drummers. He listened to the trees.

"When Alexander Henry the explorer came here in 1799, he called it Rivière du Meurleton. Split his men into three parties, headed east to fool the Cree, then circled west again towards Kootenay Plains."

As they got back in the truck, Jack hunched over the steering wheel and drew on his cigarette. The lights on the dashboard brightened his eyes.

"Found moose, deer, mountain goats, mountain sheep, even buffalo right here. The Cree and Blackfoot didn't want him trading with the Kootenays. Didn't have guns themselves, didn't want the Kootenays to either." Jack shook his head. "They knew. History matters, Trout. They knew what would happen.

"The Cree were right. The guns arrived and by 1807, when David Thompson came through Rocky on his way to the Columbia, there's no mention of buffalo at the Mirlton River, as he called it. Then, there was the battle. You heard." As Jack looked across the plains, the twin beams of the headlights silhouetted the steel skeleton of the bridge. In the distance, the ranger station was lit up too.

"The Stoneys call it the Whitegoat River. Should never name a mountain or a river after a man." Trout shivered again and yawned, his head full of history and the sound of drumming.

"You're tired." Jack pointed to the lights of the ranger station. "Your Auntie Shelagh is waiting."

Before he went to sleep that night, Trout wrote in his journal:

Tatanga Mani	Walking Buffalo	George McLean
Meurleton	Cline	Whitegoat
Joseph Cloud	Silas Moses	Paul Smallboy

In his sleep, the drummers drummed and the dancers danced. And the Stoney babies turned with him in their sleep and Red Wilson and Trout listened to the voices of the trees through his conch.

Two days later, at breakfast, they watched rain pour over the eaves and Jack joked that he'd asked Silas to perform a rain dance. They'd had more than forty days of dry weather under late summer sun. The cold and damp raised goose-bumps on Trout's arms. He wore a slicker to chop firewood and his hands were chilled and greasy with rain. But there was no rain in Nordegg, just over the range, which always got twice as much as the Kootenay Plains, Shelagh said. When she first submitted her weather reports, the meteorologist came up from Calgary to check the rain gauges because he couldn't believe two places fifty miles apart could have such different readings.

"Soil's pure glacial silt. Had it tested, came back zero," Jack said. "Zero nutrients."

His aunt and uncle were joyful that morning as the water ran off the roof.

"He asked everyone he knew in Rocky to save their shoes and old boots."

"Shoes are good compost and they anchor the moisture," said Shelagh. "Gathered all the bones I could find on Kootenay Plains, all the years of hunting camps, quite a few were buffalo.

"The boys at Nordegg helped bring in a load of peat from the bog. We mixed it all up, and that's how I got my garden. Before that, everything we ate came from the freezer or a can." Trout listened as she told him how Jack had made her an English garden thousands of miles from home and many more feet above sea level, and of how it flourished in the heat of the closed valley where even in winter it was warmer than on the lower ranges.

"That's why the tribes had their hunting camps here." Jack took his time with his coffee that morning. "Mount Cline, although it's above the tree line, was once covered with limber pine; and Red Wilson now keeps a garden at seven thousand feet." Jack told Trout how, when they'd first built the lookout, the helicopter couldn't land and he was lowered by rope with a chain saw to clear the mountaintop.

"Some of the trees, Trout, were ninety feet tall."

"Oh, yes, I could tell exactly where he was, from watching the trees fall," Shelagh interrupted.

"Anyway, there'd been a big fire in '56 and the bull-dozers couldn't cross the Cline River to Kootenay

Plains," Jack continued, moving his coffee cup to the centre of the table.

Shelagh got up to get more coffee.

"We heard about that fire," she said. "We were down at Castle Mountain then, near the area they now call the Whaleback. We'd park the car at the general store in Beaver Mines and take the dog team ten miles in."

"We often didn't get out 'til spring," said Jack.

Shelagh pulled their coffee cups into the centre of the table and refilled them.

"Forestry decided the Plains needed a ranger and so Jack applied for us to come here."

Trout's eyes flashed from his aunt to his uncle, trying to keep up with the conversation.

Clouds hung over the valley and the low ceiling dropped below the lookout. Red Wilson radioed to say he was closed in. Creeks spilled their banks and the puddles behind Trout's cabin became small ponds and overflowed. The garden was lush now and the leafy rows of cabbages, turnips and squash were crisp. On the fourth day, when the sun came out, Jack lowered the thermometer on the fire hazard sign to moderate and said they could finally go to town.

Trout, meanwhile, had started working in the barn, mucking out stalls, and dodging barn cats that wrapped themselves around his ankles as he hooked hay bales, which Jack pulled up to the loft. The work was dusty and hot, but he could feel his muscles limber and the axe now sliced through the firewood, often on the first try. Trout worked with his shirt off, and the acne on his back dried in the mid-day mountain sun. He wished for a face as leathered and brown as Silas's, and he daydreamed of Carrie. Since meeting her, his daydreams had become more complicated. Carrie's laugh stayed with him long after the Sun Dance, and he worked harder now with this small joy in his head.

"Since you're staying, better teach you how to ride," Jack said one day as they ate lunch. Trout was afraid of his uncle's horses, which towered over him, and especially of the broad-backed pack ponies that thundered past his cabin. Their muscular hocks kicked up massive hooves as they raced along the trails in the scrub bush in the riverbed. And he'd found a barn cat's stiff body one morning when he mucked out a stall, its head flattened by the hooves of the packhorses.

Jack assigned him a roan mare named Belle. Trout made friends with her, and fed her carrots from the garden. He loved her long lashes and large eyes and her sweet, open face. Jack showed Trout how to lead her, using his body, and taught him never to show fear. Trout learned to saddle and groom Belle, to trot and lope, and one day he graduated to a full gallop in the pasture while Jack watched atop the corral fence.

"You're gonna need some Western boots, but those gumboots will to have do for now," he said, as Trout brought her in, and tied the reins in a slip knot before he flipped the stirrup onto the saddle horn and uncinched her. But his boots were sweaty and his socks came off inside when he walked. Jack was right. He needed proper boots.

Shelagh woke him early, the day they went to town.

After so long in the bush, Trout found Rocky Mountain House big and noisy and muddy. Wood smoke from the wigwam burner in the lumberyard hung in the air. Trout was excited to try on new boots and jeans at the Bay. His new Western boots had inlay on the high leather tops.

"The steel shank and the heel will keep your feet in the stirrup and keep ya from getting dragged," Jack told him.

As Trout walked down the street, the stiff new jeans chafed his thighs, and he stared at the shiny toes of his boots. He revelled in the raw smell of new leather and canvas, oblivious to the people who smiled at him, a boy with new boots.

After Shelagh stopped by the post office to pick up the mail and his correspondence courses, Jack and Trout visited with the ladies in the forestry office. Jack was gregarious, and never afraid to ask someone to repeat themselves. His "Eh?", both insistent and curious, got an answer. They went across to the diner with the chief ranger, a mild-spoken office man named Vickery. Trout watched the way his uncle listened intently, his eyes on his boss's, his head cocked to funnel sound into his better ear. Jack was not afraid to ask his boss to repeat something, if he couldn't hear it over the clatter of the diner.

Trout ordered a double-cheeseburger, with fries and gravy, and was startled to hear his uncle raise his voice.

"Damn, they won't stop it?" He looked at his boss and then at Shelagh, who no longer smiled.

"Not this time, sorry," the chief ranger said. "We

got final approval." He got up to leave, and tipped his hat to Shelagh. To Trout, he didn't sound sorry at all.

"Dammit!" Jack walked on ahead and kicked at the gravel outside the coffeeshop. Trout had no idea what was going on, but Shelagh was grim-lipped.

On the long drive back, exhausted by the bustle of town, Trout soon fell asleep between his aunt and uncle. The truck rode low on its springs, filled with fifty-pound bags of dog food, supplies, and bundles of mail under the tarp.

They arrived in Nordegg too late for supper, but Frank Jones and his wife came out of the house when they pulled into the yard. Beth invited them in and poured them all coffee, even pouring some for Trout. Jack and Frank took their coffee onto the porch to talk and smoke.

"You're looking pretty fit there, young fella," Beth Jones said. "New boots?"

Trout nodded shyly.

"So what's this about you staying, Trout?" Heather Jones was slim like her father and tanned now too. Like her mother, her hair was nearly white from the summer sun, but her pale blue eyes were mocking. She was two years older than Trout, and went to school in Rocky.

"He's with us for the year," Shelagh said.

"So you can come and visit us more often, eh?" Beth teased. Trout blushed, but he liked her. Who wouldn't, he thought.

Heather laughed, as sure of herself as Trout was shy.

"With those new boots, maybe we can do a moonlight ride up to Goldeye Lake, eh Trout?"

"Sure." Trout didn't want to seem too eager. Heather winked as she walked him to the door.

"Heather." Her mother shook her head.

"We should go," Jack motioned through the screen door. "It'll be dark by the time we get back."

"I'm sorry, Jack," Frank Jones said, shaking his head, as he leaned in the truck window. Jack looked down at his lap. "But we're both old war horses." Frank patted Jack's back.

"Don't know about this one." Jack grimaced, and put the truck in gear.

"We'll do alright somehow," Frank said, before they drove out. "We always have, Jack."

All the way home, Trout's aunt and uncle sat in silence. Trout stared out the window into the dark forest. The two-way cracked with banter between Red Wilson and the lookout on Old Baldy.

As they crossed the Cline River, Trout thought he could see a faint light from the lookout. The clouds were high and the sky cold and clear, with a gibbous moon. Like a cookie with a bite out of it, Shelagh said.

When the truck pulled into the yard, all the dogs were there, waiting for them: Blondie, with her young puppies; Lady, the Samoyed and her mature pups; her mate Silver; and the St. Bernards, Dagwood, and his monstrous son, Junior, who weighed two hundred and fifty pounds, and dwarfed Jack when he stood up on the fence.

All of the dogs barked frantic greetings. Trout and

Shelagh fed them while Jack unloaded the truck. The horses ran along the fence and Belle hung her head over the top wire and snorted before she galloped off. And Trout knew that, for as long as it lasted, this was exactly where he wanted to be.

Two days later, just after lunch, Charlie and Carrie roared into the yard in a spray of gravel.

Charlie was out of breath and upset. Jack sent Trout out to saddle Belle and Dusty.

"Stay on this side of the river. Water's still high."

Carrie seemed angry as she walked with Trout to the barn. This was not the girl he'd seen at the Sun Dance. The lines in her face that had opened to laughter now shrank in a tight knot about her forehead and around her mouth.

Trout saddled Belle, but Carrie insisted on riding Dusty bareback. They set out across the dry flats that Jack had named for Carrie's grandfather, Silas, past the airstrip and the Stoney graves at the end of it. Carrie rode ahead, slipping in and out of the low willows along the North Saskatchewan River. Her hair, a long black tangle past her shoulders, shone in the August sun and the buckskin of the Sun Dance was now replaced with men's work boots, jeans and a lumberman's shirt loose at the neck.

They rode alongside each other until the ranger station was out of sight. Then Carrie slapped the reins on Dusty, and pushed her to a gallop on the open plain. She hugged the pinto with her legs and leaned forward, close to the horse's mane, a fluid rhythm of horse and rider.

Trout hung on to Belle's saddle horn as Carrie led them down the cutbanks. Trout could barely restrain Belle who tried to outrun the pinto. He was at the limits of his riding skill, but he didn't want to slow down in front of Carrie.

At the sight of the graves, Carrie suddenly heeled and circled back to the fence that sheltered the grave-yard from the plains. Trout was glad for the rest. His knees and wrists hurt from hanging on, and he was thankful for the new boots that kept his feet in the stirrups. Carrie turned to him as he rode up beside her.

"Silas's brother's kids." She pointed to the small crosses. "Died when they were babies." He watched her lips. "My cousins." She nodded to the greying plank. "And my aunt. She died giving birth to an-other one." She looked at the graves and said nothing more, but brought the pinto around.

"Let's go."

This time she loped along the riverbed until they reached the confluence of the Cline and the Sas-katchewan. Then she slid from the pony and stood overlooking the two rivers, with her hands in her jean pockets, and her back to Trout. She looped the reins of the pinto between her fingers, reminding Trout of the picture of his great-grandmother holding the reins of her horse in the same way, but with gloved hands. Carrie leaned into the pinto. Her hair tangled in the horse's mane.

Trout tethered Belle to a willow and watched Car-rie, whose eyes were fierce flashes of brown. Her jaw was set and there was something vaguely Asian about her features. Yet, there was no mistaking that she was the granddaughter of Silas Moses. She was what his mother might call plump, but she was beautiful. Trout didn't feel shy around her, nor did he feel he had to fill the air with words. Like him, she seemed comfortable with silence. They'd ridden long stretches without a word, but Trout was always aware of her presence, and her intelligence. She eyed the landscape the way Jack did, and she watched Trout without appearing to. He wondered about the source of her anger and hoped it had nothing to do with him.

"This is all gonna be underwater." She took in the range of both rivers with her gaze. "You heard about the dam?"

Trout shook his head.

"The government's putting one here. Silas sent my dad to ask your uncle for help."

He remembered the words of the chief ranger and how Jack had said damn, like a curse. But he must have been talking about the dam.

"Jack hasn't said much. But he's upset about something."

"Silas didn't like Jack when he first came here. He told us to take our horses back on the reserve," Carrie said. "Silas's brother, Norman, wouldn't go and Silas said the ranger built a fence around his house."

Trout knew that house. The abandoned one he'd explored at the end of the pasture.

"Think that was another ranger, before Jack got here." Trout defended his uncle, but he didn't know. Maybe she was right.

"He shot our horses. Then Silas spoke to him. He'd

had enough. My dad thought they'd kill each other." She toed the gravel with her boot.

Trout knew she'd spoken the truth. Dry old horse skins without brands hung on the fence beside the barn. He'd wondered who they belonged to. Jack told him the Stoneys were proud of their horses, which once ran free on Kootenay Plains.

"Jack just did what he was told." Trout turned towards Carrie.

"Silas knew that," Carrie nodded. "The government wanted us off the Kootenay Plains. But your uncle was all alone out here. My dad said a Winchester wasn't much protection."

"I know he really likes Silas." Trout watched Carrie's face and tried to understand what she was saying. "Your grandfather was nice to us at the Sun Dance. What happened?"

"The graves." She looked past Trout towards Moses flats. "Your uncle knew our language, enough anyway, so he could talk with Silas. When he found more graves, your uncle put a fence around them." She sat down on the gravel cross-legged, pulled a rollie from her jacket and lit it with a wooden match. "No one ever did that before." She took a drag and offered Trout the cigarette.

Trout sat down beside her. The gravel was cool through his jeans. "Is the dam going in for sure?" He drew on the cigarette and coughed as the harsh tobacco seared the tops of his lungs.

"We don't know. It's not the first time. When Silas was a boy there was talk of building a dam, and again in the forties when we got the reserve. But the government always stopped. Silas wants your uncle's help." She took the cigarette from Trout.

"This valley's full of sacred places. There's many people buried here." She drew on her cigarette again and peered past him down the river. "This is all I've ever known, Trout."

Trout watched the green silted water rushing past them. He felt the hairs on his arms quiver in the wind off the river. Despite the cold, he could feel Carrie's warmth.

"Silas likes you. The-one-who-watches, he called you, after the Sun Dance." She looked directly at Trout, and chuckled. He didn't blush this time. She tilted her head and squinted.

"Last time your eyes were blue, now they're green."

"Something I do, I guess." He laughed and she pushed his shoulder, then threw the end of the cigarette into the gravel and ground it out with her heel.

"I'm going away to school in Red Deer next year. I'll live with my sister."

She was so close her smoky breath warmed his face as she spoke, and Trout's field of vision filled with her lips. He felt the heat of her. Cigarette smoke mingled with the campfire scent of her shirt, horse sweat, and the musk of river mud. He sat forward and sniffed. And recognized another, more familiar scent as she leaned her shoulder into him. It was the smell of lilacs, the perfume his mother bought from a woman who came to their door selling it.

"My sister's an Avon lady," Carrie said, pushing him away. "Silas wants me to go to the university like his brother, George McLean. 'The Stoney people need lawyers, Carrie. Be a lawyer,' he says. 'Learn the Whiteman's words.'"

As she laid her head on his shoulder, Trout's hearing aid squealed like an alarm and she pulled away.

"What was that?" She looked at him,

"They do that sometimes. Interference." He took her hand. His face was red. His heart pounded. "It's not you. In school, I used to make it whistle on purpose. The teachers would go crazy thinking they were hearing things." He didn't want her to lean away from him. "My friend Kenny and I, we had a secret language. We talked without making any sounds."

He hadn't thought of Kenny for a long time, but he knew Carrie would have liked him.

"Can you read lips?" She mouthed something.

"It's going to snow, plowboy?" He grinned.

She blinked, and picked up the reins of the pony. "It's time to go, cowboy!"

"I know," he teased her.

She tugged him to his feet, and then slipped onto the back of the pinto and trotted toward the flats. As she turned to look at him, her hair blew across her face. She smiled and he was happy.

While Carrie brushed down the horses in the corral, Trout unsaddled Belle and kept his head down to hide his eyes. He knew they would reveal how he felt about Carrie and he wasn't ready for her or his aunt to know.

Carrie looked at Trout one more time before she left. "You gonna go to the Cavalcade?" she asked. He nodded. She walked toward the truck where Jack and her father were waiting. Trout's head spun in opposites of joy and loss, of Carrie Moses and the news of the flooding of the valley.

That night, over supper, Trout asked his uncle about the dam. Jack glanced at Shelagh before he answered. "It's up to the cabinet. I don't know what I can do," he said, and looked away.

Trout was disappointed. Somehow, he had imagined his uncle could fix anything.

"You could talk to the Minister at the Cavalcade." Shelagh sounded perky as she said it, but her eyes were worried.

"Jesus, Shelagh, I don't know."

Jack went out on the porch with his glass of whisky and after the dishes were done, Shelagh and Trout joined him in the cool of the screened room. The dogs stood at the front of their pens and wagged their tails.

But Jack was impatient and gulped his drink. He got up abruptly and went to the tack room in the barn. Then he came across the yard to the garage, dragging the traces for the dog sleds. Trout realized that this was what his dad did when he was angry. He'd work with his hands on something he loved, and it calmed him. At the sight of the harness, despite the absence of snow, the dogs began to bark joyously and pushed the mesh fence with their snouts and paws. The Saints, as Shelagh always called them, stood up on their hind legs, baying and woofing. Jack must have known how the dogs would greet him. He grinned at Trout and made no effort to quiet the dogs.

That night, Trout sat in the lower bunk with his

back to the wall of the fallout shelter and wrote in his journal. His own words seemed feeble as he tried to write about the dam, which he now heard as damn. He thought of Carrie, her breath on his face. And he rifled through the book of love poems his mother had given him. But this reverie baffled him. He knew something of reverie now, of which the poets spoke in words of such power and beauty. This reverie was close to madness. It was an idiot joy that numbed him and changed him at once. He wanted to find the words for her so badly, he wrote and wrote like a sweet fool. Unrequited love had struck him surely as an axe could split a log.

Although Trout was uncertain how it showed, his uncle, and his aunt especially, had smiled at him through dinner, and Shelagh hushed Jack when he started to ask about the ride. Still, probably the only thing secret about Trout's love then was what he wrote in his journal.

Trout would have given Carrie anything, so smitten was he. He would even have given her his beloved conch. If he could not find the words to say what he wanted to say, surely she could hear them in the conch.

The next morning, after breakfast, Trout worked hard to get the wood box filled, the dog runs scooped and the dogs watered. Shelagh had the steel Thermos and a sack of sandwiches waiting by the back door when Jack pulled the truck around to take Trout to Two o'clock Creek. There, they'd help the trail crew ready the campground for the David Thompson Cavalcade on the last long weekend of the summer. For Trout, work was easy now with Carrie's face before him.

Clare

My favourite time of the year has always been the fall, especially what people used to call Indian summer, when the nights are crisp with frost. After the girls went off to school, and the frost melted off the grass, I'd get the housework out of the way, and then walk along the fence behind George Abel's old run-down farm.

When we first moved here there'd been a dozen of those last-ditch farms, with root cellars dug into the hills and tumbledown barns. Now there was only one, surrounded by houses and newly-poured basements rising out of the subdivision on the hill where we'd once taken the kids tobogganing.

I'd walked out on the last strip of prairie, past the wolf willows—their fragrance always seemed tinged with sadness. And there's a quality of light about that time of year. Something about the sun being lower in the sky—a pink, sometimes yellow hue that matched the autumn. I always thought it a perfect season to die, fading with the light.

I'd walk along the beaver dam road, sitting down to rest when the baby made me tired. I liked the view of the mountains to the west and the city to the north. There was a groaner I'd sit on. A family of gophers nearby would come out of their holes to watch—their noses twitching—and stand up and chirp at me. My grandfather Locke used to say that on the homestead there were only two kinds of rocks: grinners and groaners. Groaners were the rocks he could move, and grinners were the ones that peeked and grinned, buried in the earth, daring to be moved. I'd sit there with the sun soaking into the boulder; something soft and womanly about it—my thinking rock.

The girls now took their lunches to school, so sometimes I'd bring a sandwich and a Thermos of tea. I didn't write poetry anymore, but when I was younger, sometimes I painted, mostly watercolours—oils were too expensive. I'd always meant to paint that scene. The sky so big, the blue-and-white wavy line of mountains to the west, always a few of them covered with snow, and in the foreground, the new bridge under construction over the aqua band of river and the black gash of Blackfoot Trail pushing south.

I always thought about my dad in the fall, maybe more so now that I'd decided to name the baby after him. Maybe because autumn is the leaving time, like in a poem I once read by Bliss Carmen. "There's something about October that sets the gypsy blood astir." I couldn't imagine abandoning a child. I couldn't imagine Lowell or me doing that. But my dad left us, and there wasn't a day I didn't think about that.

One night Mom and Ian came for dinner. Her steady Eddy, she called him. After dinner, Ian had taken the girls to the Dairy Bar while Mom and I sat at the dining room table surrounded by the dinner dishes. That's when I decided to tell her.

"I'm naming the baby after Dad," I said.

She looked at me over the tops of her glasses

and didn't say anything for a long time. "He lives in Bankview, you know," she said.

It was my turn to stare.

"I looked him up in the phone book and called him."

I looked him up too once, a long time ago. But I hadn't had the nerve to call.

"He's got three little girls and a boy," Mom said, biting her lower lip. "I saw them."

I didn't say anything. I didn't know what to feel.

"I got Ian to drive by." Mom laid her glasses on the table and dabbed away her tears with a dishtowel. "He looks happy, Claire."

"Did you talk to him?"

"I called him. He said, 'Don't ever phone here again,' and hung up."

"You tell Ian?"

"No. I had to call your dad. I thought maybe he'd want to meet his grandchildren."

I brushed the hair off her forehead with my hand. "Oh, Mom."

"You're not going to name the baby after him? How do you know it's a boy, anyway?" She looked hurt. "Do what you want. You always have."

"Now wait a minute. I'm not so sure now. About the name. I had no idea, Mom. It's stupid, but you know, I always thought that Dad leaving was some kind of mistake and that one day he'd realize it too and he'd come for us."

Ian's car pulled up to the curb and we could see Emily in the front seat. She had ice cream all over

her face. She was a happy, independent little mess—
and a princess.

"He'll make a good husband," I said.

"We better get this cleaned up." Mom swabbed her
eyes with the tea towel and began to clear the table.
We never talked about Dad again.

Years later, when my kids were in their teens, Mom
called one night. "Read the obituaries," she said.

I didn't have to ask. Dad's four children from his
second marriage were listed and his grandchildren.
But not me, nor my children. It was as if we'd never
existed.

Will had started to write letters home. I didn't show
them to Lowell, because the letters went on about
Jack and Shelagh, especially Jack—Jack and the horses, Jack and the forest fire, and the Sun Dance and
somebody named Red. I kept those letters for years.
I thought about Will's life, running parallel to ours,
and wondered how he was keeping up there. I remember my math teacher talking about parallel lines
and how they go on forever and never converge.

I wondered about Lowell too. He'd made foreman
at the gas plant. But the work there was almost finished, and he figured he'd be home to stay by Christmas. A man he used to work for through the John
Howard Society had offered him a foreman's job in
the city. A university was going up in the northwest
and there was new construction everywhere as the
old buildings were torn down.

Maybe convergence is an illusion and our lives

always run along parallel lines—some closer, some further apart. Like the baby inside me.

My labour pains started one day when I was out on my walk. The girls were back at school, Lowell was in Pincher Creek, and Will was at the ranger station. I dropped my sandwich and walked toward the last row of houses under construction, clutching my dress. I asked one of the men to please call a cab for me. A trickle of blood filled my shoe.

One of the workers laid a plaid car blanket on the ground beside an unfinished house and helped me lie down. A circle of tradesmen in overalls stood around me. Men like Lowell. One of them held my hand and said, 'It'll be all right lady, we called, and an ambulance's on the way'.

I could feel the blood soaking the blanket under me. I didn't want any fuss, just a cab, but the men got scared when I screamed. I could hear the siren coming for me and I prayed—dear God, I prayed for this one.

As the ambulance raced towards the hospital I thought if I was to die, I'd never see my father's grave. And I prayed for the baby. The ambulance was a Cadillac—the only Cadillacs poor people get to ride in are hearses or ambulances, Lowell used to joke. The siren was off, and I could hear "She's a girl, I'm a boy, and I love her" on the radio. I knew something wasn't right.

When we got to the hospital, the nurse rushed me into the operating room, where Dr. Speilgleman was waiting for me. He'd delivered Emily and the twins. He was always kind to me. Before he began the delivery, he leaned to my ear and said, "We'll take good care of you, Clare."

Stephen Magnus Taylor Dunlop was a beautiful baby boy with a round chubby face. He looked like Lowell in his baby pictures. I held my baby while Dr. Speilgleman stood by. Even the nurse was in tears. She took the baby from me, and Dr. Speilgleman explained that the placenta had separated. And no, my walking hadn't caused it, he assured me.

But just as I had known all along that the baby was a boy, I'd known, even in the ambulance, that something terrible had happened. I'd felt the small life leave me even when I lay bleeding on the ground at the construction site.

I came home from the hospital two weeks later. Mom was there with the girls and my friend Marnie came in to help me. Lowell came as soon as he could get away, but I sent him back. If tears helped me with my pain, work helped Lowell with his.

The tears didn't come, just then. I couldn't go out, not on my walk to the prairies. I was ashamed. I thought that what had happened was my fault, and my world closed in on me.

Thank God, for Pauline—she took right over. She brought me food in bed and got her sisters dressed and off to school with their lunches. I slept for days and days, getting up only long enough to open the drapes and peek out the window to see what time it was. I felt as though I was looking through a keyhole from a dark room into the light. I had a bad case of the dreads. When I ate, I gagged. I felt like my insides were coming up through my throat.

About a week after I came home from the hospital, the tears finally started. I cried for nearly four days and I couldn't stop. Pauline phoned the doctor and got some pills from the drugstore. I'd always prayed till then, but I'd stopped. There was a period, maybe days, maybe hours—it's all gone now—where I remember nothing, although the girls told me I was talking to them, and we even did things together. There's nothing there anymore, like my memory's been erased.

I don't know how it happened, but I found myself in the ambulance. Pauline was holding my hand and crying. I didn't recall Pauline slapping me after she called the ambulance. She told me about it years later. She'd found me on the bedroom floor. I don't remember taking the pills. But I do remember one crazy thought: that I had nothing more to lose.

It never occurred to me then that I had everything to lose: my son, my girls, my husband.

When I woke, I was in a hospital bed. An older woman lay asleep in the bed beside me. The curtains were drawn across the window. In the hall, the lights were low. I was incredibly thirsty, so I gathered my gown around me and shuffled into the hall to find a nurse. I turned into what I thought was the bathroom, through a swinging door. In the dim light I could see a narrow bed with straps across it and a black machine with a crank that looked like Lowell's battery charger and wires coming from a headset. I turned away and closed the door quickly. I knew what it was, and where the ambulance had brought me. Grandma Locke was sent to the General too, where doctors gave her shock treatments for depression. I felt weak and helpless as I turned back into the hall. It was painful to walk on the cold cement in my bare feet—I had no slippers.

A nurse peeked out a door at the end of the corridor.

"Just where do you think you're going, dear?"

"I'm thirsty."

"Let's go back to bed." She took me by the arm and walked me past the room I'd wandered into. "I'll bring you some water."

"I'm not going in there, am I?"

The nurse laughed, "It's all up to the doctors."

I drank my water through a straw. The water tasted flat and papery and I lay there wondering what they'd do to me. The nurse gave me a pill.

As I drifted back to sleep, my dreams were full of lights—my children and I were in the house. I'd hear noises in the yard and flick on the outside lights, hoping to catch the intruders. I kept asking Lowell to please put up more lights, so we'd see who was trying to break in.

In my dreams, dirty clothing and dishes piled up everywhere. When I swept the floor, more debris emerged from under the table and the chesterfield. I kept sweeping and the rooms filled up, but the girls were oblivious and I kept hearing noises in the backyard and I kept putting on the light hoping to surprise whoever it was. Pots and pans and toys were falling out of the cupboards and slowly the rooms in our house came undone—all the shelving disappeared and the rooms Lowell added were slipping away. The house went back to it's beginnings, starting all over again.

I remember, even in my dreams, not wanting to dream. I was exhausted—afraid to shut my eyes, afraid to open them.

When I woke the next day, near noon, tired and fuzzy-mouthed, Lowell lay asleep in his work clothes in the chair opposite me. I tried to sort out what happened, how I'd gotten here. I don't know what medication the doctors had prescribed for me, but everything appeared through a gauze like the bandages I'd put on my kids' cuts and bruises.

The woman in the bed next to mine was sitting up, looking out the window. "The nurse will raise the bed for you, dear." She pointed to Lowell. "He's been here since last night."

"It's okay," I smiled at her. Her speech was slurred and her wrists were bandaged. I turned away when I realized I was staring, but she only smiled back sweetly. I was ashamed and wondered what my own voice sounded like.

When the porter brought in the lunch trolley, Lowell woke up.

"We're awake, are we?" He cranked up my bed, put down the trays, and lifted the steel cover to reveal a small square of white bread with a bit of beef and gravy, and a small scoop of mashed potatoes beside a green puddle of canned peas. There was a glass of milk and a shallow dish full of purple Jell-O cubes.

Lowell tried to talk, but I shushed him and said, "Want some, honey? You must be ravenous."

He shook his head. I could see his hands were dirty—he must have driven straight here from work.

"How are the girls?" I pushed my plate away and picked at the Jell-O cubes.

Lowell watched me eat as if he'd never seen me do so before.

"Have the rest of my sandwich, okay?"

He took my plate in his lap and looked down at it as he ate. "The girls are alright," he said. "Your mom came over to help. Pauline called me. I came as soon as I could." He choked back a sob. "Catholic Family Services is going to bring in a housekeeper."

"Lowell, I want to come home."

"The doctor wants to keep you here awhile." His eyes were red.

I wanted to scream—I did not want to be quiet. Then I remembered the room with the shock machine. So, I made a very conscious decision to be clear and wide-eyed, enunciating every word. I knew they would be watching me. I also knew what the doctors said about Grandma Locke—that she was hysterical. If there's a modern day word for witch, that's it.

Grandma Locke told me a crazy story—crazy, except that it was true. A long time ago, she said, when there was still a moat around Edinburgh Castle—the Nor' Loch—it was full of sewage, and the rotting carcasses of cattle and horses. If a woman was thought to be a witch, she was thrown in the Nor' Loch. If she drowned, she was innocent. Because the devil hadn't rescued her. If she floated, she was hauled out and burned at the stake. Because she was a witch who had magic powers. I felt like those women. No matter what I did, there was no way out.

Mom claimed the shock treatments helped Grandma become normal. But I thought my grandmother became dull. As she dutifully took her pills, she stopped telling us stories. When she tried to make cookies, she burned them and she'd cry. Mom told her it was alright, but her eyes were placid water, without waves or ripples.

Lowell got up and put the plate on the bedside table. He took my hand. "I phoned Paddy MacIntyre. I never liked it down there in Pincher Creek anyway. I can start work for Paddy next week."

I let Lowell talk about work. It calmed him.

His eyes welled with tears and he turned away. "We'll be alright. I'll be home with the kids at night," he said quietly.

I could hear his mother's voice in the hall, taking charge, as always. Dot came in first, carrying a large, obviously expensive bouquet of flowers. She was followed by her friend, Mr. Jones. He stood by my side with his hat in his hand and I caught a whiff of cigar smoke from his sports jacket. His eyes were warm as he stood near the edge of the bed and talked to me.

Lowell was glad to see them. His mother fussed with the bouquet, trying out different places in the room for it. She adjusted the curtains, which were already open, to let in more light. She was scared of the darkness—I could see it in her eyes. She was afraid to look into my eyes, so she put on a shaky smile and talked to the woman in the next bed like we were both there to have our appendixes out.

The expensive bouquet embarrassed me. But I was glad she'd come. I could see her now as Lowell saw her, a lonely frightened woman. I knew that whatever I was afraid of, she was afraid of it too.

"Lavinia, the flowers are just lovely." I squeezed her hand and I used the name she liked to be called by. It had been her mother's name too.

Dot adjusted her brooch and turned abruptly to talk to Lowell. Mr. Jones took my hands in his and kissed me on the cheek before they left. Lowell's mother waved from the door, but she still couldn't look at me. Her white glove was the last thing I saw before I drifted back to sleep, with warm sunlight on my face.

Mom came with Ian after supper. She brought my suitcase with my slippers and dressing gown. I was still weak, but the sleep helped me feel a bit stronger. Mom told me Lowell had gone home to change and to get some sleep. The girls needed him more than I did anyway. Ian seemed nervous, but he helped hang my clothes while Mom read the card on the bouquet of flowers. She stuffed the card back in the vase and said nothing.

"Can I get you anything?" she asked, fidgeting in her seat. My mother was never comfortable sitting. She liked being up and about. She looked hurt, like I'd punished her.

When I took her arm, she flinched.

"Mom, I'm not like Grandma."

Mom sat on my bed and put her arm around my shoulder.

"Oh, Clare."

I could feel her tears on my neck. Ian stood at Mom's side and my mother took my hand, the one with the hospital bracelet. We all remained that way for what seemed like a long time.

"When your father left, my mother used to tell me, 'it will get better'. I didn't see how it could, ever. I thought she was so heartless then.

"But she was right. I never thought I'd be in love again, but I love Ian very much," my mother said, glancing around the hospital room.

"I didn't think I'd tell you the news here. We're getting married at Christmas and I want you at the wedding."

The bell in the hall sounded; visiting hours were over.

Ian patted my shoulder. "We'll get through this, won't we, kid?"

I nodded, trying not to cry. Mom held me tight.

The woman in the next bed had no visitors all that day. After Mom and Ian left, she turned to me and said, "You have a real nice family." I tried to smile.

I hadn't thought of that, simple as it was. What I had was enough, and whatever was missing couldn't be helped.

Trout

Archie Baptiste and his trail crew had the campsite at Two o'clock Creek ready for the David Thompson Cavalcade: stones were placed around freshly-dug fire rings, and tidy pyramids of cord wood and new log picnic tables dotted the alpine meadow. Jack nodded his approval to the trail crew as he drove through the campsite without stopping. Junior woofed in agreement from the back of the truck. Jack was moody that day and when Trout tried to talk, he merely grunted. Trout knew his uncle's mind was on the special visitors.

In the morning the creek was dry. By the time they passed the simple sign, Two o'clock Creek—Jack's handiwork, nailed to a creekside spruce—there was a fresh boiling creek under them that the truck splashed through. To Trout, the prairie boy, this was as mysterious as the valley into which they had travelled. Two o'clock Creek was dead dry in the morning, a live mountain stream by mid-afternoon, and a trickle again by nightfall.

"What makes it do that, Uncle Jack? I can see why it's called Two o'clock Creek," Trout said.

Jack pushed in the clutch and geared down. "Why don't we go look," he said. "Work's done for now."

He turned up the mountain towards a fire road. A loud thump hit the roof, and Junior's shadow filled the rear window; his paws pounded on the cab. Jack yelled at the dog to get down and he scraped to a halt. A brown bloodied shape lay across the road. Jack jumped out of the truck, and shortened the chain on the dog to keep him back.

As Jack stood over the carcass of a bull moose, he pointed to skid marks in the powder of the road. In the ditch was a heap of fresh bear scat.

"Hit it and drove off. Bear's been feeding. Somebody's lucky to be alive."

Trout looked at the body of the moose, with its fine set of antlers. Its haunches were smashed and its sides had been clawed by the bear. Its intestines looped out. A dry froth rimmed its nostrils and flies swarmed the open mouth. The tongue lolled to one side.

"This was the same moose we saw last week. He's an old one. Damn it."

Trout walked back to the truck where Jack had Shelagh on the radio.

"Roger. Watch for anybody coming through with front-end damage. Better radio the wardens at Saskatchewan Crossing. Over."

Jack handed Trout the winch hook from the front bumper and released the lock, while Trout ran with the cable. His uncle noosed it carefully around the haunches of the moose and engaged the winch, then slowly hauled the carcass towards the shoulder of the road, where they levered it into the woods with shovels.

"Animals will feed on it," Jack said.

Trout was shaken, but fascinated by the oddly beautiful, almost pre-historic-looking body of the moose. He couldn't look away. His uncle was quiet and Junior panted behind them in the truck. Jack grasped the dog's large head in his hands.

"Good boy," he said, as Junior's tongue rasped his cheeks and knocked his glasses off-kilter.

They turned up a fork in the fire road. Trout opened the log gate, and closed it behind them. As they climbed the mountain, the truck shuddered in second gear. Jack dropped into first. Boulders thudded under the truck's floor and the truck swung and bounced on its suspension.

When they arrived at the upper reaches of the creek, Trout stayed in the cab while Jack got out in midstream to winch the truck across the water, which was now up to the running boards. They crawled upwards until the road ran out in a clearing. Jack unchained Junior, took a leather pannier from the toolbox, and packed binoculars and their lunches on the dog's back.

He slung a climbing rope over his shoulders and took the Winchester from the rifle rack in the cab.

"Might have scared him off." Jack loaded shells into the Winchester and said, "Just in case we didn't. We're in the bear's house now. Probably sleeping off his dinner."

Junior ran ahead, and waited with twin ropes of slobber drooling from his jowls, a dog grin around his panting tongue.

Above Two o'clock Falls, they rested for a while. Then Jack roped Trout in as they began the final ascent. He was thankful for the rope as they slid and slipped through the scree. But they saw no bears. After a short scramble over the scree, they neared a sheer rock face where they could see the start of the underground stream that flowed from Athabasca

Glacier and that fed Two o'clock Creek. Jack pointed over the range to Banff-Jasper Park and the Great Divide.

"Where all the rivers begin," he said. Trout knew from the schoolroom maps that this was the beginning of the route of the coureur de bois, coursing down across the prairies to Hudson Bay. It was windier up here and colder than on the valley floor, but close to the rock face intense heat radiated from the sun-baked stone. Jack mopped his neck with his bandanna and Trout did the same.

Junior barked and lunged at a small tailless rodent with big ears. It slipped into the rocks and appeared again above them.

"Junior! Quiet, boy. It's a pika," Jack said, "a rock bunny." They made their way across the rocks. The St. Bernard drank from the stream. His big tongue slapped the water as his ears floated on the current. Jack crouched and motioned near the ledge. Trout could see a row of small plants and stems laid out on the rock.

"The pika's drying his food for winter and then he stores it. Like your Aunt Shelagh putting down preserves."

They were above the treeline now, between the highest point of land and sky, where the horizon opened up in front of them, and the ranger station was far to the east. Taking the binoculars from the pannier, Trout scoped the valley: Thompson Creek to the west, the Siffleur River confluence opposite Whirlpool Point, and past that, Banff National Park and Saskatchewan Crossing on the Icefields Highway. Below him lay the greying ruins of the Barnes Ranch. The wind riffled the blonde grass on Kootenay Plains, where the Plains Cree came to barter with the Kootenay, and across the river, through the trees, they could see the silver slashes of Whiterabbit and Coral Creeks. Behind them there were a dozen glaciers, Jack said, and the watershed of the North Saskatchewan.

They climbed again until they were well above the waterfall. Jack pointed to the distant white of a glacier cowled in rock.

"Here you are. Sun makes it way around. Mid-day, it hits the glacier, and melt water comes through the rock. Two o'clock Creek." Jack grinned. "Mountain Standard Time."

Trout wondered at the magic of water wrung from clouds and wind, somewhere between the highest point of land and the sky. The wind buffeted his hearing aids and he leaned in to listen, between the static of the microphones, to his uncle, who hung onto his hat. Even Junior's great ears lifted in the high mountain gusts.

"Seven hundred and forty-three square miles; this is my district," Jack shouted. "But Silas says the land doesn't belong to us. We belong to it." The grin on Jack's lips seemed formed by the wind. "Hungry?" Trout's uncle ducked against the rock face and waved him over to a sheltered ledge in the sun.

"Let's sit here." Jack squatted and took their sandwiches and Junior's dry food from the pannier.

"When I was a boy in Avoch, I'd walk by the churchyard where Alexander Mackenzie was buried.

Dreamed of following the Mackenzie River one day to the Arctic.

"Our harbour was full of boats from the Baltic taking on barrels of herring. Three-masted, square-rigged sailing ships. A beautiful sight as they went down the firth under full sail. Could see 'em from my schoolroom window. I dreamed of running away. When my dad said we were going to homestead in Canada, I could hardly wait, Trout."

Behind Jack's grey hair, hearing aids and glasses, Trout could still make out the face of an adventurous boy. Junior lay beside them, a mound of dry food between his paws, and munched with his brow furrowed as if deep in thought. Despite the sun-warmed rock at his back, Trout could feel the wind shift to the north and a shiver went down his spine. Just a few feet away from the rock ledge, the temperature dropped to chilling. He pulled his jacket collar up.

"Could never have done any of this in Scotland," Jack said. He then told Trout about how Junior's grandparents were raised by monks as rescue dogs in the Alps.

After lunch they picked their way back among the rocks and slid down the gravel. The dog, clumsy and mopey when he was penned up, was graceful in scree and broken rock, especially after Trout fed him half his sandwich. They barely kept up with his massive haunches as Junior led them back to the truck.

"Glad you asked about the creek," Jack grinned and slapped Trout's shoulder.

"I wasn't going to, Uncle Jack, but yeah," Trout said,

tired from the climb. He was now less afraid of his uncle's moods, which, unlike his mother's, didn't last.

Early that Saturday, the line of cars in the David Thompson Cavalcade pulled up to the ranger station. At the front of the line was the Minister of Highways. Trout recognized him from his pictures in the Calgary papers. He and his wife both wore glasses. She had a sheer red scarf tied around her head and his hair was slicked back. He drove a new Chevrolet pulling a fibreglass trailer shaped like a boat. Jack quipped later that it didn't look like that boat would either float or afford much shelter. The Minister shook hands with Jack and Shelagh and admired the green lawn and Shelagh's English garden, with its August blooms of bright daffy heads of bergamot and slender verbena amongst the lavender and daisies.

"When we hire a family man we get the family too," the Minister said to Jack before the cavalcade left.

Shelagh flushed at his comment. Her smile thinned and her eyes glowered, but she said nothing.

The dusty line of cars was much smaller than the Sun Dance procession that had filed out of the valley earlier, but its arrival marked the end of summer. After supper, Jack put on a fresh uniform and polished his boots before he and Trout headed to the campsite at Two o'clock Creek. Shelagh waved as they drove out of the yard.

Picnic tables had been gathered around the campsite, where a PA system was set up with a generator. Trout recognized Charlie Moses's pickup and scanned the small crowd for Carrie. Without the bright colours of the tepees and the drummers of the previous week, with only a few cars and a truck or two parked beside the forestry vehicles, the event seemed strangely without joy. His uncle disappeared and Trout tried to listen to the Minister's speech, but it was lost in the clearing despite the PA's underwater sound and staticky gurgling. Bubbles came from the politician's mouth. It had been a long time since Trout had seen those.

Eventually, the Minister raised his voice and the bubbles snapped and Trout heard him clearly.

"No, you don't want that highway, do you? You don't want a dam. You don't want a lake?" He held his hand to his ear and looked at the crowd. Trout knew the power of water and he watched the man who promised it.

"Well?" the minister said. "You don't want prosperity."

"No!" answered some of the whites sarcastically and they laughed. "Never!"

"No!" Some of the Stoneys shouted too. "No." The word echoed in Trout's ears. But the Stoneys weren't laughing.

The Minister thanked the crowd and waved before he stepped down. Confused, Trout looked for Carrie. A drummer from the Bighorn Stoneys took the Minister's place. The sun went down, the main campfire glowed and the brilliant white mantles of the Coleman lanterns ringed the clearing.

Trout felt a hand brush his elbow. He turned and saw Carrie walk by with some of the Stoney women and children, all wearing ceremonial dress. Charlie Moses took the mike to invite women and children to join in the Chicken Dance, but most of them were content to watch from the fringes. Others trailed back to their campsites, but Trout stayed to watch Carrie swirl in her bucksksin on the dusty grass, as clouds of moths circled the Coleman lanterns.

Carrie glanced sideways and pulled Trout into the dance. He found the beat, with his eyes on her feet, and he imitated her, pausing when she paused, and circling on the spot like a prairie chicken.

Cameras flashed on the dancers. Out of the corner of his eye, Trout watched Jack standing next to the Minister and Charlie Moses. All of them had drinks in their hands. Silas was nowhere to be seen. When the dance ended, Carrie left with her mother before Trout could talk to her.

After shaking hands with the Minister, Jack roared back through Two o'clock Creek, the phosphorescent green dials on the dash of the truck and the red glow of his cigarette lighting the cab. The ripe air smelled of whisky as they plummeted through the forest. As if in the belly of a dream, willow striplings whipped the outside mirrors. Jack raged. Trout held on to the door handle. He knew Jack was angry about something the Minister had said.

Suddenly, a flash blinded them as a logging truck rounded the bend. Jack cursed and swung into the cutbank. The truck swept by, inches away, its airhorn blasting loud as a locomotive. Its lights filled the truck's windshield, and then it was gone. Trout's heart skipped a beat, but Jack revved back to speed and said nothing.

After breakfast the next morning, Jack took the door panel from the forestry truck and pounded out a dent that hadn't been there the day before.

September turned the aspens at the base of Sentinel Mountain to a pale yellow, and traffic slowed to a logging truck or two every day. Each morning at eight, after the wood box was filled and the dogs were watered and fed, Trout went to the school Shelagh had set up in the dining room. A small blackboard leaned on a chair against the wall. Trout sat at the end of the table facing his aunt. Through the windows he could see the dogs asleep in their pens. In the kitchen, the constant static of the two-way radio hissed and crackled, and the radiant heat of the woodstove warmed the room. As he wrote his lessons, his aunt paused to check on the oven. At ten they stopped and, if he wasn't on patrol, Jack joined them for tea and buns or thick slices of buttered bread, spread with spoonfuls of Saskatoon and blackberry preserves from the bushes in Shelagh's garden.

Somedays, if Trout got ahead in his schoolwork, he spent the afternoon with Jack. One day, after inspecting the logging at Whiterabbit Creek, Jack took Trout to hike the trail to Siffleur Falls.

"It's *Sif-fleur*, Trout, a French word, like *fleur de lis*," Jack said, before showing him the split between the rock formations that shaped the river's course. Trout knew his uncle's education ended in the ninth grade. "Don't talk like a Yankee."

Siffleur Canyon was gouged in a schism of rock: on one side, contained by the hard, nearly-vertical limestone of the ancient seabed that set a straight course for the river and, on the other, a steep bank of soft shale eroded by millions of years of current. They hiked the trail along the top of the gorge to Siffleur Falls, where the air was sweet and wet in the brief September heat. Squatting on the lip of the waterfall, they watched the torrent that dropped over the sheer ledge.

"Thousands of fossils down there." Trout felt the thunder of the frothing white water driven through the rock chute.

"Part of what's called the Banff formation. Runs all through here. Sandwiches of soft and hard rock that wear away. Erosion uncovers the fossils," Jack shouted over the roar of the swift green water. A small rainbow formed over the falls.

"Too bad there's no way to get you any, Trout." Jack pivoted on his heels. "Don't get too close. Two years ago a man fell in; we couldn't recover his body. I found him later, on a sandbar behind the Upper Saskatchewan." Jack shook his head. "He had two little kids. Jesus."

"Jesus," Trout echoed under his breath.

As they hiked back down the canyon, Jack said, "There's fossils at Onion Lake above Ram Falls. Maybe we can get you some there. Called Hummingbird Reef. Nine hundred feet thick, maybe thirty miles long on the bottom of the Devonian Sea." Jack laughed.

"A coral reef in the mountains?" Trout asked. "Can we go there?"

"We could. Have to go in on horseback over the pass. It's covered with coral and snails. Maybe next spring." Jack gestured over the gorge and the western range, "You're on the bottom of the sea in these mountains, Trout."

Another day they stopped at the ruins of the old Kootenay settlement. As they walked through the tall grasses, Jack taught Trout the names: wildrye, bentgrass, blue gramma and sweetgrass. All along the creek were clumps of mountain timothy, broken circles of stone and strewn logs, sunk in the white glacial silt lapped by waves of wildrye and brome. Trout would have walked right over the teepee rings had Jack not stopped him.

"The Kootenay died here. Sometime in the 1840s, they got smallpox. From wearing the white man's clothing."

Trout plucked a ripe stem of wildrye, tugging it from the mother plant. He fingered the silky purple head and sucked on the straw, crushing the sweet pulp to draw out the moisture.

"You can eat the head too," Jack said, separating the kernels. "The Stoneys used it for food. You have to watch out it's not black. Ergot. Eat a little and you lose your fingernails." Trout grimaced and Jack laughed. "Eat a lot and you lose your internal organs—gangrene." Jack popped the seeds in his mouth and chewed them the way Kenny Dawes chewed the wheat they'd found spilled from the grain cars along the C.P.R. tracks.

"Actually, it's not bad," Trout said, surprised.

"I want to mark this with a fence. Once Silas Moses and I are gone, Trout, there'll be no one to remember what happened here. A lot didn't get written down." Jack toed a stone with his boot.

"Silas's not well. He's ninety, and news of the dam hasn't helped." Jack turned to go back to the truck. The afternoon wind, warmed by the sun, blew dry and hot across Kootenay Plains, but Trout shivered. The valley would be under water again, if the dam were built.

Trout was silent as Jack pointed out formations on the valley wall along the base of Sentinel Mountain, the vertical layers of soft and hard rock shorn away by the creeks running off the sunslope. "Flatirons." Trout stared at the grey points of limestone between the spillways of scree above the treeline, and recalled the heavy old-fashioned irons in the basement after his great-auntie died. Flatiron was an old name for something even older. Everything here had a name, a story.

Elliott Peak above them was named after Elliott Barnes who lived on the Kadoona Tinda ranch. His long-empty cabin, with its set of deer antlers above the plank door and its fireplace with a shale mantelpiece, stood forlornly in the centre of tumbledown corrals. A picture in the ranger station showed Barnes cleaning his rifle, a lever action Winchester like Jack's, his hair slick, his buckskin shirt fringed along the yoke and beaded at the shoulders. He was wearing a cartridge belt and a skinning knife hung at his waist. A real frontiersman, Jack said.

Just over the river were the ruins of Tom Wilson's trading post on Whiterabbit Creek. Wilson rode in from Lake Louise in 1888, led by the Kootenays, Jack said. All of them were gone now: Wilson, and Barnes, who left in nineteen o' five, and the Kootenays too. The valley was full of their ghosts, and his Auntie too was gone. Trout was glad for the crackle of the two-way and the modern-day voice of the rangers calling Nordegg.

Back in the classroom, Shelagh led Trout through Shakespeare, and her bright English enunciation sang through the house: "A bit-ter fo-ol!" as she read from *Lear*.

Trout stood at the table and played back to her: "Doest thou know the difference my boy, between a bit-ter fool and a sweet one."

Trout rooted always for the Fool, who, in his riddled wisdom, sword-danced between idiocy and genius, between madness and clarity. If Kenny was a bitter fool, he himself was a sweet one, Trout thought, but sometimes, they switched roles. In the kitchen, brown-topped loaves cooled on the counter and on the stove, Shelagh's broth of barley and ground beef simmered. Shakespeare never smelled so good.

He memorized the soliloquy and recited it to Jack, who sat in his living room chair with the bearskin to his left and the cougar, its chin rested on a shelf, to his right. The tawny head watched with staring eyes and bared fangs. Jack's pipe smoke curled luxuriously as Trout recited, his face puckered and his eyebrows stern:

"Have more than thou showest,
Speak less than thou knowest,
Lend less than thou owest,
Ride more than thou goest,
Learn more than thou trowest,
Set less than thou throwest;
Leave thy drink and thy whore,
And keep in-a-door,
And thou shalt have more
Then two tens to a score."

"Whore, like in 'ore'," Shelagh prompted, "Not who're as in 'sewer'," she insisted. Jack stifled a laugh behind the back of his hand at Shelagh's correction, but applauded loudly. He poured himself a dram of Scotch, and one for his wife, and then offered one to Trout. Shelagh pursed her lips, but said nothing.

"A wee one for the wee scholar," he said of the sour mash that seared Trout's throat, but that increased his appreciation of poetry as the night went on. Jack lowered the lights and closed the fireplace damper, and then he recited Robbie Burns. His voice was as rugged as his wife's was polished. Listening to him, Trout felt there was hope for his own ragged voice too.

Jack hammed it, his accent growing more Scottish with each whisky. His glottal 'och sprayed now. He stood and addressed an imaginary mouse as he looked over the handles of the plough that uncovered it. Trout caught a whiff of the great windy farts of the draft horse as Jack slapped its brown haunches with the traces.

"To A Mouse," he declaimed. He cupped an imaginary mouse in his hands, and opened them to squint between his fingers:

"Wee, slecket, cowran, tim'rous beastie,
O, what a panic's in thy breastie!
Thou need na start awa sae hasty,
Wi' bickering brattle!
I wad be laith to rin an' chase thee,
Wi' murd'ring pattle!"

He turned to the bear and the cougar, the palm of his hand turned upwards. Trout, inspired by the whisky now, watched the wee mouse sitting on its wee haunches. It stared at them all, as Jack's voice deepened with impossible woe:

"I am truly sorry Man's dominion
Has broken Nature's social union,
An' justifies that ill opinion,
Which makes thee startle,
At me, thy poor, earth-born companion,
An' fellow-mortal!"

The unsentimental version of "To a Mouse" lurched forward between Jack's wracking smoker's cough and his raised shot glass. It ended with:

"But Mousie, thou art no thy-lane,
In proving foresight may be vain:
The best laid schemes o' Mice and Men,
Gang aft agley,

An' lea'e us nought but grief an' pain,
For promis'd joy!"

Jack bowed and Shelagh and Trout applauded. The half-deaf Scotsman's voice was a great glottal rumble, and Trout could hear departing thunderclaps and distant howitzers, and the music of the Cree, among the mid-Atlantic burr of Scots-English mixed with the rambling patois of the backcountry ranger and cowboy.

"One more dram," Jack offered all around. Trout was now thoroughly converted to poetry and whisky.

Together the three of them sang "Auld Lang Syne" and "Loch Lomond." Shelagh strummed her guitar, urging Trout: "Sing dear boy, sing. You've got to sing." When they finished, she cupped her hand against the chimney of the kerosene lamp, for the last word was always Shelagh's, and she snuffed out the light. "Bed."

The words, the poems, and the songs were incomprehensible to Trout. The next day, light-headed with whisky, he sought them in the polished glass case that contained Jack's small proud library, among the carpentry and geology texts. Somewhere between the field guides and the complete works of Robert Louis Stevenson, Grey Owl's *Tales of an Empty Cabin* and *Songs of a Sourdough*, he found the worn copy of *Poems, Chiefly in the Scottish Dialect*, its margins flecked with flying V's like geese pencilled by a child, the key words underlined in its glossary.

In his uncle's voice, poetry was as real as a waterfall, as practical as a doorjamb. His aunt's "po-em" was a two-syllable word, lovely and affected, while his uncle's rhymed with home.

That fall, Trout's tongue loosened, lightened of the thickness that had plagued him all his young life. While feeding the dogs, he sang to them, his rude voice swelling in the rough songs he made up and the finer ones he'd learned. He hummed the lows he could hear, and the highs the dogs or Belle heard for him. When their ears flattened he softened those notes until the animals relaxed. Even the dog choir listened now, as did the horses. Slowly he learned to sing and Shelagh showed him how to strum chords on her old Epiphone with the huge sound box that he balanced on his knees. Trout practiced in the fallout shelter to spare his aunt and uncle, and discovered that the conch sounded low enough for him to hear, when he blew through its broken crown.

Frustrated one day because Shelagh always had to tune the guitar, he remembered the science lesson in which he'd learned that sound consisted of vibrations, and the cochlea conducted sound through bone. He gripped the metal pitch pipe between his teeth, dropped his chin to the guitar, and felt the vibrations as he strummed. He turned the pegs and went in and out of tune. The notes he could not hear, he could feel. The flats buzzed, the sharps hurt. When he matched the ring of the high E through his teeth and his chin, the reverberations rang in his cochlea. Then he played "Auld Lang Syne," on Jack's Chromatic harmonica, after biting down onto the chrome case until he could "hear".

And he began to find the sounds he couldn't hear.

He placed his fingers along the taut wire fence as it buzzed in the wind. And he felt the guitar strings resonate as he strummed it open, without chords. He leaned with his chest on the fender of the Ford to hear the carburettor as he tuned it.

"That's it," Jack instructed. Each slight turn of the screwdriver changed the pitch of the engine as it faltered or revved through his chest and fingers. Trout hummed with the truck, for the first time nearly on key. And he found comfort in the lessons his aunt and his uncle gave him.

They sang and they ate, and, like the dogs in their pens, they waited for snow.

Clare

I stayed nearly three weeks in the General Hospital, until I was moved to a larger room that I shared with two other women: a former nurse who joked about us being in the loony bin, and a woman who was a psychology teacher at my old high school. Someone asked her one day, "What are you in for?"

"Life," she smiled. "I'm not very good at it." We all snickered.

No one there looked crazy. Sure, there were one or two who were different, something I'd been called all my life. The serious cases were sent to the big mental hospital in a town north of here. She's gone to Ponoka, people would say, and it had a faraway sound, like she's gone to Mars. They sent the kids strung out on drugs to the Apollo ward. Most of the patients looked like my neighbours—housewives, ordinary women—which just goes to show. Some talked to themselves. Others were medicated into a trance. Most were women. I remember checking my own face in the mirror and thinking how we all looked hungry on the ward. The white fluorescent light pulsing off the shiny green walls darkened the shadows of my face and lightened the whites of my eyes like stage make-up.

Lowell wanted to keep the girls away from the hospital. One or two of the patients paced up and down the ward, sliding along the wall for balance and one of my room-mates calmly said Adolph Hitler spoke to her through the walls, in code. She made it sound so normal. I agreed with Lowell, it would be too frightening for the girls. Now everyone goes on the talk shows—even movie stars bravely talk about their breakdowns, or about going to the Betty Ford clinic, but I was terribly embarrassed to be at this hospital.

The housekeeper Lowell had hired was working out fine. The girls liked Mrs. Jonsgaard, who was an old-fashioned Danish woman with six kids of her own. I was worried about the money because I knew Lowell's new job wouldn't pay what he earned at Pincher Creek. He told me how he brought blueprints home every night now. I felt so selfish and lonely up there in that ward overlooking a park and the zoo across the river. When the snow came in November, I watched all the kids come running out of school and setting their lunch pails down to make snow angels, running and stamping circles in the fresh snow. It was still bright and sunny. One boy played by himself in the corner of the playground. When he turned my way, I waved to him from the big window of the lounge at the end of the hall, where we were allowed to smoke.

The boy in the playground squinted and shaded his eyes with his mitted hand straight over his eyebrows the way my son did. I'd taken my make-up mirror out and now I flashed it in the sun. The boy was still looking in my direction, so I sent a message to him, for fun. Another boy joined him while the first one pointed towards me. Three shorts, three longs, three shorts—Morse code—like the instructions had said in the signaller's kit we'd got for Will one Christmas.

SOS—Save our Ship, or some said, Save Our Souls. The newcomer slugged the other boy in the shoulder and they both went back to playing, oblivious to the message I'd flashed them. I missed Will terribly but I knew Jack and Shelagh's was where he should be. His letters gave no indication of missing us even though he said he did. He talked of the life he had there, the forest fire, the dances and the teepees. Shelagh wrote how proud she was of him and that they loved having him, how good it was for Jack. After the death of his son, Jack blamed himself for a long time and turned bitter. In a strange way, I knew he had a second chance with my son, and I wanted that for him too.

The psychiatrist said I was to rest, but I couldn't sleep and had to be sedated. Sometimes the feeling of choking came back to me. It felt as though my womb was coming up through my gullet. I couldn't trust my sense of taste or smell. Everything seemed off. It was the same feeling that I'd had before I took the sleeping pills. I'd asked the psychiatrist about the shock treatment and the machine down the hall, hoping he'd say I was fine and I wouldn't need it, but he just nodded and kept writing on his clipboard. That scared me. I didn't dare tell him about Grandma Locke. He'd have written that down too. How she'd been in a depression ever since she came to Canada in 1927, with six children. I think she missed the old country, the winding, busy streets of Paisley, the little trains running into the countryside, she told me, to Loch Ness, to Glasgow and Edinburgh. Instead, she was stuck on the homestead in the bush, with three more babies coming one after another, until there were nine. She never regretted the children, but they eat you up, she'd said, and there's just no one to talk to. She'd tell me how everyone in Paisley came to walk the High Street and to visit on Saturday morning with their prams. Everything was a walk or train ride away.

Something snapped the first time shortly after they were married, Mom told me, while they were still in Scotland. Grandpa trained as an engineer before the First World War and worked in the Coates thread factory in Paisley. He came from a farm family; she was a city girl. She stayed home with the kids. She grew jealous. He was a handsome man with red hair, tall and thin, who wore a Harris Tweed jacket even to the factory. There were women working with him and maybe there was something to worry about. And who ever knows what goes on inside a marriage except the couple themselves.

But one day Grandma Locke waited outside the factory gates, and, as the shift came out, told anyone who would listen that her husband had syphilis. The gate man came to get Grandpa and he went to her. She was weeping. That's how Mom always said it—not crying, but weeping. I don't believe Grandpa was doing any of the things that Grandma thought he was. But I know how fears can grow and take over a person until the shadows that lurk everywhere are full of terror.

Then the first war broke out. Grandpa went to France and was gassed at Ypres. When he came home, the doctors told him he couldn't go back to the factory, so he became a gamekeeper. "To the laird of

Rosshaugh on the Black Isle. Near the fishing village of Avoch situated on Moray Firth in eastern Ross-shire. Home of Clan Mackenzie," he'd tell me.

I can hear him still. I thought it a romantic and wonderful place by the way he described it. When I first read *Lady Chatterley's Lover* I saw my grandpa as Mellors, the gamekeeper, a man of the same circumstances and generation and my grandma as a poorer Lady Chatterley, though I couldn't quite see Grandpa saying those words. His John Thomas. Her Lady Jane.

I cast Grandma Locke as the Lady of Rosshaugh. She was a tiny beauty with her blonde hair plaited behind her neck and a musical voice, and that laugh that Grandpa said could charm a bird out of its feathers.

Grandpa was especially good to us after Dad left. During the last few summers of the war, once the crops were in the ground, he'd come down to Calgary on business and stay for a few days in a rooming house in Victoria Park by the Stampede grounds. Grandma stayed behind on the farm and took care of the chickens and the cows. Mom and I rode the train to Olds, with the coach cars full of British and Canadian soldiers on furlough from training at Suffield and Penhold. We'd spend two weeks with my grandparents on the homestead, a summer ritual during the war years. We'd pack Grandpa's tent, along with some pots and pans, and ride in the back of the Model A truck with their old blind border collie, Bobbie, all the way to Sylvan Lake to camp.

Sitting around the campfire, Grandpa told stories of the old country. Like the time he got Jack, who was ten, a summer job on Lanny Macleod's farm. Lanny was a miser, even amongst Scots. Two weeks later wee Jack returned with his bundle on his shoulder saying he wouldn't go back. But Grandpa reminded Jack he'd promised to stay the summer.

"Dad, I'll not want to be goin' back. The first week a sheep was drowned and Lanny Macleod sent me for a bag of salt to make braxy from 'em."

Braxy, I gather, was a type of pickled meat.

"The second week a pig died and I got sent for some more salt to cure 'em and make braxy, which is all they eat on Lanny Macleod's farm, Dad."

Grandpa interrupted. "You can't always eat what you want at other people's houses, Jack."

"But, you don't understand. Last night Lanny Macleod's old mother died. No, Dad! I'm not goin' back."

During his visits to the city, Grandpa would take me to Riley Park, where I'd splash in the pool. He'd carefully fold his tweed jacket, tuck his tie in the pocket and unbutton his shirt to his chest, which had red hair too, with flecks of white. He'd sit in the shade of the cottonwood trees smoking his pipe. He looked younger than fifty, with wavy red hair which turned gold, like his beard, in the sun. Women flirted with him, but he was a solid Scottish Presbyterian and even when it was clear that their marriage was long over, he stayed loyal to his wife. After a while she wouldn't even leave the farm to visit her daughters. My grandma hadn't wanted to be a farmer's wife. Her boys were all overseas. They'd joined up to get off the farm, the younger ones lying about their age, all of them tall, except for wee Jack. But all Grandma Locke told were ghost stories that sent me off to bed, pulling my blanket over my head—every shadow on the tent a ghost. Isolation makes a fear so much bigger—you think you're the only one who's afraid. And how a person tells a story tells so much about them.

The last time I saw Grandpa was in the Colonel Belcher Hospital. I was fourteen years old that summer. His hair was still tinged with red, but his beard and temples were almost completely grey. The wards were full of veterans from both wars. Uncle Jack came in from the Highwood Ranger station where he was posted and stayed with us. We went together to visit Grandpa and pushed his wheelchair through the ward. He'd talk to the other vets, patting their hands, offering prayers, even as he knew he was dying himself. Vimy, he'd say of one, as we left. The Somme, of another—where his brother had died. His voice choked around the word. Passchendale, after another, in a hushed tone, offering up the names of the battles like the Stations of the Cross, and he rubbed his eyes with his fist before tears could start. Uncle Jack said nothing, but he guided the chair and shook hands with each of the vets. Between them all, they'd seen so much of war.

In the final week of Grandpa's life, the visits to the vets stopped. Grandpa closed his eyes and his breathing became harder, magnified in the quiet room until it sounded like roaring. Then he'd gulp and gasp like he was drowning. Uncle Jack and I watched at his side. Every little noise in the street came through the open window. The electric trolleys on Fourth Street, the light daytime traffic, the distant slamming of car doors. Across the street in Memorial Park, a bronze statue of a soldier riding a horse faced the hospital where some of the patients sat sunning in wheelchairs and smoked. My grandfather's breath rose and sank, counting out the hours between the distant sounds behind us. Then he blinked.

"We'll go up to Sylvan Lake in the new Studebaker," he whispered.

Uncle Jack touched my arm and said, "Go call your mother, tell her to come now."

By the time I got back, Grandpa was gone. He was fifty-three years old in the summer of 1948—the youngest person to die in our family. The gas finally killed him thirty years after he breathed it.

For a long time, I didn't think I needed or wanted a father, but I missed my grandpa. We all need love.

One day Ian MacGrenaghan, Mom's boyfriend, showed up at the General just before lunch, dressed in his blue fireman's uniform, holding his captain's hat in his hands. His red hair was swept back and slicked with Brylcream. It reminded me of my grandfather's, though his was parted on the side and brushed dry.

"I'm taking my daughter for a walk. Any problem with that?" Ian said to the head nurse. He wrapped me in his greatcoat and whisked me off the ward before she could protest. He was a man used to being obeyed. He'd brought me a carton of cigarettes and a box of Chicken on the Way. We sat in his car in the hospital parking lot, eating fried chicken and corn fritters.

"You won't get better on hospital food, Clare. This

is okay, but I sure miss Hooley Furnoe's cooking. He was right around the corner from the Number One fire hall when I started."

"Chicken Inn?" I laughed. "I went to school with his son, Steven."

Hooley Furnoe, who was from South Carolina, ran the Chicken Inn. His was the only black family in our neighbourhood. In grade six his son, Steven, was taken out of class and sent to the school near Chinatown. Steven will be more comfortable there, the teacher said. We all knew it was because he was black.

Hooley's father sold more than chicken. Chicken Inn had the most beautiful girls in town upstairs. Even the mayor and the police chief were rumoured to take more than corn fritters there.

"You get yourself better, Clare. Your mother and I can wait to get married." Ian squeezed my arm. The car reeked of fried chicken. "I better take you back upstairs so that old battleaxe doesn't give you grief." He hugged me before he left and winked at the head nurse on his way out.

Christmas was coming, and I wanted to be home with my girls on Christmas morning. Shelagh had written to say that once the snow came, they sometimes didn't get out 'til late March, or even later some years, so I knew I wouldn't see my son, but I was determined to be there at city hall with Mom and Ian before the New Year. I wanted to get better, but I still didn't know what was wrong with me. A bad case of life? Maybe the cure for living, is living.

One day the doctor came in. "You can go," he said.

I was glad to be free of the ward and back home. We had agreed—my doctor, Lowell and I—that the housekeeper would come in two mornings a week until I got back on my feet, but I sent her home after the first week. I wanted my home back and there's nothing worse than having someone else in your kitchen. I couldn't find anything. Even then, everything looked different, not just the fading light of December, but the snow in the street. I've always found December the cruellest month, full of longing and disappointment—the short, short days and the long nights. For my girls' sake, I made a fuss over Christmas, though it reminded me of the father and the family I thought I didn't have. Instead, I preferred to plan New Year's, arranging for a babysitter, and getting Lowell's suit dry-cleaned.

After the long darkness of December, the turning of the calendar brought longer days and the slow ascent into January, light and spring. My grandpa used to pull down the poplar buds and show them to me, tender and green under their casings. Almost spring, he'd say, while all around a whiteout swirled. Sometimes, he said, the trees were fooled by a Chinook wind—where the temperature rose in hours, driven by the warm breeze off the Pacific—and the sap would rise with the thermometer. Then the inevitable cold snap came, and the sap froze and sometimes exploded through the trunk in a nasty frost boil—you can see these on the trees along Memorial Drive. In the bush, he said, you could hear that frost crack like gunfire as the temperature dropped.

The year Grandpa died, Grandma Locke sold the

farm after all the crops were in. All her daughters except Mom had married farmers with places of their own, and none of the boys wanted the farm. We moved her into a tiny apartment in the Beltline—a walk-up with a two-burner stove. She gave us all the household items we wanted and auctioned off the rest. The hall closet of the farmhouse was full of shoes and boots and, up top, the fly rods and creels—hers and Grandpa's—piled beside the calfskin Bible with all the family births dutifully entered. She brewed root beer in that closet, an old country recipe, with herbs gathered out on the prairie. Once or twice, the root beer bottles exploded—glass in everyone's shoes. The Psalms and epiphanies, the names of the disciples in the family Bible are, for me, forever scented with root beer. There was something divine about that.

And whatever we gave her for Christmas found its way back to us another Christmas or through the cousins—the same gift passed on, like a chain letter, always new to the next person. She'd send us home with Red Rose tea boxes, lined with waxed paper and filled to the brim with sugared fingers of golden shortbread. When the kids started school, she came out on the bus to visit, a Hudson's Bay shopping bag in each hand. Always a gift in her purse for the little ones, and two dozen cinnamon buns that she'd gotten up at four in the morning to make, still warm, wrapped in waxed paper and tea towels.

Each time I hugged her at the door, even with her coat and her purse, she got lighter and lighter. She was hollow in my arms. There was less of her each time, until I thought we'd go to visit her apartment one day and it would be abandoned, only bits of moss and bone left behind. But she outlived Grandpa by nearly seven years, until Mom and my uncles put her in a nursing home in Bowness, the year before she died.

As I put out the baby crib and clothes for the Salvation Army, I wondered about my grandmother, but I wanted to get on. My health was back and it was hard to believe I'd ever done what I had. I never wanted to be that black or fatigued again. As if my body was stone, and even to lift my eyelids was an exertion. I started my Christmas baking, stacking layers of butter tarts, pies and squares in the freezer. I made plans for the New Year, not just New Year's Eve—I wanted to work downtown. Lowell's new job didn't pay nearly as much as the one at the gas plant, and the girls were old enough now to let themselves in after school.

The twins moved through the neighbourhood like a single unit, trying out for different sports teams. Because of the new subdivision, there was a covered rink with a Zamboni and ball teams and field hockey for girls, volleyball at the school, and track and field. They got their love of sports from Lowell, who was a swimmer once. Emily took after her brother, and me—she was a reader, and a brooder. I knew Pauline would probably leave home as soon as she could.

I took a job gift-wrapping parcels for ten days before Christmas, and got to know the woman who ran the Bay cafeteria. After the holidays, I got work there making sandwiches. I was glad to be back downtown during the day. I left the house before breakfast, but

was home most days to greet the girls when they returned from school.

It was an easy, automatic kind of job. I liked the
girls I worked with, and the laughing and joking. They
were my age or older and not that different from the
women on the ward, except that we all wore hairnets.
I got promoted to salads. Emily calls them my salad
days now. It felt good to be busy with work, but I
didn't want to run away from what had happened, so
I started seeing a counsellor my doctor recommend-
ed. I kept thinking of my grandma—in the end she
had nothing. I didn't want to end up like that—alone
in a tiny flat, my children all elsewhere.

I worked hard, reading all those self-help books.
Emily, when we cleared out the basement, rifled
through them with me: *I'm Okay, You're Okay, the
Luscher Color Test, Psycho-Cybernetics.* We found my
Carole King and Helen Reddy albums beside the old
flip-top stereo.

"Mom, 'I Am Woman'?" Emily held up the album
by its corner. "Retro."

We plugged in Pauline's old stereo and listened
to the scratchy track of "If You Need Me." My kids
grew up on that song. Emily hummed along without
even realizing. When things were bad, we'd play that
song over and over.

Retro—a funny word, that. There's a band called
the Dino Martinis that Pauline goes to hear. She
likes to wear my old dresses—they're back in style.
The big band music of my youth is back too. The
other day we took our lawn chairs and went to watch
the General Hospital being blown up. The explosives

went off along the floors like the strings of babyfinger firecrackers that Lowell used to bring the kids from Chestemere Lake, and then suddenly the whole place fell in on itself. Everyone applauded and cheered. Some people had video cameras, like we were watching Haley's comet or something. Calgarians don't like the old. Most are newcomers now and maybe it reminds them that they haven't been here long. But who'd thought we'd see the fall of the General? Some of the times I'd spent there, though—I wasn't sorry to see it go.

Mom and Ian got married at City Hall. Lowell and I were there, along with two of Ian's boys. Afterwards, we all went for lunch at Chicken on the Way because Ian had to get back to the firehall. His crew tied tin cans and old shoes behind the pumper truck and hung a sign, Just Married, to tease him.

Mom moved in with him in the house he owned next door to his mother, in one of the old Calgary neighbourhoods just off Centre Street and 16th Avenue, behind Chesney's Hardware and the Beacon Hotel. There was no fence between the two houses. Planks ran between the garden rows and out to the saskatoon bushes, raspberry canes and rhubarb patch.

On Boxing Day, he and Mom held an open house. His married sons and his crew from the fire hall came. Ian poured drinks behind the bar and cracked jokes while Mom fussed in the kitchen, running downstairs with trays of turkey sandwiches.

His sons were wary at first, but Ian introduced me

to everyone as his daughter. Mom was the happiest I'd ever seen her. Like this was the love they'd spent their lives getting ready for—not a minute too soon for either of them. And my children had a grandfather.

Trout

In the week leading up to Thanksgiving, the last visitors came to the Upper Saskatchewan Ranger Station as Jack got it ready for winter: the propane truck; the honey wagon that came to empty the septic tank; and the Royalite truck which topped up the diesel for the generator. Trout took breaks from his lessons to watch them trundle away across Moses Flats over the Cline to Rocky. With the fire season ended, the helicopter flew Red Wilson off the mountain, and Archie Baptiste honked as the forestry three-ton towing the trail crew's trailer passed the station. Trout took his first helicopter ride with Jack up to Cline lookout.

The trip up was as short as a ride at the Stampede midway. They'd barely fastened their safety buckles in the three-seater before the small Bell helicopter lifted nose down and banked over the ranger station. Through the plexiglass bubble, Trout watched the river below. Rocks and trees blurred as the machine moved up the mountain, and came into focus again when Bud Anders eased the helicopter onto the small timber pad braced on the side of the overhang.

Red Wilson's small cabin stood on the top of the mountain beside a garden patch, now bare. There was a barrel for water, and another for gasoline for the generator that powered the lights and radio. The fire lookout was a square-windowed room on top of the cabin. From there, Trout scoped the Saskatchewan River valley with high-powered binoculars. He could see the horses and dogs behind the outbuildings of the Upper Saskatchewan, and the airstrip beside it.

Jack showed him how to read the co-ordinates on the map table below the fire finder, pinpointing the Pinto Lake fire to show how Red located it for the fire crew. Trout peered at his own cabin three thousand feet below, a grey smudge against the yellows and browns of the muskeg that surrounded it. To the west he could see the open range of Kootenay Plains and the old Barnes ranch. To the east, Whiterabbit Creek and Tom Wilson's old trading post surrounded by the abandoned cabins of the Stoneys. In front of him, the Cline wound down to its confluence on the Saskatchewan, breaking out of the woods onto the gravel bar.

His heart raced as he squinted through the firefinder towards the Bighorn Reserve, just out of range to the east. He thought of Carrie Moses constantly, and felt her smoky breath on his face. Her black hair and brown eyes tormented him. In his dreams, she was always just out of reach. Her laughter goaded him when he pursued her on horseback, his arms around the mare's neck, his hands grasping at the horse's mane as it slipped through his fingers.

Jack called Trout to nail plywood on the windows. A chipmunk, feeding on shelled peanuts that Red Wilson had left behind, watched from the woodpile. A wary herd of mountain goats grazed near the garden. Their white coats made them a perfect target for the hunters swarming the valley below. Only the high altitude and an impassable fire road afforded them protection.

On the trip down, Trout could feel the solid timber of the landing pad slip out from under the helicopter. White-tailed deer scattered in the alpine meadow below at the sound of the chopper. The river panned below him, while the plexiglas cabin came eye-level with the snow-caps of Sentinel Mountain as the pilot flew directly at it, then banked east and around. The nose tilted in a large spiral before he landed the chopper in front of the ranger station. Trout's legs trembled with excitement. He still hadn't met Red Wilson, but Jack assured him he would, next spring. For weeks afterwards, Trout floated high above the Kootenay Plains in his dreams, as close to being a bird as he would ever get.

Shelagh and Trout continued their lessons in the dining room school. Jack made trips to Rocky, during one of which he took two of Blondie's puppies to meet their new owners, who had driven in from Calgary. The mother dog moped for awhile in her pen, then turned her attention to the remaining puppy, which now tagged behind her everywhere. On the return trip, Jack packed the truck's box full of bags of dog food and flour—winter supplies for the basement storeroom. On another trip, Jack brought back a side of beef for the freezer, parcelled in crisp butcher wrap and wax-pencilled—chuck, round, porterhouse, T-bone, burger—along with boxes of canned goods, that Trout stowed in the freezer or piled on the shelves outside the fallout shelter.

The day before Thanksgiving, the three of them stripped the last garden rows, turned the soil, leaving large broken clods on top, and packed burlap bags of carrots, potatoes and turnips, then hauled them to the root cellar.

"Put one bag of each on the truck, Trout. After breakfast tomorrow, we'll go see Silas." Jack was mostly quiet. Hunting season kept him busy on weekends. With the departure of Archie Baptiste and Red Wilson, he was now alone in the district, with the nearest help at Nordegg or from the Mounties in Rocky. As a precaution, he rode with his revolver beside him on the front seat of the truck, or the Winchester in the saddle scabbard, if he was out on horse patrol.

The Bighorn Reserve was home to fifteen families of the Wesley band of Stoneys, who came over the Dolomite River pass from Morley flats before the turn of the century. Jack told Trout that the Indian agent there had chastised them for killing one of their own cows when they were hungry.

Past the Cline River there were shiny new culverts over the creeks. Red-tagged survey stakes lined the ditches and piles of brush and stumps awaited burning along the highway as it approached Kootenay Plains. As he turned off the new gravel highway, Jack followed the rutted dirt road along the Bighorn River and stopped at two green-and-white-painted log buildings. One was a schoolhouse, and the other was a teacher's residence with a Canadian flag out front. The teacher came out to greet them. On the slope below, a dozen plain board houses were scattered through the woods with footpaths criss-crossing between them. Wood smoke drifted from the

chimneys. Jack said there were no radios or telephones on the reserve.

Trout waited in the truck while his uncle talked
to the schoolteacher, a tall man with brown hair and
glasses. Jack thanked him, started up the truck and
drove on until the road ended in a clearing, where
there was a white cook tent lashed to a timber frame.
Smoke rose from the stovepipe, and in front there
were animal skins, stretched and drying. Trout recognized Carrie's mother, Sarah, dressed in a print
dress with a lumberman's shirt pulled over top. She
was wearing high moccasins and butchering a deer.
Another carcass hung by its hind legs from a tree, its
throat slit. Sarah looked up and greeted Jack shyly,
wiping her cheek with the back of her hand.

Inside the cook tent, Silas Moses lay on a camp
cot, his braids white against the green canvas. The
old man smiled and gripped the bag of turnips Trout
carried, sitting up on the cot to admire them. With
Sarah's help, Trout got the other bags to the tent as
the two men talked. Then she motioned him outside.
She gestured towards the river.

"She's with her father." She didn't smile, but waved
him on.

Along the river, Trout found a broad clearing full
of anthills, where a group of men, along with Charlie
Moses and his daughter, stacked poles, which were
being skidded out of the bush by a horse. A smudge
fire burned nearby to keep away the mosquitoes.

"Jack here?" Charlie Moses said. Trout nodded.
He wasn't sure if Carrie was glad to see him. Charlie
started down the trail towards the cook tent.

"Follow me," Carrie said. She bushwhacked along the river, then turned back towards the road into the reserve. A rough lean-to and corral stood beside a small board house that Trout assumed was her parents'. In the window were kerosene lamps. The corral held a short-legged paint mare and its colt. Trout had never seen a horse quite like this one. She was little, almost as small as a pony, but she looked tough and fast. She had a big head, a long neck, and large flared nostrils. Her hooves were large, with tufted fetlocks. Jack had told Trout that the Plains Indians rode wild horses they claimed were descended from those of Sitting Bull, and some of the Stoneys believed the remnants of that herd still wandered here.

Trout watched in admiration as Carrie climbed into the corral, slipped a halter over the mare's muzzle and put a blanket on its back. The horse calmed under her touch. Trout pulled open the gate rails so Carrie could ride the mare through. Its colt followed, nuzzling the mother's haunches.

"Wait on the fence," Carrie said.

Trout straddled the top rail, while Carrie brought the mare alongside. "C'mon," she said. He slid on and wrapped his arms around her waist.

The mare dropped down a cutbank to the river. Its colt skidded beside it. Carrie reined side to side, stepping the horse gently down the soft silt. Trout's stomach flattened against Carrie's back and her breasts slipped over his hands, which were knitted across her belt. Her back was muscular and the horse's gait lurched through her body. Trout buried his nose in her hair and tried to control his breathing.

"Scared?" Her laughter swelled until he could feel it rumble through her back. "We can go back. My dad's got a saddle."

"It's okay," Trout lied, and tried not to grasp her waist too hard. He loved how her voice's bass hummed through his chest. It didn't matter what she said, it was so delicious just to feel her voice as he leaned into her.

When they reached the confluence of the Bighorn, Trout tied up the mare, and Carrie spread the saddle blanket out on the gravel. Along the river, the wind was cold, the fast water green with glacial silt. Most of the aspens were already bare.

With the sun behind her, Trout couldn't see Carrie's face without squinting, so he closed his eyes, and breathed in the smell of her: horseflesh, sweat, pine sap and smoke.

"C'mon out of the wind." She pulled him down to the blanket. "It's warm here."

Trout laid down alongside her, his elbow pressed into the blanket, his arm holding his head level with hers. His leg quivered, and he put his hand on it.

"Something wrong with it?" Carrie laughed.

"It's nothing,"

"You hear anything yet?"

Trout stared.

"The dam?"

He shook his head.

"My dad got a letter from the government," Carrie said. "I read it to him. The teacher helped me write to the government."

Trout nodded.

"We'll have to wait," Carrie said. "The teacher told us not to worry." Carrie sat up on the blanket and snatched a strand of mountain timothy, its head like a small furry grass hot dog. It reassured Trout to know the names of the vegetation that surrounded him.

Carrie feathered the grassy head on the ridge of Trout's nose. He blushed. As she twirled it under his nostrils, he began to sneeze, and scratched like a pup with ants on its muzzle. He sat up and turned away, angry that she'd teased him, and that he was not in control of his body. He had no name for what was happening to him.

"Here." She bent and plucked a small flat pebble from the river. She dried it on her shirt and began to move it around on her nose, and then on his, rotating and flipping it over. Miraculously, the dry stone appeared wet, shiny with nose oil.

She brought her face close to his, and her breath seeped into his mouth. He looked in her eyes. She turned away. For all her teasing, she was as shy as he was. Blood pounded in his ears as he placed his hand on her neck. She pulled away. He turned the volume down on his hearing aids, so they wouldn't whistle when she was close. He placed her free hand on his neck. He smelled the sweet pine resin from the logging. She placed the nose stone in his hand and closed his fingers around it.

Trout pulled Carrie to him. Their noses bumped, and he mashed his mouth on hers. He'd wanted to kiss her ever since the Chicken Dance. The river wind blew around her neck, over his face and down his chest through his open shirt collar, under his jean jacket. He shivered. They stayed that way for several moments. Neither of them knew what to do next. They were slowly suffocating taking shorter and shorter breaths, until they laid down again. They faced each other and gasped. Then both of them laughed. Trout stroked Carrie's cheeks and she touched his chest, tracing a line over his shoulders to his jaw. This time she leaned toward him. Her lips brushed his roughly and then planted on his mouth. Trout felt his jeans chafing him as he pressed himself against her. Suddenly, she pulled away.

"Hear that?"

Trout shook his head and turned up his hearing aids. His radar was back.

"Truck horn. We better go."

He went to kiss her once more, but she turned her head and he tasted the smoke on her cheek. His tongue was flecked with the salt of her skin. Trout wished for a saddle on the ride back. Carrie insisted he ride while she led the mare. The colt trailed behind as Carrie led them back up to the truck. Trout could feel his grossly inflated testicles chafe on his jeans and each step reminded him of something Kenny had once described. Blue balls. But Trout was exultant—one of the new words his aunt taught him. He had kissed Carrie Moses and she'd kissed him back. He wondered if his balls really had turned blue.

Silas came out of the cook tent and, with Carrie's help, placed his bag of turnips against a tree. Leaning on a pine staff, he peered into the cab of the truck. The shoulders of his buckskin shirt were level with the window and his white braids framed his face as he spoke to Jack.

"Bring me stone," Silas said, tapping on the door. "I make you the pipe" His voice was tired, but he waved as Jack backed out to the road. Carrie stood beside the mare and the colt. Sarah stared at Carrie, and then at Trout, while Charlie Moses turned back towards the tent.

As Jack drove past the board houses on the road out, two black dogs followed the truck up to the highway. Children stopped to watch and Trout waved at them.

When the truck crossed the Bighorn River, the radio snapped and cracked.

"Come in Clearwater Car Four, this is X78278 calling Clearwater Car Four. Do you read me?"

Jack frowned. "Clearwater Car Four, go ahead Shelagh."

"We've been trying to reach you. Got a man down at Whitegoat Creek."

"We're on our way. Is the helicopter available? Over."

"He's on standby. Frank Jones is on his way from Nordegg and the hospital at Rocky's been notified. X78278 out."

"Clearwater Car Four over and out." Jack placed the mike on the dash. "Jesus."

They pulled onto the gravel highway and the speedometer needle leapt to seventy-five.

"What'd you take off for? Remember what we talked about?" Jack looked straight ahead. "Jesus, this is why." He pointed to the radio.

"I'm sorry, Uncle Jack." Trout worried the nose stone in his jacket pocket. He didn't blame his uncle. Still, he waited several miles before he asked. "Can I come?" he said, to the windshield, afraid to see the no in his uncle's face. Jack didn't react at first. Trout watched out of the corner of his eye. Jack was mulling it over.

"We'll get Junior," Jack finally said, like he hadn't heard Trout. "We've got about three hours of light. If this guy's where I think he is, we've got a climb." Trout heard the we, and relaxed.

Jack raced down the highway, dodging the construction barriers and vehicles, slowing slightly as the gravel ran out on the forestry road.

He turned to Trout. "She's Silas's grand-daughter. He's my friend. I'd like to keep it that way. You understand?"

Trout said yes, but to what, he had no idea. He would have said yes to anything anybody asked him right then, he was so happy. First, Carrie's kiss, and now he was joining the men in a search.

When Jack drove into the yard, Shelagh had Junior harnessed and chained to the fence, his packed pannier beside him. The big St. Bernard strained on its chain and its tail flapped wildly at the sight of the truck. In the front office, a hunter in a red canvas coat paced while Jack checked the maps and Trout came upstairs with his gear from the fallout shelter. The smell of roasting turkey filled the house. Then the radio barked.

"Clearwater Car Four to Clearwater Car One."

"Clearwater One, go ahead."

"Frank, we'll meet you at Whitegoat Cabin, over."

"Be there in about twenty minutes, over."

"Roger, Clearwater Four out."

The ranger's cabin, nestled alongside Whitegoat Creek, stood at the base of the mountain where the hunter had fallen. His friend, a man named Turner, had hiked out, leaving another man with the injured one. In his panic, Turner hadn't blazed a trail out, and couldn't show Jack a route to take. He pointed vaguely above the treeline, above one of the flatirons. As the man walked to his car to get extra clothes, Jack turned to Trout.

"You won't find elk up that high. Probably scared 'em right over the range into the next valley." He shook his head and pointed to the map, which he'd spread on the hood of the truck.

"Here's what we'll do when Frank gets here. Since there's four of us, I'll lead with the dog. We'll make a grid, and then one section at a time, we'll sweep across the mountain. Once we've eliminated an area, we'll move up. Let's spread out—Frank and me on the outside, you and that guy inside, okay?"

Trout struggled into his pack and pulled on his gloves and toque. The sun had dimmed behind Mount Sentinel and the air was already cold.

Frank arrived and Jack briefed him before the search party set out through the forest, traversing the range. They swept one grid at a time up the mountain. It was slow, but the hunter had no idea where his friend had fallen. All he could tell them was that he'd fallen off a ledge onto the scree, and he was badly hurt.

Once off the leash, Junior was calm. He searched the slope and waited for the men, reading Jack's cues. The dog's pannier was loaded with food and first aid supplies. Jack carried the radio, which he turned off, to conserve the battery. Soon the forest floor tilted, and the trek became slippery. Trout's boots skidded on the dry needles and silt. His breath shortened in the rarefied air, and the oversized pack frame, meant for a man, thumped against his tailbone, but he said nothing.

Trout removed his toque; sweat speckled his forehead. Turner kept repeating, "I can't believe it." Jack and Frank looked at each other without saying anything. Turner was still panicked, but they needed everyone now that the sun was down. Frost formed on the rims of Trout's glasses. He wondered if the man would be found alive. Jack had taught him about exposure. Each hour meant it was less likely the injured man would be found alive.

By ten o'clock, the search party was still only part way up the mountain. The moon rose in a clear sky, and they squatted among the spruce and rested. Jack tied up Junior and broke out sandwiches and a thermos of tea from the pannier. At first, Turner wouldn't take any food, he was too proud and embarrassed, but Jack insisted that he eat.

"Whatever happened to that little keg you had for your dog's neck, Jack? A little brandy would be real nice right now," Frank said, clouds of steam rising from his mouth into the small clearing.

"Ate one hell of a lot of pickled herring to empty that barrel," Jack said. Junior sensed they were talking about him, and he licked Jack's face, nearly knocking his hat off.

But when the searchers began climbing again, deadfall scattered over the scree slowed their progress. They picked their way along, following the erratic shards lit up by the beams from their flashlights. Trout's eyes became keen in the moonlight. He'd never seen such brightness of stars and moon. Around them, night animals roamed—bear, cougar, porcupine and skunk—but he was unafraid. The search party rested more often now.

"One slip and we'll have two rescues on our hands," Frank said to Turner, who wanted to go faster. The rangers kept the search slow and methodical, sweeping first one grid, then the next.

At midnight, Jack radioed out. Shelagh sounded bright and alert. The transmission crackled in the forest night.

"X78278 to mobile, I read you loud and clear, over."

"We're almost there, over."

"Roger, I think I can see your lights from here, Jack. I'll stand by when you need me, over and out."

Trout was giddy from lack of sleep, and from the tea and sandwiches that had fuelled him. He placed one foot in front of the other, following behind the dog and his uncle. No one talked now. Turner seemed resigned to the pace. At two o'clock in the morning they stopped once more at the base of a flatiron. Frank built a small, quick fire to warm them, and the flames reflected off the sheer rock face, radiating light and heat. Frank's face glowed in the fire. Soundlessly, he moved from the fire to gather wood, and the search party warmed themselves. Then, signalling that it was time to move on, Frank kicked in the fire and pissed on the small coals.

The searchers scrambled over rockslides that reached into the woods far below them. They were above the tree line now. Cold air pinched Trout's cheeks. He felt he had been gone for a long time. Carrie seemed part of a distant dream. In Trout's delirium, Stoney spirits guided them—which ones, he didn't know. Manitou? Coyote? He was beyond exhaustion. If he ever saw Carrie again, he'd ask her about the spirits, but Jack said the Bighorn Stoneys were Methodists. It didn't make sense, but Trout had left sense behind hours ago. He lumbered now, half-asleep on his feet, still thrilled by Carrie's touch just hours before. He wanted to lie down, but Jack didn't stop.

Suddenly, Junior started barking. A man shouted. When the luminescent glow of his watch dial read four-thirty in the morning, Trout saw a light flare in front of him. He was suddenly wide awake, oblivious of the cold. The injured man lay sprawled on the scree; his friend hovered over him, shining a flashlight on his face. Junior stood guard beside the man, and barked loudly.

Scrambling in the gravel, Jack leashed the dog. Trout dropped his packboard and held Junior's collar, while Jack kneeled beside the hunter. Turner and the hunter's friend shone flashlights on the injured man, as the rangers attended to his injuries. Trout could see that the man was older, and tall. His face was bruised and cut.

The man's foot was turned backward and his leg was twisted under him. Frank straightened the mangled leg and Jack eased splints into place. The injured man groaned in pain. His plaid bush jacket was torn, and a jagged bone poked through his bloodied pants. Trout looked at the high ledge from which the man had fallen. The scree must have saved him by cushioning his fall.

Once the man was stabilized, Jack covered him with a blanket. "Gonna need a doctor and a stretcher," Jack said.

"I'll stay with him. Can't do anything more tonight." Frank said. "Have Shelagh rouse Beth. She'll call Rocky for a helicopter in the morning."

Jack followed a game trail that ran parallel to a creek and then dropped down the mountain to Whitegoat Cabin. It wasn't far. Trout followed; the adrenaline surge had charged his blood and warmed him. At the cabin, Jack untied the wire bundling the mattresses to the ceiling and unrolled them onto the iron cots. Trout split kindling and stoked the fire in the stove. They hung their damp clothes in front of the stove and his uncle got dry food for Junior.

"Might as well get a couple hours sleep. Helicopter can't get here 'til morning."

At daybreak, Trout jolted awake. The stove clattered as Jack made breakfast. Thick coffee, sweetened with brown sugar and powdered milk, scalded Trout's throat. Jack boiled oatmeal and spooned it into three bowls, diluting Junior's portion with powdered milk. There was no table in the ranger's cabin, only a rough counter on a cement floor, doorless cupboards, and stumps for sitting. Trout spooned brown sugar and dry milk into the tin bowl that warmed his hands and was grateful for the thick mess that filled his stomach. In the searing light of morning, his eyes were red and tight from lack of sleep.

They left the St. Bernard at the cabin and hiked back up. Jack scouted a landing site in a clearing down the mountain from the injured man. When the familiar turquoise-and-white helicopter came over the range from Rocky, Jack radioed the pilot to land in the clearing. The tail rotor of the helicopter clipped the brush around them, and missed the aspens by inches. Jack ducked below the spinning rotor and held on to his cap as he ran to get the stretcher. The doctor lugged a first aid kit and jogged behind. Trout followed them with the radio.

In daylight, they were at the rescue site in minutes. The injured man's eyes were open now, but dulled with pain and hypothermia. His skin was the colour of cigarette ash. The ledge he'd fallen from stood seventy-five feet above them. His legs were so swollen the doctor had to cut his pants away.

"Both your legs are broken," the doctor said, as he sedated the man and cut his boots open with a pair of surgical snips.

"Those are expensive boots," Turner muttered.

"And this is a million dollar rescue operation," Frank Jones said. Turner was silent.

It took all of the men, lifting carefully, to get the

injured hunter onto the stretcher. Frank tied an anchor rope around his waist to keep the stretcher from sliding, as the men clambered down the mountain. The injured man moaned, as the stretcher jolted and bounced. Frank strained on the rope to keep the stretcher level, while Jack led the search party out to the landing site.

Back at the helicopter, the pilot had cut down the small aspens for take-off. The stretcher wouldn't fit in the helicopter, so the injured man was placed on the floor, curled around the pilot's seat. The doctor climbed in over him.

The helicopter lifted a few feet, hovered and teetered as the rotor pounded the air. The pilot shook his head and set it back down. The doctor got out. On the second try, the helicopter cleared the meadow, and headed down to Whitegoat Cabin. Jack motioned to the doctor and Trout to follow him. When they got to a small alpine meadow below the cabin, the chopper was waiting. This time, with the doctor on board, the pilot pulled up in a long, easy glide over the creek, grazing the treetops.

"Some pilot," Frank Jones said, before he left for Nordegg.

"Some team," Jack replied, and clapped Trout on the shoulder. They watched the hunters' car spin out on the gravel road, racing the helicopter back to Rocky Mountain House.

When Trout and Jack sat down that night to an early dinner of hot turkey sandwiches, Shelagh told them the good news. Beth had radioed to say the man was going to live.

"Broke both legs and his sternum, though," she nodded, as she crossed her knife and fork. "Lucky fellow, that one."

"Usually they aren't, in the mountains." Jack shrugged. "Shock alone should have killed him."

Jack didn't say grace that night. There wasn't much talk around the table, but Trout found a small glass of Scotch next to his tomato juice, when he sat down. Jack raised his glass to Shelagh, and to Trout, and clinked glasses with them in a silent toast. They forked turkey, ladled gravy, and spooned cranberries onto the thick rich bread, steadily eating slice after slice.

For dessert, there was a deep pie of pumpkin and sweet potato, with whipped cream. Amen to a prayer, unspoken but answered.

Clare

Just before Christmas, I took a job wrapping gifts at the Hudson's Bay store. I was downtown again, and most of the kids I worked with were university students. There was a kind of happy desperation among all of us. Everyone was working to make money for Christmas. It was fast, easy work, just a few hours each day, and the days went by quickly. I had little time to think about anything. One night a week I stayed downtown and took my supper in the cafeteria. The gift-wrap shop was next to Toy Town, and the "sheriff" there was smart and funny. The young sales girls giggled when he came by. I'd never known many men outside my marriage, and I was fascinated by him. One night he asked if I'd join him for supper.

Nolan Isakovitch looked like a Mod, with his zippered calf-high boots, and his button-collared shirt under his suede sports jacket. We met for coffee before work at the Java Cafe. It was a place I wouldn't have gone—later it would be full of heads and freaks, as they called themselves, but then it was mostly old beatniks, some of whom I recognized from my short stay in high school. Nolan lit my cigarette with a fancy gold lighter. He'd gone to my old school, Western Canada High, and was in the drama club, as I had been. He'd acted in a few local theatre productions, mostly bit parts at MAC 14. He was taking theatre courses at the university.

With the money I made at the gift-wrap shop, and with my staff discount, Nolan helped me pick gifts for my kids at the Bay. Nolan had a better eye for fashion than I ever did. Some of the sales girls were "hitting on" him. But he'd already told me about going up the stairs at our old high school with a copy of James Baldwin's *Giovanni's Room*, when his English teacher came up behind and slapped him hard on the back of the head with a roll book. "Why are you reading that trash," the teacher shouted. Nolan met the man at a gay swimming party two years later. The teacher was married, with children. Nolan lived a double life—by day he worked in the toy department. By night he was an actor, and a gay man.

"I've been acting all my life," he told me once. "My mother doesn't even know." He gave me an ironic smirk. He hadn't told her, yet he trusted me.

"I'm such a disappointment to her," he said. "First, I'm not a dentist, and now, this." He spread his arms wide in mock exasperation.

"She must know."

"Maybe. In any case, I'm tired of pretending."

It made me wonder about my own kids and what I'd do, if one of them was gay. I had wondered about Will and his friendship with the Dawes boy. The twins never married—it finally dawned on me why. But for far too long I just wanted to believe they were tomboys, and they'd grow out of it.

I enjoyed those times with Nolan, and I started to think about going back to school. But Lowell and I needed the money from my job. And I dreaded having to go back to my old high school, where the night school courses were held. Nolan said he'd help me. We'd laughed about all our old teachers, like the legendary math teacher with a bulldog's snarl, who barked at us if we weren't paying attention, and flung chalk at our heads.

Things were fine until one of Lowell's crew walked by the Java Cafe. Nolan was flirtatious, holding hands with me, playing James Bond, all the while making eyes at the male waiter. He was so bitterly acerbic and ironic. I had a sort of crush on him. Maybe because he was safe.

Lowell was waiting up when I got home that night, his blueprints and briefcase open in front of him on the dining room table. I'd always meant to tell him about Nolan, but I'd held back because of what he'd done to Roly Faro.

"You mind telling me what's going on?" Lowell spoke in a monotone and stared at the protractors and triangles spread out on the table. The geometry case I'd gotten him lay open in front of him, and the brass compass with a pencil stub lay beside it. Then, he threw the case at the wall and swept the blueprints and the plastic triangles to the floor. I was frightened.

"You asked me, now I'm asking you." Lowell put his head in his hands. "Is there somebody else?"

"What are you talking about?"

"Please don't bullshit me, Clare."

I could hear Emily stirring in her room. The twins and Pauline now slept downstairs.

"I hear from my crew my wife's in the Java Cafe holding hands with some guy. You know what kind of place that is? They were ready to haul him out of there for me."

"The girls are sleeping." I sat facing him. "I've got a friend, Lowell."

"Some friend."

It felt like a betrayal, but I had to say it."He's a fruit, Lowell."

Lowell didn't react—I didn't think he'd heard me. "A queer."

"Why'd you hide it then, Clare?"

"I know what you did to Roly Faro, Lowell." He blinked. "I was afraid."

"That was a long time ago, and I'm fed up going over and over this.

"You hurt him, Lowell. I was already in love with you."

"You let me find out. You didn't tell me. Just like now."

"I was afraid, Lowell. I had no one to talk to. I wanted a friend."

Lowell was stung by that. He took off his glasses and wiped his eyes with the back of his hand.

"If he's a friend, like you say, then invite him for dinner."

I thought for a moment and then said, "Okay, I'll ask him."

Lowell bent over to pick up his blueprints, his neck muscles corded. I picked up the brass box and put the geometry set back together. We were facing each other, but he wouldn't look me at me. I'd hurt him. Maybe I wasn't very good at living.

"The church has couples' weekends," I said. Lowell stared at the mark in the wall where the geometry box had hit the wall. "Will you come with me?"

I extended my hand, not knowing if he'd take it. Before he could, I heard the slow rasp of Emily's door opening. "Mom?"

Lowell took her back to bed, while I watched from the doorway of her room. He tucked Chico, her pyjama dog, in beside her. Her dark curls fanned out on the pillow next to Chico's tawny face, with its stitched-tee nose and brown button eyes. Lowell kissed her forehead. "It's alright, love," he whispered. "Go back to sleep."

I worked harder that Christmas than I ever had before. The twins put up lights and Emily helped me make arrangements for the table. We got a little red-roofed white plastic church with a tiny bulb inside that lit up the stained glass windows, and a music box that played "Silent Night." I set it among a grove of miniature pine trees and plastic lambs, all floating on a cloud of cotton-batting snow. Lowell climbed up onto the roof of the house to put up our plywood cut-out of Santa going down the chimney with a sack of presents over his shoulder.

Pauline worked at the Dairy Bar a couple of nights a week. My kids all worked from an early age. The twins delivered the *Star Weekly*—the first girls in our neighbourhood to do so. I knew there wouldn't be another Christmas like this. The girls were all getting too old for family holidays. Pauline wanted no part of the decorations, but she helped me with the baking. Her boss at the Dairy Bar had her cooking now, and handling the cash when he wasn't there.

We made up a parcel to send to Will in Rocky Mountain House, and I took it all the way to the main post office downtown to make sure it got to him on time. Christmas always made me think of the war years. Everything was rationed then, and Mom would stockpile sugar, going without it in her tea or oatmeal, so she'd have it for her baking. Grandpa would bring us parcels of butter, wrapped in waxed paper. Mom would open them on the kitchen table, and we all admired the golden blocks. Nobody had much, so Mom made shortbread and packed it in Red Rose tea boxes for gifts, as her mother had done. I set out in the snow, like one of the wise men, with tea boxes of shortbread for my teachers, and for Mrs. Laverty, my tap dance instructor.

Those years affected us forever, like the Depression had affected my mom. She had what she called a Depression fridge. It was full of bits of everything. Nothing too small to wrap in waxed paper. Margarine containers with a spoonful of mashed potatoes and peas, tin cans full of bacon grease, long after everyone used cooking oil. Kitchen shelves full of empty jars and drawers of plastic bags all washed and saved—just in case.

Neither Lowell nor I'd ever gone hungry, but we'd never had too much either. That came out in little ways. When the kids weren't looking, I'd spread butter on Wonderbread, lay down a half-inch of brown sugar, and crimp it all between my fingers until the sugar and butter oozed together. Lowell liked to plop a thick pat of butter in his tomato soup, a silky yellow island melting as he spooned it down. Or when I broiled his steak on Friday night, he put a pat of butter on his mashed potatoes and another on the steak.

For years, we drank our coffee with condensed milk and spoonfuls of sugar. Long before double-double. Sometimes, for breakfast, he'd have corn flakes with brown sugar and condensed milk, making a mash as thick as fudge.

And we always had a freezer. Lowell would have a side of beef butchered. Our kids never went without. That Christmas was no different. The union sent Lowell home with a turkey after the kids' Christmas party—the girls each got a nurse's bag, with a plastic stethoscope and a needle. The boys typically got carpenter's kits with a boy-sized hammer and saw. We didn't have much, but we had enough. On my last day at the Bay, I met Nolan for supper in the cafeteria.

"You said you liked poetry." He handed me a slim white package, immaculately tied in a red satin ribbon. I looked at the cover: *Howl.*

"Allen Ginsberg," he whispered, as he looked around, mocking. "It's a conspiracy. We're everywhere."

"I feel so stupid. My present has butter in it. I'd forgotten."

"Clare, I got us the special." Nolan pointed to the blackboard. Pork Schnitzel. "My mother doesn't bake. The housekeeper does." He laughed bitterly. "With lots of butter."

Nolan picked up his meat on his fork and waved it, as he read out loud from the book. "I saw the best minds of my generation destroyed by madness, starving hysterical naked."

Right there in the Bay cafeteria, oblivious to all the Christmas shoppers with their bags of gifts, in his cowboy vest and hat, with his tin sheriff's badge, Nolan declaimed, swirling his pork schnitzel to the beat.

"Dragging themselves through the negro streets looking for an angry fix."

He read the poem as if he was Allen Ginsberg—all the pain and passion shutting out everything around us. It certainly wasn't anything like the poetry I had known. Nolan and I ate fingers of shortbread and read poetry in the basement cafeteria of the Bay. Afterwards, I told him about my grandmother and her recipes, and about my mother, and about the golden blocks of butter from my grandfather's cows. Nolan made anything seem possible and fun.

He did come for dinner in the New Year. "Cool guy, Mom," Pauline said, after he left. Lowell was tense with him at first, but they both liked jazz, and a few weeks later, they ended up going to the Blind Onion together. Nolan invited us both to the Musicians and Actors' Club, which was a drafty old boozecan on 1st, across the railway tracks. Lowell liked the idea of going to an underground place and meeting all the local musicians.

Nolan and Lowell were both outcasts. I've been drawn to that type all my life. Perhaps that's why, of all my children, I felt most drawn to Emily and Will.

Trout

November's snow, when it finally came to Kootenay plains, quickly melted by mid-day. The logging trucks, coated with muddy silt, stopped in front of the ranger station to put on chains for the journey past the Cline into Rocky. There was heavy snow in Nordegg, and the plow was out between the town and the end of the gravel highway. Shelagh and Beth monitored its progress on the two-way radio. Charlie Moses passed without slowing on his way to his traplines at Whiterabbit Creek.

Jack still went out on patrol, usually in the truck, or sometimes on horseback when he surveyed the elk herds that had come back down off the mountains once the hunters had left. He returned at supper with a story about a pack of wolves being trailed by a lone calico barn cat, which had wandered off and joined them three years earlier. The wolves apparently accepted the cat, he said.

Trout spent his mornings with Shelagh, studying Shakespeare and Coleridge or, more tortuously, math. Afternoons, he went out with Jack to patrol the range, or to do maintenance work on the barn, or on the dogsleds. Short days were made shorter still by the shadows cast by the mountains under low clouds, their brute rock waves tipped with more new snow. The Upper Saskatchewan seemed remote.

Those times he was gloomy, and he missed Kenny and his sisters. But to admit that to himself made him feel even worse, and so Trout didn't. He'd read through everything in the house. When mail came, he rummaged through it, looking for letters addressed to him. His grandmother, Dot, who wrote only notes, always sent some kind of sweet. Yet he already had enough of those, thanks to Shelagh, who stocked the storeroom with lemon and cherry sugar candies, caramels and toffee, bonbons, bulleyes, poppycock. And she baked pans of date or chocolate squares, with mint from the garden, each cut in a careful grid, stacked on plates piled high at tea.

Trout read and reread his mail, and peered behind and under the words to mine everything, just in case he'd missed anything. He'd learned that from Shelagh's lessons. So much, she'd told him, is conveyed by what is not said, like in Shakespeare's plays—the things that remain off stage, encrypted in silence.

Trout treasured those letters piled up on his window ledge, weighed down by the conch. When his mother's letter came, he didn't recognize that it was from her, because the handwriting on the envelope was so erratic and strained.

"There is no way to say this," she'd written. Her words were frail. The loops of her j's and l's, usually so open and graceful, were tight curves. Trout breathed deeply before the tears started.

"It was a boy," his mother wrote. "I lost him."

Trout wished she hadn't told him, but he knew she needed him to hear. He wished he could have been home to help her.

When Jack leaned on the doorway of the fallout shelter, Trout knew that Shelagh and his uncle already knew about his mother's miscarriage. An envelope in his mother's handwriting had come for them in the same mail. Because of the long delay between the time letters were written, posted and picked up at the post office in Rocky, letters were not always received in the order in which they were mailed. Three weeks' mail often came at once, dumped on the kitchen table by Jack. Time was out of sequence, to be pieced together by reading and rereading.

"Want to come to Whirlpool Point," Jack asked, when he had Trout's attention. "We'll go get Silas's pipe stone."

The next afternoon, they drove to a bend of the North Saskatchewan River, opposite the Siffleur confluence, where a whirlpool churned in the wide green band of water. No cars passed the station now, and there was a sign saying: Road Closed Beyond this Point at the eastern gate to Banff National Park, which was locked after the first snowfall closed the passes. The road turned from gravel to slick bare rock. Danger signs marked the ascent from both sides. During the summer, on their way to Saskatchewan Crossing, Jack had cursed when they saw a sedan with two of its wheels balanced over the ledge. The weight of the driver and passenger was all that kept the vehicle from plunging into the holy place where the Stoneys gathered pipestone. Jack and Trout had winched them back from the brink.

When he'd offered to make the pipe, Silas had asked specifically for Whirlpool Point stone. Jack parked the truck near the top of the Point. Sun soaked the silt dunes, which were warm to the touch. Jack found an anchor tree and sat Trout down with his back braced in at the base, and his feet wedged into its roots. Roped in, Jack stepped lightly over the cliff, facing the rock, and called out, "On belay!" He rappelled, feeding rope through the carabiner cinched at his waist. On his back he wore a small pack that held a rock hammer. Trout released the rope. Jack pushed off again with the tips of his toes and, mid-way down, found his rock. He was surrounded by battered limber pines with corkscrew trunks that clawed the cliff. The wind strummed the taut rope in Trout's hands. Chunks of rock showered into the whirlpool, as Jack hammered at the cliff face.

Jack worked crevices and toe-jambs as he climbed. The rope, carefully looped by Trout beside the limber pine, held him. Trout was glad for the leverage of the anchor tree, for he knew that without it, he could not hold his uncle. The placid surface of the river below hid the green cyclone of the undertow that would keep a body down for days.

Trout murmured the prayer that he saw each morning, that was embroidered in petit point and hung on the kitchen wall of the ranger station. "God grant me the Serenity to accept the things I cannot change."

Trout pulled the rope tight around his waist, and kept the line taut, as Jack had shown him, using the tree like a pulley brake, should he slip. Jack trusted him now, more than Trout trusted himself.

"The Courage to change the things I can and the Wisdom to know the difference," Trout said to himself, as his uncle appeared over the ledge.

Jack dusted himself off, Trout coiled the rope,

careful not to step on it, and left it ready for an emergency, the way his uncle had taught him.

On the drive back, Jack hummed a bagpipe air, and Trout hefted the biggest of the soft grey-and-white stones back and forth in his hands. He wanted to keep one, to make a marker for the brother he would never know. His mother would like that. For now, he mouthed the words to the prayer for Serenity, Courage and Wisdom, over and over to Jack's beat. It helped him whenever he thought about his mother's letter.

That night in his journal, Trout mapped a triangle. On top, Serenity. In the left corner, Courage and in the right, Wisdom. In the middle, he put a question mark.

Now, he touched each point of the triangle with his fingers, and waited for the echo of his prayer. The contraption man had told him that the deaf hear everything twice: the sound that is incomplete, and then the sound echoed, imagined and completed. Watch their eyes, he'd said. We call it the telephone effect. They don't look at you, because they are listening to the listening. In their minds, he'd said, they're putting it all together. And listening thus to the listening, Trout fell asleep that night.

The week before Christmas, with the snow pack building on the nearby peaks, on Moses Flats, and all down Kootenay Plains, dry snow fell on top of wet. The wind flattened the drifts into frozen sheets, shiny and hard as a mirror. When the sun came out, Trout was dazzled. His eyes narrowed to slits. The muddy track in front of the house froze and wrenched the wheel from Jack's hands now, when he ran patrols west to the logging camp above Whiterabbit Creek.

December's brittle silence fell upon the Upper Saskatchewan, breached only by the dogs' barking. Jack stepped out with the coiled snakeskin whip that hung at the door. When the dogs continued to bark at a herd of deer that dashed across the plains, he shook the whip once and commanded, "Down." One by one, the dogs sulked back to their snow-capped houses.

In the close quarters of the station, Jack and Shelagh bickered occasionally, but mostly they bantered good-naturedly, before sinking once more into the silence the mountains shouldered on them.

Christmas morning came and Trout welcomed the bright interruption, when they all unwrapped their gifts in the living room under the gaze of the grinning cougar and the upside down bear. All of the gifts, except the ones from his aunt and uncle, were wrapped in brown paper, with a colourful patch of stamps in the left-hand corner, seared by the postmaster's black ink. Jack must have slipped the packages into the house on his last trip from Nordegg, after stopping at the Bighorn to deliver gifts of tea, tobacco, and sweet biscuits—Shelagh's name for her cookies—for his friend Silas Moses, and the elders, Joe Pee Beaver and Jacob House.

Jack's daughter, who lived in Edmonton, had sent him a plaid tie and matching stockings in the clan tartan "For Robbie Burns' Day, Dad," the bright card said. Trout got a Marine Band harmonica in a cardboard casket and a songbook from Shelagh. Jack gave him a pair of bearspaw snowshoes and a reversible down vest. "Red side out in hunting season," Jack laughed and winked at Shelagh. "Don't want ya gettin' mistaken for a bear." Trout had gotten Jack a boxed set of Paul Kane prints from the gift shop in Rocky, and given Shelagh finger picks, and a new capo for the Epiphone. His Grandma Ruby had sent him a brand new five-dollar bill. Dot had gotten him a bone-handled pocketknife, with a fork and spoon on it. "For the trail," her card said.

A large package, wrapped by his mother, the flourishes of her handwriting bolder now since the baby's death, contained a small tabletop telescope on a tripod. Trout could use it to spy back at Red Wilson. In the same parcel, was a smaller gift. "Love, the girls," the card said, followed by a gentle dig, "Just in case you forgot: Pauline, Emily, Chris and Liz." They had each signed in their own handwriting.

Trout missed his sisters, but he also brooded when Jack went off to the Bighorn by himself. Trout had no idea what he should give to Carrie, or how he would get his gift to her. His shyness wouldn't allow him to ask Jack to take it along. He was afraid of drawing attention to his feelings for Carrie.

Kootenay Plains seemed as windswept and vast as the Gobi desert of which he'd read in his correspondence lessons. Snow crystals sharp as sand grazed his nose when he was out in the yard. Calgary now seemed as distant as Tibet. Trout was lonely. Kenny was in the Don Bosco Home for Boys, and Trout hadn't heard from him in months. Kenny wasn't a letter writer anyway, and the nearest phone was ninety miles away. Trout ached for the yells of his sisters when they played.

"So don't forget us," one final note said, in Pauline's handwriting. There were times he both loved and hated her. Her note had come folded like origami on top of the shells, all wrapped in sheets of newsprint and, beside them, the candy jar Auntie had left her. He poured the miniature shells into the jar: cowries, cones, limpets and whelks, along with miniature scallops and razor clams. Carefully culled by her, these were the small jewels of his collection. The bell-shaped jar was her sole heirloom from their auntie. He would never have thought of this: sea candies.

Shelagh rotated and admired the jar in her hands. "You've got the world in there, dear boy. When I was a girl, before the war, Mum and I would go to Brighton. I collected sea shells too, but these are much prettier." Shelagh's voice put a snap in "much".

That night, Trout put the candy jar of shells beside the conch on the window ledge, beside his growing cache of letters. He saved the wadded newsprint from the *Calgary Herald* that the shells had come wrapped in. Later, he ironed out the creases in the newsprint with the heel of his hand, to read the weeks-old news from his far away home.

Boxing Day morning after breakfast, he and Jack drove out to check the precipitation gauge at the headwaters of Cataract Creek. In the woods, as they snowshoed along the creek, deep powder covered the meandering pools of water open even in the cold of the mountains. Jack nearly broke through, stepping back just as a snow bridge gave way. Trout was grateful for the bearspaw snowshoes they wore; they were nimble-footed, unlike the long-tailed Algonquians Jack swore against. Although the trees around them were buried under snow, Trout was cosy in his new down vest, deerskin mittens, and his toque.

When they reached the headwaters of Cataract Creek, Jack tramped the snow in a shallow bowl and cut short stakes, building a raft on which he made a fire, while Trout gathered spruce boughs for them to sit on.

"Keep your snowshoes on. It's at least a good twenty feet deep here," Jack laughed. "Wouldn't find you 'til spring."

The fire cracked and popped. They ate thick turkey sandwiches, and slabs of Shelagh's mince pie washed down with tea. The tin mug scalded Trout's bare hands, and the smoke from the fire stung his face. Except for the tops of trees poking up around them, they might have been on the light side of the moon. Burled and scalloped snow smoothed out the ridges and scree under them.

On the trip out, they made good time on the packed trail. Then, Jack put his forefinger to his lips and said, "Shhh." Thirty paces in, a ridge sheltered a large spruce. Its lower branches were cowled in ice. In the shallow under the tree, Trout saw twin jets of steam. The vapour had risen from the bole of the tree and coated its perimeter.

Jack tapped Trout's arm. "Bear," he said. As they slipped back to the trail, Trout turned to admire the snow cave that protected the lone sleeper. Crystal ridges rimmed the hole where the bear slept.

Two weeks later, when Jack and Trout returned to Cataract Creek, the bear tree was blanketed in heavy new snow. The bear had gone elsewhere, Jack said. They sometimes moved house several times in a winter.

On New Years' Eve, Trout was invited to Nordegg, but he chose to stay behind at the ranger station. He had the two-way radio there so he could call out if necessary. The dogs needed care, and besides, he knew Heather Jones was away with her boyfriend in Rocky, and the other rangers' children were small. Shelagh left the kerosene fridge full of snacks and enough food for four meals, since she and Jack would stay overnight with Frank and Beth Jones.

After they'd left the yard, Trout snooped around Jack's office. Trout had no fascination for the guns, not even the Luger smuggled back from Germany and hidden in the second drawer of Jack's desk. The bottles of Johnny Walker and Glenfiddich in the liquor cabinet were another matter. He poured a small tumbler of the good stuff, and mixed it with tap water. He gulped it as he settled in front of the Grundig. With its antenna wire running out the window, and strung across the yard to the radio tower, the Grundig linked Trout to the outside world that night.

Removing his hearing aids, Trout got up, brought the bottle to the table and poured another Scotch, this time without water. He jammed in the rado's hard earplug, just like the one from his old contraption. He'd always been wired, Trout laughed to himself, tipsy with Scotch and giddy at the thought of having the place all to himself. He flicked the dial, and caught waves of static, sonic belches and otherworldly klaxons. He cranked up the volume and reached out to the world—through the wire, across the yard, past Rocky, south through Calgary and Lethbridge, Great Falls, and Kalispell, all the way to Mon-tan-a. Trout played the vowels and consonants over his tongue, lightened now by the alcohol. He listened awhile to the country stations and poured more Scotch into his glass. Down the spine of the Great Divide to the Sierras he searched, bouncing off the clouds to pull in San Francisco and Los Angeles, then shifting his search east, the mid-west accents counting down New Year in between the music. He leaned into the radio and strained to hear, but he'd learned patience now.

He'd caught something. He twisted the dial and tuned it until he heard, for the first time, a blue howl from way down in Tallahatchee County, which he knew was somewhere deep in the Mississippi Delta. It was a caterwaul of a sound—that word he'd found in his dictionary, new and fine, unattached to anything, until now. A deep blue caterwaul, blown from Chicago's Southside, a soulful wail born in the heart of Africa, brought over on the slaver's bloody ships, chanted on the chain gangs, burnished in the juke joints of the South. Freighted clackety-clack north of the Mason-Dixon Line on up through Memphis, amped up and drummed out on the Windy City's Southside. He drank his uncle's Scotch and listened as the sound whispered and shouted, called and called back, a rangy caterwaul pulled through a thin brass plate. Its nimble reeds fluttering, thin as paper matches, bending down those blue notes. Blowing and blocking those reeds with a machine-gun tongue, reaching into the gut, and taking the sound back again through Chicago, Memphis, Port Au Prince, and the distant African shores, back and forward across night, oceans and time.

Trout had recognized the instrument and the sound instantly, of which he'd made a crude imitation days earlier. Blowing in his new Hohner Marine Band harmonica, he had tried songs he'd never heard, as he'd bitten down on the chrome case. His clumsy tongue had fingered the wooden plate, sandwiched between the brass reeds, as he played along with Shelagh's records: "Frankie and Johnny", over and over, following the instructions for the harmonica. Two fat lips over the soundboard, blow and draw arrows, a simple notation of the music he tried for: "Freight Train" and "St. James's Infirmary".

But this faraway player blew his harmonica and sang with a voice that dispelled the flood. When fishes sang, Trout thought, surely this would be their tune, deep and blue. The bluesman on the radio played to him on New Year's Eve, hit the high notes, raced along the diatonic scale to the lows, dah-dah-dah-dah-wa-wa-wa-wa, and a stomp, and back up to the highs Trout couldn't hear, but he knew were there, twice in a beat.

"Counting down to the New Year on WLOT, you're listening to Sonny Boy Williamson. King of the Blues Harmonica, the Mississippi saxophone, here on the Blues Rundown with the Hossman. Brought to you by the folks at Randy's Records here in Nashville. The Hossman says, Come on down now to Randy's Records for all your records. If Randy doesn't have it, you don't want it." There was a crackle, and the sound drifted away. Trout twisted the round dial, chasing over the wire after it. But it was gone.

Trout wanted that low down sound, that mourned love, that sang and swung at the end of a wire attached to his heart. It coursed along his jaw, through the bone pan of his cochlea, into the old reptile brain, down his spine to his feet, dancing them, and flooding his small heart.

As the New Year wound down, Trout unplugged from the radio, put down the hard earphone button, picked up his harmonica, and sat in front of the record player cranked up high. After one more Scotch, he practiced past midnight, trying for that sound, that blue wail. He ached for Carrie Moses, as he clamped his teeth down hard on the Hohner's tin sandwich. His tongue too blunt to block the notes he didn't want; his ears too dense to hear the high ones, he blew and pulled large on the sound anyway. His red cheeks sank and bellowed as he played a wail swallowed up by the mountains. The dogs in their pens and the bear in its snow cave slept. The party was elsewhere that night, but here was music, crude, but music nonetheless, as Trout sang about the girl he loved. Like the man on the radio, that Sonny Boy Williamson.

Trout fell asleep a few hours into the New Year, the needle on the record player bumping again and

331

again, his harmonica still in his hand. In his dreams he played grand, Sonny Boy Williamson and the band behind him, and the girl he loved in front, all the high notes rang sweet and clear. For in his dreams, he heard everything.

Clare

Lowell brushed my eyelids with his lips before he left that morning. The scent of shaving cream filled the bedroom, and I heard the car pull away. My girls were already up after their dad went off to a job. In those days the trades worked Saturdays. I could hear the television and the Saturday morning cartoons. I lay there as long as I could, before joining the girls in the living room for coffee. The February winds blew against the house, and snow drifted across the yard. One of the neighbours, who ran a gravel business, was under his dump truck with a pan of burning oil, trying to thaw the engine block. The rest of the neighbours had electrical cords hooped over the sidewalks, running from the houses to the block heaters in their cars.

By noon, the sun broke through and a grey Chinook arch crossed the sky behind the house, pink streaks rising from it. The eavetroughs began to drip as snow melted on the roof. I made the girls soup and grilled cheese sandwiches, the slap of butter on the grill smoking the air. As the sky warmed, children next door ran out to play. I walked with the twins and Emily to Safeway.

In Israel, Nolan had said, they're called the witches' winds. They turn everyone's moods black, and suicides increase. The Chinooks didn't affect me that way. They just sent me out to the edge of the prairie to wander with my kids, welcoming the warm blast of wind in our faces. I carried our coats. The twins pelted each other with wet sloppy snowballs, and Emily and I joined in. Across the road, some boys had dammed the gutter on the hill and the water backed up until the bus smashed through, unleashing a torrent of brown slushy water. The Chinook always brings the first hope of spring. It's a short rush of delirium as life thaws again. No matter what the groundhog says, spring is on its way.

I took the girls to the bakery for a round of long-johns with rich caramel icing. I bought steaks for Lowell and me, and hamburger to make meatloaf for the girls—their favourite—in celebration of the Chinook.

Jack and Shelagh had sent pictures of Will sitting on a horse, wearing his new cowboy boots. He looked stronger than he ever had, and handsome in the way my grandfather was, with the same red hair. Undeniably a Locke, Mom chimed in, when she saw the pictures. But a child is the product of both parents, and all the people before them. Will was as much a Dunlop, I knew. He had Lowell's baby face and glasses. In his letters to his sisters, he told them about the animals, and about his adventures. His letters were no longer illegible and garbled. Will told them stories of all the new experiences he'd had—the places he'd seen and the people he'd encountered.

I couldn't forget something Jack had once said to me, when Will was little. Jack and I had talked about the deafness. And that's how we said it. The deafness, not his deafness, as if that were too personal. His affliction too immediate to admit. He's going to have a difficult time of it, Jack told me when Will was first tested and got the hearing aid—Lowell called it his contraption. Everyone else said how this hearing aid would fix it, and how much Will would improve. But Jack had said, try it on for a day or two, wear it around the house and out to the store. So I did. As I wore the body aid around the house, the sound was awful, brassy and loud. All the noises—and they were noises—came at me all at once and were jumbled together. After a while, everything irritated me. Sharp sounds made me jump. The aid rubbed against my dress and produced static. If two people were talking at once—and with a house full of kids, this happened all the time—I couldn't pick out anyone. The loud ticking of the grandfather clock in the front room distracted from the sound of the television. Everything was amplified equally, democratically. It was chaos.

Outside, it was worse. The squealing of car brakes frightened me. There were sounds missing that I knew should be there, like the chirping of birds. The wind across the prairies sounded like crumpled wrapping paper. I began to lose my sense of balance. And people stared when I went downtown, commenting even when I could hear them. Some of the store people raised their voices, trying to be helpful but exaggerating their words, as if I was simple. Emily, when she was in university, talked about projection—how people project their own fears onto someone else.

Another word Emily used was denial. *They're in denial, Mom.* And I think that's the way we were in the fifties about so many things. If we refused to see it, if we projected enough warm good feelings on it, then by God, it must be so. I was in denial about Will's deafness, and how it affected him. Uncle Jack wasn't. I tore the wire out of my ear after only a few hours. I never forgot Jack's lesson.

As the girls and I made our way home that day in the Chinook wind that lifted our spirits, we visited Pauline at the Dairy Bar. She gave us an order of French fries right out of the sizzling fryer, hot oil and vinegar seeping through the bottom of the bag. I knew Will would never hear any of this as my daughters did. But I was grateful that he'd been given a year with Jack and Shelagh, who taught him and took care of him as if he were their own. Will's Christmas test scores were high. I wanted to run back to the school and tell them. My life and my faith had taught me to be cautious, not to take anything for granted. But after all we'd been through, I was happy. The fresh smell of damp clothes on the line, the jumble of my kid's wet boots on the back landing, and the girls excitment about meatloaf all made me smile. When we got back home, I fixed myself a rum and coke and made coleslaw and a casserole of scalloped potatoes.

That night, when Lowell came home, I ran him a bath and brought him a rye and ginger ale—all he ever drank. I grilled steaks in the gas broiler in the bottom of the stove. We ate our supper; even Pauline laughed with her father. Sometimes, she let her guard down for an hour or two. I'd bought a chocolate birthday cake, not because it was anyone's birthday, but because I wanted to celebrate. After supper, we pushed the table and chairs aside and took turns dancing, mostly over and over to "Blue Suede Shoes".

Lowell loved Elvis. All of us did the Twist and the Mashed Potato, dances Pauline had taught the girls.

After the girls were asleep and Pauline had gone to spend the night at a girlfriend's house, Lowell and I lay in our bed watching the drapes at the window fluttering in the breeze. Lowell pulled me onto him, running his hands up and down my back, lifting my breasts, weighing them in his hands like apples. My grandfather showed us how to pick the tart green apples that grew on the farm. Careful, Grandpa said, lift them up, and away from the stem. Don't tug them, Clare, and they'll float right off the tree, he said. Even then I knew he was talking not about apples, but about love.

My life swirled around me. After we made love, and Lowell lay asleep beside me, I thought of my Grandmother Locke. She had what mom called her fey way—a touch that could calm a child or an animal. My grandmother had told me of the time when Grandpa, desperate because the well had ran dry, came to her with a newly cut Y of willow. He didn't believe in old country superstitions like water witching, but he asked her, "Will you?"

She told us that a crowbar or coathanger would have worked just as well. Anything that was handy would carry the pulse of the water below; she'd learned this as a child. In one of the houses they lived in back home, "Auchtermuchtie drumna drochit— our wee house in the hill," she'd say, she hadn't been able to sleep because she heard things. Her mother thought it was ghosts, but when a man came to exorcise the house, he'd found an underground stream running under my grandmother's bedroom. Her iron bedframe had picked up the pulse of the water vibrating all around her.

"You have the gift," the man said to Grandma Locke, and showed her how to dowse for water. She found water on the homestead alright, though the first well was saline and couldn't be used. But that turned out to be the most lucrative well—not for my grandparents, but for the people who bought the farm after Grandpa died. When the oil companies came through, they drilled over the first well, pumping out salt water from the Devonian Sea, where all the oil lay.

Grandma didn't talk about any of this when Grandpa was around, but sometimes she'd read tea leaves for Mom and me, laughing, and even wrapping her head in a bandana like a fortune-teller. The news she read in the tea leaves was always good. But shortly after I met Lowell, I went to Grandma Locke and asked for a reading. I hadn't told her about Lowell, but after she read the tea leaves, her brow crumpled, and all she would say is, "Ye'll ken when ye ken—you'll know when you know." No matter how hard I pressed, she shook her head and changed the topic.

After that, I stopped reading horoscopes in the newspaper. But once in a while, when we were alone, I'd ask Grandma to read the tea leaves for me again. She would shudder and shoosh me away, "Ach, a' wa wie ye, Clare."

Before she died, I tried one more time. She whispered, "Ye'll ken tha noo." I forgot about it for a while, but my mind always came back to what she had said. Usually in the happiest moments, with the spring wind in the air, and Lowell sleeping beside me. I'd lie awake with the streetlamp's glow casting shadows of the lilac bushes across the drapes. I'd always believed in premonitions. I think it's a lost animal sense that protects us from danger. Or it's a combination of all the other senses that guides us, even in our dreams. I'd gone down to the river once, with Lowell's hunting knife, and cut myself a pliant Y of willow. I tucked it under my coat and brought it back to the house. When the neighbours were away at work, I dowsed the yard, going back and forth across it. At first, I didn't feel anything, but eventually, I could feel a slight pull up my arms, through the back of my hands. My hands began to move ever so slightly on their own. I threw the willow branch in the old oil drum where we burned garbage. That night I asked Lowell to show me where the water line was. The notch I'd made on the fence matched up exactly with the spot where the pipe came into the house. I never told Lowell what I'd done, just that a man from the city had been around and I needed to know.

And now the feeling, like the slight pulse that came from the ground, centred on my family. The more I concentrated, the less I knew. But in those rare moments when I could disentangle from my day-to-day life, first the sense turned on my husband and then on my son. I was scared at how premonitions, like dreams, can feel so real. In the waking world, I'd laugh at these premonitions, but a doubt remained.

If I let it, it would consume me. So I pushed those thoughts away.

I never told anyone about my kooky thoughts except Nolan. I was too busy with my job and an evening class that was held at my old high school lab, with its smells of musty wood and formaldehyde, and the gooseneck taps and gas jets for the Bunsen burners. That wing of the school had tall windows that opened outward, like doors. When I was younger, the boys in my class would jump down from those windows to the ground, six feet below, and slip over to the pool hall when the teachers turned their back to the class.

But this time, school was different. With Nolan's help, I saw a place for everything, even algebra and logarithms, which had once seemed joyless and dry. English was always my favourite subject, and I had a lovely teacher. I was discovering parts of me that had been left behind in the scramble to be a wife and mother. But I didn't forget my girls. Every Sunday I made the week's dinners ahead of time, so that they had hot meals on those nights when I wasn't home. Lowell seemed to recognize my need to go back to school, although he didn't do housework—most men didn't, then. Not like my daughter's husband. He makes us breakfast every Sunday morning—giant omelettes, or pancakes by the dozen, with sausage or bacon grilled on the barbeque.

But the crazy thoughts I'd had crept back. The black phantom shapes, as liquid and dark as the appearances of our dead cat, who, if I looked twice, disappeared and reappeared in the periphery of my vision. When I told Nolan about my premonition and the water witching, he didn't laugh. Instead, the next week after work, he took me to a small cafe I'd never noticed before, The European. It had goulash, paprikash and ragout on the menu. In the front window, between the pots of ivy and pointed mother-in-law's tongue, a sign read: *Miss Ena—Reader of Stars.* We took the back stairs up to a room above the café, led there by the owner's wife, a slight dark-haired woman whom Nolan knew. Downstairs she was the hostess; upstairs, she was Miss Ena. I was disappointed because, other than an overweight silver tabby sleeping upside down in an overstuffed chair, and the card table with four chairs, the room was so ordinary. But Miss Ena sat down at the card table, and gestured to Nolan and me to do the same. I sat opposite her. There was a beauty mark on her cheek. Her grey-streaked hair, which had been pulled back off her face when we came into the restaurant, now hung past her shoulders, creating the effect of a hood. She wore silver bangles on her wrists, and hoop earrings. Her eyes and skin were reminiscent of a younger beauty. Miss Ena was still striking. She was a Roma, a gypsy, Nolan said.

A small wick floating in a red jar of oil sputtered when she put a match to it. The lamplight transformed the room, and in the background, the cat purred like an idiot. I almost wanted to laugh. But shadows changed the fortune-teller's face. She took the Tarot cards out of their velvet cloth wrap, and then shuffled the deck, fanning the cards out on the table in front of us.

Miss Ena peered into my eyes and turned over the cards, one by one. I don't remember them all, just the bony, bent skeleton of Death, the Pope, the Knight of Cups and the Fool. She spoke in a low voice of fire and air, past and future influences. Her face was fixed on mine, reading me, as much as the cards. Her eyes were clever and curious. She may as well have said, abracadabra. I couldn't listen anymore. I reached into my purse and put some money on the table. "It's okay," I said to her. "Thank you."

Nolan touched my elbow. "What's wrong?"

I pushed past him and gathered my coat. "I have to go." On the street, I looked at him. "It's like voodoo. And knowing won't help, Nolan."

As I rode the bus home that night, everything seemed to be changing again, even the colour of the streetlights, and the faces of the people beside me. They were both familiar and strange, as though I hadn't really seen them before. When I got off the bus, the priest's black car was parked outside a neighbour's house, where all of the upstairs lights were on. The priest's words no longer helped me now. All the so-called facts could fall one way, and the very next day in a clearer light, another. As a little girl, I'd watched my grandfather candle eggs on the farm, turning them in front of the light to see the embryo, and from every angle, there was a different story. There were never just two sides to anything, but many, and layers within them, shimmering in darkness and light.

I came away from Miss Ena shaken, and no closer either to peace or to a clearer understanding of my premonitions.

"Think we got enough snow now," Jack said, one day after lunch. "Let's take the dogs for a run tomorrow." The routine of chores, and the short hours of daylight left Trout little time to explore outside. Some days, he'd take one of the St. Bernard pups on a chain leash and let it pull him through the pasture. As Shelagh had promised, Trout had gotten used to the cold, going out most days with only a wool shirt under his down vest.

By mid-February, small avalanches had started to thunder down Sentinel Mountain, dropping between the flatirons. Large plates of snow broke off and slid into the trees. But Kootenay Plains was often swept bare, white for a few days at most, and the wind ploughed the snow into the woods on the sides of the valley floor. Charlie Moses waved when he drove past on his way to his trapline. But Carrie was not with him, and Trout pined for her.

After supper, Jack checked the sled in the garage and showed Trout how the runners were built to flex against the cross-braces, which were lashed with rawhide. Jack demonstrated the iron brake that dropped down behind the sled to stop it. Traces and leather collars for each dog lay on the floor. Silver, the Samoyed, would lead, Jack said. And two generations of St. Bernards would pull. Wheel dogs, Jack explained. The two-hundred-and-fifty-pound Junior would take up the rear, behind his father, Dagwood.

Next morning, Jack lashed the sled on the truck.

As Trout collected the dogs, the pens were in an uproar. The whole dog village had turned out. The Sams, as Shelagh called them, bounced on all fours into the air, while the Saints stood up with their massive front paws leaning against the top rail of the pens.

"Goin' to work are we, boys?" Jack teased the big dogs, and grinned as they shook the truck with the weight of their enthusiasm. They woofed wildly, and licked Trout's hands and face. Silver rode in the cab beside Trout, while Jack drove towards the staging area on Whiterabbit Creek. Trout had never seen happier dogs.

The tires spun and Jack shifted into low as they crossed the icy planks of the logging bridge. Following Charlie Moses's tracks, Jack came to a stop in front of the firegate at Whiterabbit. After they had unloaded the sled, Jack pounded its iron brake into the frozen ground with an axe.

"Hold their collars," Jack said, and showed Trout how to assemble the team, with Silver in front.

"You can ride, for the first while, 'til we get into the woods." Jack handed Trout the lead rope and climbed into the sled. "When we stop, hang on to this, and drive the brake into the ground. If these guys get away, they'll go for miles."

Jack stepped on the tail runners and gave the command. "Silver, hike-up!"

With a powerful lurch, the sled jumped into motion. The wheel dogs pulled and Silver led the way, while Jack coaxed his team along. "Hike-up, boys." The dogs broke into a trot through the woods; the big paws of the Saints snowshoed on the crusted snow.

Trout watched the open river ridged with broken ice, and felt as happy as the dogs were. His breath frosted on his toque and on the loose strands of his hair. Kootenay Plains here was an open run of brittle blonde grass and thin snow, spotted with animal tracks leading into the woods. The wind stung Trout's face, and the dog team's breath fogged the air. Jack leaned into the turns, and then stepped down from the tail runners to run with his dogs. He pushed from behind on inclines, and tapped the brake on the downslopes to keep the sled from overtaking the dog team.

Tom Wilson's old trading post was a grey collection of corrals, with a new tripod of pine poles for bleeding deer, and a hitching post. Two cabins were still standing, while the rest were in ruins. On the edge of the clearing was a turnaround with horse tracks, along with a set of stretching frames for hides, which indicated Charlie's trapping camp. The dog sled skidded to a stop. No smoke rose from either cabin's chimney. Trout jumped out, clutching the lead, and tapped the brake into the ground with an axe. Jack separated the dogs and tied them off on the corral fence.

While Jack went down to the creek with a bucket to fetch water for the dogs, Trout built a fire in the fireplace, in the bare cabin. The fire warmed the dirt floor, and the old musk of log walls filled the room. A grey sheep skull and a rack of deer antlers hung above the stone mantelpiece. Jack never went on the trail without his billycan, made simply from a small lard pail that did duty as water bucket, lunch pail and stewpot. Trout heated frozen blocks of stew that sizzled in the pail, smoking and blinding him as he leaned over the fire.

He and Jack ate hungrily, dunking fists full of Shelagh's bread in the stew, eating out of the tin cups they'd packed in. The cabin had one cracked window, which was overlaid with cobwebs. Cold light seeped in around the door and through the loose planks of the roof.

"Silas's father built these cabins for Tom Wilson, who said he'd come here if he had a cabin to sell supplies from," Jack said. "But, there wasn't enough money to be made on Kootenay Plains."

Jack swished water around in his cup, to clean it, and tossed the water into the fire. "Wilson pulled out in 1906, according to Silas. Gave the cabins back to the Stoneys. Their own cabins. Nice of him, eh? The bugger."

Jack picked up the bucket of steaming water. "Tea?"

Trout threw the greasy water from his own cup into the fire.

"Been their winter camp for seventy years." Jack sipped his tea and reached for his cigarettes. "My boss isn't crazy about it." The cabin filled with cigarette smoke, and Trout inhaled, smoking vicariously.

"What he doesn't know won't hurt him." Jack threw his cigarette butt into the coals and drank the last of the tea. "Better not let the dogs get cooled down," he said.

Trout kicked in the fire and poured the last of the tea water on it. Jack brought in a bundle of firewood to replace what they'd used.

From the front porch, Trout surveyed the Whiterabbit range. The dogs barked, their tails thrashing,
their grins as large as Jack's now. His uncle said, "So,
think you can drive 'em back?"

"I'm ready," Trout laughed at the challenge. He
stood on the rear runners, while Jack sat in the sled
and held the lead rope, with the camp pack at his
feet.

"Remember what I said. They'll be tired," Jack
said.

When Trout gave them the command, the dogs
began trotting up the now-broken trail. They made
good time going back out. Trout used body English on the corners, and Jack leaned with him. Trout
helped push the sled on the hills and ran alongside,
as his uncle had.

When they were almost half-way back to the truck,
the dogs started barking. Then, the team took off. The
sled jerked as the dogs raced to a gallop. Before Trout
could slow the dogs, the sled was flying over the trail.
He shouted at the team to stop. Jack strained on the
lead rope, but the dogs were oblivious to his efforts.

"Jesus," Jack shouted. "Look!"

At the base of a nearby hill, a herd of wild horses
broke away, leaving a flying stream of snow in their
wake. There were a dozen or more of them: chestnuts,
greys and pintos, most with the distinctive short neck
and large head, like the one Carrie had ridden at the
Bighorn. Trout watched them in awe, more pony than
horse, with their short legs spinning under them.

"Stand on the brake," Jack said to Trout. "Stand
hard."

Trout jumped on the iron brake, but he was too light to hold it down. The brake kicked back and bounced over the surface of the frozen ground, while the dogs ran flat out. Their tails flagged behind them as they chased the horses over the plains. At the sight of the dog sled closing in, the horses veered into the woods.

"Ride 'em out," Jack yelled, leaning from side to side to steady the sled as it careened over the trail. "Hang on. Let 'em run."

Cold tears and fear blinded Trout. The sled handles pounded his hands through his deerskin mitts. Circles of sweat formed under his arms as he jockeyed the sled side to side, but the rubber soles of his felt-pacs kept him on the runners.

Suddenly, the horses turned onto a narrow path into deep snow, before disappearing through a gap in the range.

The dogs began to slow down as the herd outdistanced them. The sled sank into the drifts.

"Stand on it, Trout. Hold the brake," Jack shouted. He hopped out and pulled on the traces of the wheel dogs as they hit the deep snow.

Jack seemed angry, and Trout thought he'd whip the dogs. But instead, he took Silver's head firmly in his hands. "Silver, Jesus."

The dogs all slunk in their harnesses at the tone of Jack's voice, but moments later, their tails wagged and they were eager to go again.

"Some ride, eh?" Jack laughed. He uncased the binoculars and peered up the gap. "Nothing. Gone like ghosts. Never seen my dogs take off like that before." He shook his head. "Silas told me about a herd of wild horses who lived here years ago. Descendants of Sitting Bull's war ponies. Thought he was teasing me. Must have been a dozen of 'em. We won't see anything like that again in a lifetime, Trout."

Trout traded places with Jack on the sled, and Jack drove the tired dogs back to the trail. By the time they got to the staging area, the sun was setting. Trout's pants were frozen to his legs. Jack warmed up the truck, while Trout loaded the dogs. Silver leapt into the front seat and put his head on Trout's lap, his ears down and his nose to the door. "You did alright, Trout," Jack confided, when he got in. "I couldn't have held 'em back either."

Then the Motorola crackled with Shelagh's voice. "X78278 calling Clearwater Car Four. Do you read me? Come in, Jack."

"Clearwater Four, go ahead, Shelagh."

"There's been an accident at the lumber camp. They're on their way here now. Need you to take him to Rocky. Over."

"Roger. We're just leaving Whiterabbit fire road. How bad is it? Over."

"We've got a fatality. Mill saw split. Over."

"Shit," Jack hung the mike down before he spoke into it. "Who is it?"

The radio was quiet.

"Frenchie Baptiste. Over."

Jack dropped the mike to his knee as he shifted over the logging bridge. He picked it up again. "We're on our way. Clearwater Four out."

"X78278 out. Sorry, Jack."

Jack hooked the mike back on the radio. He ruffled Silver's back and the dog turned to him.

"Archie's brother, Andy—they call him Frenchie. Friend of mine. I'm going to have to tell his mother. Jesus."

At the ranger station, under the yard light, a truck waited with a tarp over the back. Jack lifted the canvas, took one look under it, and immediately dropped it again. He stumbled backwards, retched in the snow and wiped his mouth on the cuff of his jacket before going to the garage. Shelagh put the dogs in their pens, while Jack backed his station wagon up to the flatbed. The loggers lifted the tarp and rolled the body onto it. Jack lowered the back seat. The men hoisted the tarp and the station wagon sank on its springs. The wrapped body had to be bent sideways to fit in the back. The body didn't seem real to Trout—more like one of the parcels they got from town.

Shelagh handed Jack his suit on a hanger. "I radioed Frank. He'll meet you at the Bighorn Bridge and lead the way. The Mounties will be waiting in Rocky." She hugged him briefly. The loggers stared at their feet before getting in their truck and turning back to the lumber camp.

After the station wagon left, the cold night closed in, and the yard light cast squat shadows on the snow. Shelagh helped Trout lift the sled from the truck. He knew not to tell her for now about his ride, the dogs or the wild horses. Instead, Trout kept his aunt company while she looked out the window.

Later that night he helped her wash the supper

dishes. He felt her soapy hand on his head, stroking his hair, but she said nothing. He knew now it was always that close. That death could come out of the shadows to take them.

When Jack returned from Frenchie Baptiste's funeral, he told them how a splinter of saw had speared the sawyer's neck, catching him in mid-breath as he gasped something to a guy beside him. Seven times, Jack had told the story—to Frank, Charlie Moses and to other visitors, each time shifting details until he found the story that matched the man he knew. How the dying sawyer carefully removed his wallet from his pants, found the pictures of his family, placed them on a bench beside him, then stared down at the needle of saw that was ending his life. "Oh, shit," were his last words, Jack said. No-one laughed.

In the weeks following Frenchie's death, Trout wandered, after his lessons, out to the dog pens, where the south-facing runs were sunny and dry. The doggy smell of fur and dung wafted from the thawing earth as Trout napped with his back on the warm wood of the doghouses. Blondie slept beside him, her eyes mournful, her head heavy between her large paws, goofy and clumsy in her step, like Trout was sometimes. Her remaining puppies whimpered and nuzzled his hands. They all snored together in the sweet heat of March, without flies and wasps to torment them.

Jack sharpened tools and built gates for the fire roads. The new season came quickly, and in the house, Shelagh marked Trout's correspondence lessons and filed her weather reports. The two-way radio remained quiet in the dog days of early spring, which still saw snow on the high peaks. On one of those days, the dogs scrambled to the fence and raised dog hell in greeting when a truck pulled into the yard.

Trout stumbled as he walked, his eyes fuzzy with sleep, his legs numbed from dogs sleeping on them. Charlie Moses's pickup was parked at the back door. Jack walked up to it, and the two men went into the house. Jack waved to Carrie, who was waiting in the cab, and signalled her to join them. It had been months since he'd last seen her, but Trout had thought about her all the time they were apart. Living without television to measure time here had only heightened the urgency of his ache. And without transportation, he had no way of reaching her. Yet, he walked slowly towards the house, not wanting to seem over-eager. He stopped to swat dust from his jeans, and brushed his unruly hair with his fingers. Jack had promised him a barber-shop haircut on the next trip into Rocky, after they'd both suffered Shelagh's attempts with the scissors, which left them with nicked ears and bumpy heads.

Carrie was inside, sitting in Trout's chair. Her father, Charlie, sat next to Jack. Charlie smoothed out a letter that had clearly been read and refolded many times. Shelagh made tea and sliced bread. Carrie fidgeted, but she was quiet. Her eyes followed Trout's as he poured her tea. He wanted a sign from her, something to let him know that the months of waiting, and his longing for her, mattered somehow. Like the nose stone she'd given him, polished to a high sheen, which he'd replenished with his own oily nose. But

Carrie said nothing, just looked quietly at her father, and at the letter that lay open in front of Jack.

Trout got an extra chair from the dining room. Carrie moved over for him, and he smiled glumly at her. Jack read the letter aloud. His face flushed, as it did when he'd been drinking. While Shelagh poured tea and put plates of food in front of them, her eyes mirrored Jack's. The Minister of Highways thanked the Wesley band for their support for the dam. The dam had now been approved, and surveying would start soon on the easterly end of Kootenay Plains. There would be jobs for the Stoneys in the clearing of the land, the Minister promised. Jack's hands shook as he read the letter out loud. Shelagh bunched her tea towel in her lap, her lips set. Carrie drank her tea, but politely refused Trout's offer of chocolate squares.

"The dam's going in Tarshishner Creek Gorge," Jack said. "Three miles right above the reserve. They're clearing all the way back, this side of Kootenay Plains. Jesus." Jack stared at Shelagh. He slumped, exhausted, in his chair and dropped the letter. They sat in silence. Finally, Jack spoke again. "The ranger station's in the way." Shelagh got up and banged the big iron plates off the stovetop, shoving pickets of wood into the fire.

Charlie reached under his chair and brought out an old grey flour sack, which he placed on the table. He untied the leather thong that kept it closed, and carefully unwrapped protective paper, revealing a book. Trout saw that it was a family Bible, its covers curled and worn from use, like the one in his Great-

Grandmother Locke's hall closet. Charlie took a picture from the sack and laid it beside the Bible.

"You keep this for me, Jack. If the dam breaks. . ."

Trout recognized the picture as a calendar reproduction of the signing of Treaty Seven in 1877. He'd seen the original in the little museum at Calgary Brewery.

"My grandfather, Joe Pee Beaver." Charlie tapped his finger on the picture and pointed at a chief standing next to the Governor General. "The Queen promised." Charlie nodded and passed the Bible to Jack. "You read. Our land."

As Jack opened the Bible, dust motes rose from it and followed the light from the windows. Charlie shook his head. "It's my grandfather's. From the missionary."

"It's in Cree."

Charlie said nothing.

"From John McDougall, the missionary?" Jack said. Charlie Moses nodded, his chin on his chest, his eyes straight ahead. "I'll keep it for you, Charlie. But I'm going to lose my place too."

Trout watched the two men. In his correspondence lessons, Trout had learned about the great missionaries, Father Lacombe and John McDougall, who brought religion to the Indians and tried to make them into farmers. Jack said religion took the fight out of the Stoney. And that was how Jack looked now, defeated. Carrie, too, said nothing. Shelagh cleared away the food.

"Why don't you show Carrie the dogs," Shelagh suggested.

Jack looked at Trout. "Stay in the yard, okay?"

Trout blushed and remembered his uncle's talk about his friendship with Silas Moses.

Carrie walked ahead of Trout, past the dog pens, and slipped easily between the strands of barbed wire around the barn. Trout jogged to catch up and hopped onto the corral fence.

"Want to ride?"

Carrie shook her head. She looked as though she wanted to cry. Instead, she reached up and pulled the hair away from her face. Then she took Trout's hand and pulled him down from the top rail of the corral fence.

"Your aunt said to show me the dogs," Carrie said. "Better do what you're told." Even Trout could hear the flat nasal voice of someone who had been crying.

As they circled the barn and headed towards the dog pens, pungent swamp gas puffed from the mud under their feet. Carrie stopped and stared at him. "Help me, Trout." A tear welled in the corner of her eye.

Trout lifted his hand to her face to brush the tear away, but she snuffed it with the back of her hand. She stood so close, he could feel her body heat.

"Where will the horses go?" she asked.

Trout ached as he saw the pain in her face. He had somewhere to go. He could leave Kootenay Plains. She could not.

Carrie looked back at the house. "Better show me the dogs, like your aunt said."

As Trout unlatched the gate to the Samoyed pens, he saw Shelagh watching them from the dining room. The light from the kitchen, where Jack and Charlie sat talking, framed her body in the window. Carrie hefted a St. Bernard pup in her arms, like a giant fur baby. She puckered a kiss on his wet nose, and gently blew into his snout, until he licked her face. Trout envied the pup. He would gladly have worn a fur suit for Carrie.

Shelagh shouted something from the back landing, and gestured to Trout and Carrie to come back to the house. They saw Charlie and Jack out back, talking with their heads down. Even from that distance, Trout could read the language of their bodies.

As Charlie's truck left the yard, neither Carrie nor her father waved. When Trout went to the house, the Cree Bible lay open on the table, and the creased print of Treaty Seven lay beside it, among the clutter of cutlery, the green tobacco can and cigarette papers. Jack and Shelagh stayed in the yard for a long time. That night, they fed the dogs together. Jack never fed the dogs. It was Trout's job. There was bread and soup for supper. Later, the dirge of the bagpipes rose in the yard as his uncle played battle hymns from another century.

And Trout didn't write in his journal that night. He put the conch to his ear. He heard the words of Charlie Moses: If the dam breaks. This was what the priest at the small church in Ogden had meant by Old Testament: as in the plague of locusts, or The Flood. But Trout knew, there was no Noah and no Ark to rescue them on Kootenay Plains.

Clare

That Easter I'd cooked a ham that the girls decorated with pineapple rings and maraschino cherries We baked hot cross buns together. I had a really interesting English teacher at night school then, a petite Greek girl right out of university, who wore a leatherette mini skirt.

Eirene had told the class that the bun's cross actually represented the four quarters of the moon, and it was an homage to the moon goddess Diana, dating back to ancient Greece. Eirene also talked obsessively about love, quoting one of her favourite poets, Percy Bysshe Shelley:

"One word is too often profaned
For me to profane it."

She'd turn accusingly, pointing her finger at us:

"One feeling too falsely disdained
For thee to disdain it."

We were all adults and we were in that class because we wanted to be there. She fed our adult hunger. We could hardly wait to get to her class each Thursday night.

Some nights, Eirene would meet me before class in a steakhouse run by a Lebanese man across from the school, where she took her supper. "Have you thought about university, Clare?" Her small white hands were exquisite in expression. That was how she talked, expressively and generously. Her hands calmed imaginary waves, then commanded the wind, as she'd done when we studied *The Tempest*. For days afterward, my own hands, nicked and nobby from the cafeteria work, would flutter in imitation, and I searched the cosmetic counters at the Bay, trying out perfumes until I found the one that she wore.

One night, an older man in the class disagreed with her on a silly point that had nothing to do with anything but his ego. She was a woman unlike any other I'd met. Or he had met, I'm sure.

"Really?" she said to him. "How interesting." She tilted her head, and her eyebrows rose in irony. That was all she had to do to plant doubt in him before she moved on. She could have easily humiliated him.

As Emily and the twins made hot cross buns, I told them Eirene's story of the moon goddess Diana and the other goddesses: the Great Mother, keeper of us all. The Stone Mother, whose gaze could turn a man to stone. The Muses who inspire us to poetry, to song, and whose voices the Sirens took, luring ancient sailors to wreck their ships on the rocky islands of the Mediterranean. And the Death Mother who leads us through the hereafter. Literature is history's heart, and poetry its blood, she told us. Her slight hands pulling us towards her. We all loved her, and on the last day of class, some students brought gifts for her. They also brought cameras, so they could have their pictures taken with her. We gave her a standing ova- tion, but she shushed us.

Easter was always the second spring after the Chinook, the season of hope, leading finally into the first green in the roots of the lawn and the buds of the lilac outside our window. The snow was gone, and the five feathery green spears of the spruce trees were now visible. Each of my kids had brought one home from school on Arbour Day, in a baby food jar, and we'd planted them in the garden. The chicken wire fences around them were plugged with dead leaves and newsprint waiting to be cleaned—that was Will's job.

Shelagh called from Rocky that week, and put Will on the phone, though he couldn't hear me because the hearing aids wouldn't work with the phone. So Shelagh translated for him. I told him of the plan. We agreed he'd come home once his lessons were done. He'd made progress and was ahead in all his subjects, Shelagh had said. He'd likely go to an advanced class in high school now. I was so proud—after all he'd been through.

Lowell announced over dinner that Will could work with him on the weekends as his helper. When summer came, he could use Will full-time. There was a panel truck at the Texaco that would carry their tools. Dunlop and Son, Lowell wrote on a note pad, trying out the words, and he smiled as he said them. Lowell was tired of being foreman, working long hours for someone else, and wanted to go out on his own. At first, I nodded because I knew Lowell would do it anyway, no matter what I said. And that was what the boys in our neighbourhood did, often quitting school to follow their dads into the railway shops, as brakemen or engineers for the C.P.R., into the meat packing plants or on construction, like Lowell. But I worried Will might not want to join his father.

"Will's not quitting school," I said.

"He won't have to." Lowell closed his briefcase. "Just on the weekends. We'll let him decide after he finishes. Can you see him doing otherwise?"

"No. He's got the stubbornness of the both of us," I said.

Lowell laughed. When we argued, he'd tell me: let's start by assuming we're both right, Clare.

After supper, Lowell and I sipped Amaretto with our coffee and smoked cigarettes, while the girls cleared up. Times like these, I felt like we were a couple of millionaires. Pauline bossed the girls around good-naturedly, with the thwack of tea towels as they batted each other's bottoms. Lowell grinned into his coffee, and I watched the street through the big window we'd put in earlier, scrap from a building he'd worked on. Some of our neighbour's girls walked home from evening mass in their Easter clothes, pastel pink and yellow ribbons in their hair. The Dawes boy, Kenny, shuffled by, shoulders slouched in his windbreaker, a new group of boys with him, a cigarette in his hand. Tough and angry looking, Kenny was home for the weekend. He was a hero now, sent to the home for boys. Kenny saw me and waved curtly, but he smiled, as he went on his way—to trouble, I was sure.

Ken Dawes Sr. had left. I'd run into Ivy Dawes, and she told me Kenny was coming home to live with her. She'd kept the rented house, little else. But at least she had that, and her Kenny back, she sighed. I looked at Kenny walking by, short like his father, brushing the lick of hair from his forehead, with an angry hand. And I saw a little boy again, and wanted to sweep him up in my arms. I thought of my own son, what we'd do when he got home. I wanted a birthday party for Will. I wondered who he'd be now. His letters were not from the boy who'd left us—that seemed so long ago.

Too short for the podium the other teachers used, Eirene stood in front of it when she taught. "In Greek, my name means 'peace'," she began. "Daughter of Zeus and Themis, one of the three Horae. Their daughters were goddesses and keepers of the seasons and of nature. Zeus is father and king of gods and men, brother of Poseidon, god of the sea. Themis personifies the Divine and is revealer of what must occur, of destiny. She received the oracle of Delphi from her mother, Gali, and passed it to Apollo.

"Apollo's shrine and oracle of Delphi were known throughout the ancient world. He is the patron of poetry and music. He is also leader of the Muses. There are nine Muses, born at Pieria at the base of Mount Olympus. Their father was Zeus and their mother, another of his wives—Mnemosyne, goddess of memory."

Eirene stretched to write on the board:

Calliope, Muse of epic poetry
Euterpe, of lyric poetry
Erato, of erotic poetry and mime
Polyhymnia, of the sacred hymn
Melpomene, of tragedy

Thalia, of comedy
Terpischore, of choral dance and song
Clio, of history
Urania, of astronomy

After she'd written the names on the board, Eirene faced us, carefully pronouncing each name, showing us where to put the stress on the syllables. She continued, "These are the Muses that call out to us," she said, "if we let them."

I was so grateful, and relieved. For the first time, the voices I'd heard all my life had names. And in Eirene's class, gods and goddesses became as real as my own children. While Eirene told us of her mythical parents, she also spoke of her real ones, Niko and Ourania, who ran a pizzeria in Bowness called Nick's. She mimicked her mother, wagging a finger at Eirene's miniskirt and saying, in a Greek accent, "Eirene, what is that, a belt? Where is your skirt?" Her father called himself Nick the Grick, she said, but was fiercely proud of his heritage. She clearly loved her parents. Their names, she told us, represent a marriage of victory and sky.

One night Eirene invited the class to an opening at Clouds N' Water Gallery on Ninth Avenue, in an old warehouse. Her boyfriend was a sculptor, and we all received rice paper invitations inked with a fine brush—I recognized the calligraphy from Eirene's roll book. Nolan and I went to the apartment she shared with her boyfriend. Not many couples lived together then, or shacked up, as Lowell put it.

Robert was a professor at the university. All the

rooms on the main floor of their old two storey house were filled with books—even the kitchen held shelves of cook books, alongside the woks and colourful jars of seeds and rice. According to Eirene, Robert was part of the Underground Railroad, bringing draft-resistors to safety in Canada. Upstairs, I heard a record playing, a jazz tune; the notes reached down into the living room as we ate. When the music stopped, Eirene called upstairs and a young man came down. I don't remember his name, but he was from a fishing village near New Bedford, Massachusetts. He told us how he'd played a song for the border guard at Coutts. He thought he'd be turned back at the border, after travelling for days on the train. But the Canadian guard relented, and let him into our country on the basis of a song by Johnny Cash. It hadn't been a record we'd heard coming from upstairs, but a Portuguese fisherman's son, a jazz musician—and a draft dodger, the first of many to arrive in Calgary.

Everywhere, in those years, kids had begun to march against the war in Vietnam. On my way to work one day, I watched some of them take part in a die-in. There were die-ins, love-ins and be-ins, on the Eighth Avenue mall in front of the Bay. All of the kids wore gas masks, protesting against pollution and smog, lying down in front of buses and stopping traffic. Eirene told us that she had seen, on television one night, students in Athens demonstrating in front of the American embassy. The placards they carried called for "Eirene." "They were marching for me," she said, smiling wryly.

The art gallery was full of dinosaur sculptures assembled from automobile parts, The exhibit, called B/Ad Lands, had one piece with a muffler for a body, an oil can for a head and a large coiled spring for a neck. It was labelled Alberta Sore-Us ReX. After wine and cheese, and a talk by the sculptor, we sat at small shaky tables with tea lights on them.

A tall, bearded man with a grey mane stood up at the podium, pinched his cigarette and blew smoke. Then he declaimed: "Ode to a Fly." He peered through bushy eyebrows and flashed us a wicked grin. "Holy, holy, holy. Progeny of dung," he intoned, sheaves of paper trembling in his hands. "Son of the son of the son of the fly, the same fly that alighted on the flesh of Christ, and who tasted the blood at Calvary, watches me now with the same segmented eyes that witnessed the stoning and the crucifixion."

No one laughed. We all leaned forward, nodding earnestly as he read. When he had finished, he lit a match, set the poem on fire, and let it disintegrate to ash. He whispered, "Fuck poetry."

A much younger man stood up. He took out some poems, written on parchment, from his shoulder bag. His thin hands held the parchment delicately. He chanted OM between each line, and let each page flutter to the floor. And after each poem, he shouted, "I shed these words like flesh, and I shed each garment like false flesh."

Soon, he was standing nude in only his shoes, and his woollen work socks, like the ones Lowell wore.

"I am naked. I am free," he said.

His was not the worst poetry of the night, and he got the most applause—mostly from Nolan, who nudged me and whispered, "Not enormously talented, but certainly enormous, nonetheless." I slapped Nolan's shoulder.

Eirene and I became close friends after the course ended, meeting sometimes at Al's Steakhouse, or at the Java Café. I confided in her about Lowell's past, and told her the story of Roly Faro, and the balcony where we practiced Romeo and Juliet.

Eirene had a poem or story for everything. She began telling me a story about Lord Byron—something about his wild hair—and sighed dramatically: "Remember thee! Remember thee!" Eirene loved being centre stage, and recited not only to me, but to the others in the cafe, her gaze taking in all of them slyly.

"Remember thee! Ay, doubt it not.
Thy husband too shall think of thee!"

Heads turned at the nearby tables, and Eirene played to the crowd. People nodded at this beautiful woman, the tilt of her dark head, her inflection, her red lips, and the spin she put on her fingertips, as she spoke. Lowell said I had a crush on her. I'd laughed then, but now I think he was right. Though really, I wanted to be her. For weeks afterward, I practiced those lines in front of the mirror in our bedroom:

"But neither shalt thou be forgot,
Thou false to him, thou fiend to me!"

Tumbling the syllables like wine over my lips, I

swirled them around my tongue and cheeks. These lines troubled and calmed me. How we can reveal our fiendish sides to others, but not to the ones we love. What marriage does to us!

Eirene and her friends were so much a part of that time for me, and soon there was an excitement in Calgary that had nothing to do with oil or money. Later, her boyfriend Robert talked of the Movement. On the street corner in front of the Bay, *The Georgia Strait,* an underground newspaper, was sold by a bearded man who played a harmonica. Hitchhikers, with their thumbs out, lined the highway to Banff or wandered the Eighth Avenue Mall with backpacks and guitars. Kids in bandannas and denim coveralls from all over the world sang in the street. Everyone, it seemed, was on the road.

One night, Lowell brought home one of his crew, a young apprentice from Michigan, whose father had disowned him because he'd avoided the draft. The young American wore his hair in a short ponytail, and wore a peace pendant under his denim shirt. He told us about the rallies against the Vietnam War, and I thought of my grandfather. Each war was supposed to be the last one. The First World War was once called the Great War, until the Second World War came along and we stopped numbering them.

Lowell's crew was hard on the young man from Michigan at first, taunting him about his hair and offering to cut it with a pair of tin-snips, hazing him. But he ignored them and went right on working—Lowell said he was one of the best workers he'd ever seen. After we invited the young man for supper, the crew left him alone. Lowell was smart that way—he understood his men. But I wondered what my grandfather would have made of it, this marching for peace—a war on war. I like to think he would have said, Clare, this is what we were fighting for. But I also knew that my kids were graduating into a future different from any we had ever known.

The three of them jolted along in the truck's cab—
Shelagh wearing a dress, Jack in his uniform, Trout
in his good pants—for their first trip into Rocky together since the fall. The road beyond the Cline was
treacherous still, and the steering wheel shuddered
in Jack's hands from the frozen ruts left on the road
by the logging trucks. At the Bighorn, they stopped
to visit Silas Moses. Trout and Jack dragged sacks of
turnips and potatoes to the small cabin Silas shared
with Charlie's family.

As Silas waved them in, Trout saw that the cabin
was a clean, spare place, decorated with a few pictures of grown children and grandchildren. One of
the pictures showed three men, a younger, handsome
Silas in braids and felt Stetson, and two other Stoney
hunters, standing in the snow in front of a tepee. Six
bighorn sheeps' heads lay on the ground in front of
them. Silas stood with a carbine jutting from his hip,
and one of the others cradled a Winchester. They
all wore bandoleers of cartridges over the shoulders
of their deerskin shirts. Kootenay Plains, 1904, was
inked in the corner of the picture that hung above a
small shelf with a Bible and some papers and other
books. Carrie wasn't around. Trout wanted to ask
where she was, but no one mentioned her, and he
knew not to say anything. Her buckskin skirt was
hanging on a hook inside a bedroom. He wanted to
touch it, to take something of her with him, if he
could not see her.

Carrie's mother, Sarah, made coffee on the small wood stove and cooked frybread. In their going-to-town clothes, Jack and Sheila were overdressed, but Silas and Sarah welcomed them. Sarah seemed apologetic as she told Jack: "Charlie's at his trapline. Carrie too." Before they sat down to eat, she showed Shelagh the beadwork on her deerskin jackets and mittens, which were spread across an iron bed with a fur cover.

Silas motioned to Trout to sit beside him at the small table so he could hear the conversation. The old man moved slowly, and his hands quivered as he spoke. He took a grey stone pipe from a shelf. It was the soapstone from Whirlpool Point, buffed and oiled to a sheen—very different from the rough rock Jack had taken out on his climb.

Silas reached for a beaded pouch. Tamping the pipe, he struck a match and put it to the bowl. Tobacco strands flared as he pulled in air. He passed the pipe to Jack.

"Silas, this is a fine pipe," Jack said, and coughed. "Helluva draw."

Silas let the smoke drift from his nostrils before he spoke. "Now it's yours. To smoke among your friends."

Leaving the two men to talk, Sarah called Trout and Shelagh outside to admire the sleek wolverine and wolf pelts she had stretched on frames. A little while later, the cabin door opened. Jack came out first, followed by Silas, who was more stooped now than he had been the summer before. The hand Silas extended to Trout seemed frail, but his grip was still powerful.

Jack held the stone pipe and said quietly, to Silas, "I'll do anything I can."

Silas raised his white brows, but his eyes were sharp. "The pipe is not a payment," he said, shaking his head. "It is a gift of friendship, like the turnips." He pointed to the sacks beside the door.

Jack clasped the old chief's hand; then he returned to the truck, where Shelagh and Trout were waiting.

On the way home, Jack slowed at Nordegg and tooted his horn as they passed Frank Jones's place.

"Silas says the band council's hired a young fellow from Calgary to help them organize against the dam. A social worker," Jack snorted. "Not a lawyer. But they'd need an army of 'em."

In Rocky, Jack stopped at the post office. Trout took his bundle of mail lessons to the wicket and picked up big envelopes of new ones. Jack parked the truck at the Hudson's Bay store, and they all got out in front of the windows lined with Easter eggs and chocolate rabbits. Shelagh ordered supplies at the Bay, while Jack took Trout to the hearing aid dealer.

"Gonna need new tubing in these, young fella," the man said to Trout. With his oiled grey hair, he looked like the contraption man's slicker cousin. He cleaned Jack's ear moulds, and gently heated the new tubing for Trout's with a match until it bent into shape. Without their hearing aids, neither Jack nor Trout talked.

The hearing aid dealer was rotund, and wore suspenders and gold spectacles, like a beardless Santa

Claus. When the repairs were completed, Trout and Jack inserted their hearing aids. The dealer gave Jack a brochure and handed Trout a dummy aid about the size of a quarter. "You might want to look at this, boys," the dealer said. "It's the coming thing, Jack."

The pink lump of plastic was tinted the same colour as Trout's conch shell, with a dial and a tiny microphone on its side. "Just got her in the mail," the dealer said, handing the hearing aid to Jack, who weighed it in his hands. "Weighs less than an ounce."

"How much?" Jack looked wary.

"That's the catch." The dealer wrote the price on the brochure. Jack shook his head.

"If a guy were to buy two, I can do better on the price."

"Let me think about it. We'll just take batteries for now," Jack said. "Don't know when we'll get back into town."

Trout held the small aid. Its skin was smooth and almost human. It would be nearly invisible in his ear. The dealer held out his hand and took back the hearing aid, but he winked at Trout as Jack headed out the door.

At the café, Shelagh and Trout sat in a window booth and waited while Jack met with his boss in the Forestry office. As Shelagh sorted mail and newspapers, Trout saw the Mountaineer's headline: 'Work Ok'd on Dam.' They had nearly finished eating, when Jack came in. He threw his cap on the seat cushion.

"Clearing's starting this summer. We're gonna have to move, Shelagh.

"I know, Jack. Look at this." She slid the Rocky paper across the table.

Jack scanned the article. "Jesus, Shelagh."

"We have your pension. We'll manage."

"We always have," Jack said, but he looked tired.

Trout's aunt and uncle drank their coffee in silence. Trout felt as though he shouldn't be there, but when they finished, Shelagh put her arm around his shoulder and said, "Maybe we should phone your mom."

The payphone was outside the real estate office. Shelagh chatted with his mother while Trout waited with his hearing aid unplugged, and Jack talked to the realtor. Trout's newly cleaned ear moulds dangled by their fresh tubing as he held the contraption of glasses and hearing aid in his hands. His head felt stuffy, and his vision blurred. Without his hearing aids and his glasses, all his senses were dull, and he was disoriented.

When he finally spoke with his mother, her words slipped out of his reach. And then, a truck passed and the wind rasped over the telephone receiver and her words were gone completely.

His mother had told Trout that she loved him. He'd heard that. He'd blushed then, too shy to tell her that he loved her too. But he missed her, and he nodded in agreement.

A logging truck geared down to enter the lumberyard, and backfired. Trout could hear nothing then, so he said goodbye. Through the confusion of sounds, he had been able to hear his sisters' excited voices in the kitchen back home. Unlike Carrie and her family, he had somewhere to go.

Jack started the truck and followed the real estate agent's car to the outskirts of town, where a country road ended at a two-storey farmhouse with a barn. Trout saw a small greenhouse on the property. Shelagh and Jack followed the broad yoke of the realtor's western suit into the farmhouse, while Trout paced out the horse pasture.

Back at the Upper Saskatchewan, Trout went down to his room while his aunt and uncle stayed up and talked, with the brochures from the realtor spread on the table, like maps of their future. Trout sat at his desk and laid out all his papers, his letters, the candy jar of shells, and the nose stone that Carrie had given him. He held each in turn, then picked up his beloved conch and the photographs of his great-great-grandmother, Bean, with her horse. All of these objects comforted him.

Later, Trout slipped into taut dreams in which he swam and gasped for air. Later still, he woke to icy water lapping at his feet. The river had risen during the night, and flowed past the dog pens and across the yard. Water had poured in through the open window of the fallout shelter, drenching Trout's books and letters. He heard Shelagh shout a warning he couldn't make out. He fumbled for his hearing aids, on the bedside table, worrying that they were soaked. Then he sat up with a start as his feet touched the iron bed rail, cold and real—unlike the water that he'd dreamed was surely coming for them. Shelagh was calling him for breakfast.

As they ate breakfast that morning, Jack announced

that it was time to open up the backcountry cabins and patrol for winter damage. "Think you're ready to come on horse patrol? You can get the horses ready," Jack said. "You may never get another chance."

Trout currycombed the horses and set up the saddles and tack on the corral fence. As Jack roped the packboxes onto the packsaddles, Trout steadied the broad-backed ponies. The hemp lines that Jack had tied pulled against themselves—rope logic, an engineered contradiction of tension and give. Of all the knots that his uncle had taught him, Trout's favourite was the diamond hitch, which was not tied but thrown. He used it to batten down the lumpy tent roll atop the rigid packframe.

When the horses were ready, Jack nudged Star with his heels. The two pack ponies were in tow behind him. Trout, riding Babe, took up the rear, and they left the yard at a trot. The dogs watched silently from their pens. Shelagh waved from the kitchen, and the pack train cut across Moses Flats towards the Cline River.

As they crossed and recrossed the Cline, the horses' bellies skimmed the water until they began the ascent to Pinto Lake along a spiny ridge. Trout marvelled at the intelligence of the horses' feet. Even as the pack horses slipped on the scree under their heavy load, their four legs were always better placed on the trail than his two would have been.

Grey snowbanks towered over the trail above them, but the riverbank on the south-facing slope was alive with April's new warmth. At the top of the gorge, he saw the river below still rising as the day's temperature climbed. The pack train broke out of the woods, onto the range below Pinto Lake, startling a herd of Bighorn sheep. A ram leapt from the low roof of the ranger's cabin and stared at them for a moment before taking to the woods. An open pitch of water, dark and hard as lapis, skirted a jagged platter of ice that moved with the wind on the south shore.

Jack opened the single small window to dry out the cabin, and stoked the airtight stove. In the high country, one side of a stream was still deep in winter, while the other was edging into spring, with patches of green growth emerging through the snow. Jack had prepared for a spring blizzard, packing double down sleeping bags, and extra layers of clothing. He kept the rifle close beside him, and told Trout to stay close to the cabin. They ate lunch on the sunny porch, reclining on their saddle blankets, while the belled and hobbled horses grazed nearby.

Jack pointed across the lake. "I know her," he said. A brown bear sniffed the wind, and squinted at the horses. "She's got a cub nearby."

After lunch, Jack and Trout hiked up the lake, staying close to the south shore, where the trail was clear of snow. The sow had reappeared behind them, and she now fished in the open water while her tiny cub waited in safety at the edge of the woods. "We'll stay out of her way," Jack said, and Trout nodded, always mindful now of where he was.

The burnt ridge of last summer's Pinto Lake fire hung under the low sky, the blackened tips of the trees stark against the snowcaps. Trout walked behind Jack, who was quiet now, both of them dwarfed by the range and sky as they picked their way over the trail. In the high country, everything seemed far away. To conserve batteries, Jack turned on the radio only to report their arrival at the Pinto Lake camp, and again after supper, before they turned in.

The airtight warmed the small cabin. They sat on their sleeping bags and ate their supper of fried potatoes, Spam and beans, all heated in the billycan.

Before they went to bed, Jack pulled a flask of whisky from the packbox. "To sweeten your dreams," he said, and poured a solid shot into Trout's mug.

A kerosene lamp hung from the low ceiling of the cabin. Its filmy glass cast their faces in smoky shadows. Jack doused the lamp early and insisted that they get some sleep. Tomorrow they'd have a long ride ahead of them, he said.

All through the night, Trout jolted awake whenever he sensed movements outside the cabin. His hearing aids were tucked inside his boots, so he couldn't hear clearly. The stove had died hours before. Jack's icy nose poked from his mummy bag and he slept peacefully. Trout lay wide awake. The cabin shifted, buffeted by gusts of wind. Under him, Trout felt the slow grinding of the rock plates, and the waves of ancient seas that washed into his sleep, when it finally came. He heard the grunts of Muskawa and her cub. But in the back of his dreams, he knew the food tins were safely burned, and the packboxes of food were hoisted high in the trees above the cabin, out of reach of the bears. And Jack's Winchester lay between their sleeping bags, just in case.

The next day, Jack led the pack train to the headwaters of the Whitegoat wilderness. Trout breathed in the smell of wind and snow. The high sharp air had not yet warmed enough to release the resin and musk of the forest floor. But the bruised grasses they rode over sent up a dusty, dry smell, alpine spice to his nose. Aspen buds brushed his face and scented the air, rarefied and clean as the lake, a liquid form of the wind which shook the Douglas firs around them. Jack spoke little on this trip. He sometimes pointed to landmarks or game trails, but he told no more stories.

After four days out, the pack train descended onto Kootenay Plains. Trout looked forward to a real bath. His quick cold dips in alpine lakes had left his body smoky and horse rank. Trout loped homeward, slouched low in the saddle. As the horses rounded the last ridge of the Cline, where the plains opened up, Trout saw the yellow trucks stretched in a line beside the ranger station. Red-tagged survey stakes ran through the old Stoney settlement and between the fenced-in graves. Men with tripods measured for the clearing east of Moses Flats.

Jack's jaw clenched around his cold briar pipe. He nudged Star up to a trot and the pack train cut through the surveyor's sight line. The surveyors stopped to wave. Jack gave them a cursory nod and rode into the yard. A small green Jeep with a distinctive whiplash radio antenna, spare wheel, and green Jerry can, waited beside the bunkhouse. Trout knew from the radio talk that the Jeep was Clearwater Car One, and it belonged to the chief ranger. It was the same kind that General Douglas MacArthur drove in the Sunday afternoon battles Trout had watched on television, back home in Calgary, that were narrated by Walter Cronkite. The Jeep, with the Forest Service crest on its door, was a vehicle Jack had declared pretty much useless in the backcountry: its four-wheel drive was prone to breakdowns; there was no room for tools or dogs; and it had a small gas tank.

Jack pitched the saddles and blankets onto the corral fence to air them out. "You take care of the horses. We got company," he said to Trout. Jack walked across the yard to meet his boss, Vickery, who stood on the back steps of the ranger station. Trout watched them from the corral while he sorted the tack and emptied the packboxes. As the two rangers went into the house, Trout knew already that Vickery wasn't welcome.

At dinner, Jack fussed with shot glasses, and Shelagh retrieved treats from the freezer. Usually, Jack and Shelagh burbled with pent-up talk when they had company, after months of only each other to talk to, but that day, they said very little. Trout read the cold flash of Jack's eyes.

During the next few weeks, Jack and Shelagh sat at the kitchen table, their bankbooks and papers before them, as they figured and refigured their finances. Sometimes, Trout heard them argue and Jack would go off the next day in the truck, but always he was back by supper.

On their more frequent trips to Rocky now, Trout saw the approaching convoys of silver construction trailers and flatbeds of Euclids and D-9 Cats, with their bladed grins, travelling this side of the Bighorn.

And the blasting for the new highway had started again on the rock walls of the valley. Charlie Moses hadn't been by in weeks. Jack and Shelagh had decided they would stay one more season at the Upper Saskatchewan. The place in town wouldn't be ready, and there was work to be done on Kootenay Plains. Although, when Jack dawdled over his coffee after breakfast, Shelagh didn't rush him.

When Easter came, Trout received a card from his mother—her handwriting was steadier now. He was glad to hear from her during this season of change. But in the high country, seasons were different than the sunny yard in Calgary. Winter lingered here and could return in a moment. The nights were icy, and most of the ponds were still frozen. The high passes wouldn't be open, Jack said, until well after the garden was planted, on the May long weekend. There were two seasons here, prolonged winter and brief summer. Trout knew he would be gone before the next summer came.

That night, Shelagh cooked a roast for Vickery, but on the sideboard, the rolled-up maps of the clearing waited. Trout was sent to bed early. From his bedroom, he could see the light on in the ranger's office, where Roald Vickery worked over his maps. The man was nice enough to Trout, asking him about his studies and his sisters. But he was a determined man, Trout thought. And the men in yellow trucks were his invading army.

The smell of wood smoke in Trout's rank clothes filled the fallout shelter. He lay in the dark with his hearing aids on, listening like a spy, hoping to catch a clue as to what would happen in the morning.

Clare

Early one Saturday morning that spring, I woke up to find Lowell and the girls gone. As I made myself breakfast, a blue truck pulled up in front of the garage Lowell had built at the side of our house. The truck had belonged to the general store owner, who'd passed away. It had sat at the Texaco station until Lowell bought it and brought it home that morning. He was so proud of it. After breakfast, Emily and I piled in beside him on the cracked front seat, which was as big as our chesterfield, while the twins sat on milk crates in the back. We pulled off the main road across the prairie and drove down to the river park.

The carpenters worked on Saturdays, and the sounds of their hammers disappeared only when Lowell took the truck over the hill to the river, and along the last band of yellow grass. Bulldozed piles of burning wolf willow and poplar filled the air with smoke, but in the run along the river, crocuses bloomed. On the river bank, trees were open, alive and green again. A new shopping centre was going in, and work had started on a bridge to the north of us. We would no longer be isolated from the city, or have to make the long drive downtown.

When we first moved here, deer came up from the river banks, along with jackrabbits and grouse. Once in a while, lynx or bobcat tracks crossed the yard. But it had been years since I'd seen any wildlife. The city was spreading south and east; new rows of houses moved out towards the river. All of the open prairie was nearly gone, and we no longer heard the shrill whistling of gophers.

The old truck took us easily over the hill, down into the bottomland, and back up again. Lowell had always loved his cars and tinkering in his garage, but this truck was special.

All that night, Lowell worked on the truck. I watched him through the window in the garage, ripping out the old floor of the truck, and welding in a new one. Lowell was a builder, a doer. Our yard was full of the things he'd made—including the garage itself and the wading pool for the kids. The chicken coop, which he'd towed home one day behind a tractor, was now a giant playhouse for the girls. He'd covered it in new siding, dry-walled it, and added windows and an aluminum screen door, all of which he'd scavenged.

By Sunday afternoon, Lowell had put up shelves in the truck for his tools and welded a rack on top for the ladders. Jerry Riley, an old sign painter, a rounder Lowell knew from the Cecil, showed up just before supper. His hands were shaky, but Lowell poured him a rye. By nine o'clock that night he had painted a sign on the sides of the truck in bright yellow letters announcing: L. C. Dunlop and Son. He even put a flourish on the D and the S. No one smirked now. "He's a worker," one of the neighbours said to me later. "Grant him that."

But my life didn't converge with Lowell's anymore—I was busy with the girls and the house. My friendship with Eirene and her boyfriend, and with

Nolan, too, took me further away from my husband. People like them didn't live in our neighbourhood.

I see it clearly now, but back then I just pushed on, working and taking my class. My doctor was pleased with my progress. Although, sometimes, a greasy black shadow crossed my mind, always slinking around the periphery like a black sludge, there one moment and gone the next. I didn't tell anyone. I didn't want to go back to that ward at the General.

I didn't see much of my family then. Mom and Ian were busy, driving out to Water Valley, or Caroline, to fish on his days off. Nolan had a new friend, Ali. I put my energy into school and my job—the girls didn't need me the same way anymore, except maybe Emily, and they were all independent girls. Shelagh had written to say that there would be changes at the ranger station, and she asked if Lowell could come and get Will before the tourist season started on the long weekend in May. Will's courses were nearly done. He could write the departmental exams with the other kids at the high school downtown, Shelagh said.

Lowell must have told his mother Will was coming home, because she phoned one day to offer to have him stay at her house, which was two blocks from the high school.

"But, Mom, it's his decision," Lowell told Dot— the first time I'd heard him speak that way to her. He said it louder the second time. "It's up to him." She hung up on him.

"Where's her friend, Mr. Jones, these days?" I asked.

"Busy, so she says." Lowell shook his head. Other than Christmas and birthday presents for the girls, we hadn't heard from Dot since Will left. Dot didn't drive, and she also didn't take the bus, especially not the Ogden bus.

One day I got a call from Eirene's husband. I was flattered, a university professor calling me. There was to be a demonstration in front of the U.S. Consulate against the war in Vietnam, and Robert asked if I would come. Eirene told me people were marching everywhere now and going to jail for what they believed in. She didn't call them kids, but they were. It was such a brave thing for them to do then. I thought they were right to protest against the war.

One of my cousins had signed up for the U. S. Marine Corps. Six months before Gerald Ford declared that the war in Vietnam was over, my cousin was M.I.A—a polite way of saying he was dead, and they didn't know where the hell he was. So when Robert invited me, I said yes.

There weren't many of us at the demonstration—people were afraid, or just didn't care. This was Calgary, and the war so far away. Someone burned a small American flag on the front steps of the American Consulate. It seemed such a feeble gesture, given all the news stories of bombers pounding the Vietnamese with napalm that exploded in the air, and stuck to the skin as it burned. I thought of my babies, when I heard that.

In the end, though, I didn't agree with the burning of the flag. The anti-war protester who did it, a ruddy boy from Louisiana whom I'd met earlier, got into a shouting match with the Consul. Things got tense for a while until the police arrived.

I knew the issues weren't as simple as the protesters claimed, or as the newspapers depicted them. And I thought of how my own people had also fought each other.

My grandmother used to tell us a story that her great-grandmother had told her, about the Highland Clearances. How the people were run off their land by Highland regiments, sent out from Edinburgh Castle. The people were so fiercely loyal to their clan chiefs—like children, my grandmother said—that when the orders came down, Scot attacked Scot. Always, she said, a Scottish regiment was sent against its own people. When the Highlanders wouldn't abandon their tenant farms—some of them stayed in their crofts, bolted the doors and boarded the windows—the Highland regiments were ordered to set fire to the roofs. The soldiers burned the crofters out and they fled, destitute and starving, to the coast or poured into Glasgow.

Grandma Locke said that as the slave trade died, the empty slave ships picked the crofters off the coast and offered them passage to the New World. The crofters had to sign a lien for their passage that took years to pay off, rendering them virtual slaves. They were crammed by the hundreds in the holds of slave ships, Grandma Locke said. Many of them died. Some ended up in Nova Scotia or the southern United States. Others settled in Barbados, fighting against the British for their independence—Red Legs, they were called, because their bare legs, in kilts, burned in the Caribbean sun. Later, the Highlanders joined the crofters in their own fight for freedom.

A few years ago, Jack and Shelagh went to our family reunion in South Carolina. One of the Caribbean cousins showed up there. His name was Andy McNaughton. He had red hair and blue eyes, an island accent, and skin as black as Newcastle coal. It shocked the southern cousins, my Uncle Jack said, but Andy McNaughton was family, just the same.

I thought of the men, withered and bent in their wheelchairs, whom my grandfather knew in the Colonel Belcher—they'd gone proudly to the first war, the Great War, with the pipe bands playing them a farewell at the C.P.R. station. We'll be back by Christmas, they'd all thought.

My grandfather's eyes were filled with grief as he told us about the French general at Verdun who ordered his men, "*On ne passe pas.*" They will not pass. His voice choked. "No surrender. No retreat. Die where you stand. A million French and German men died on one square mile." It was the only war story he ever told me. "What have we done?" Grandpa asked me. "This, I cannot forget, Clare. And for the love of God, I want to." I wiped his eyes for him.

What's done keeps getting done over and over again, I thought, as I watched a police car take away the anti-war demonstrator. The American Consul went back inside. The burnt flag and torn signs were removed by a groundskeeper. It was as though nothing had happened.

The Friday of the May long weekend, the twins had all the camping equipment stacked in a neat pyramid on the floor of the garage. Even Emily had helped, carrying pillows and packages of buns. Lowell had left work early that day, and backed the station wagon into the garage—the panel truck was too slow and too old to make the trip to Rocky Mountain House, he said.

"Why don't you take the girls," I'd suggested. We both understood that did not include Pauline, who was now a teenager, with a job at the Dairy Bar Drive-in. Already, the boys were coming by to see her, which made Lowell nervous. I reminded him of how he himself had been at their age.

The stack of supplies grew, as the girls helped load the station wagon with the tent and their bags. Bring warm clothes, Shelagh had said, it gets cold here in May. Don't worry about cooking, I'll feed them, she'd insisted. I didn't want them showing up empty-handed.

The next morning at five, Lowell pulled out of the driveway. The car was like a modern day wagon train, with Emily in the front and the twins waving from the back seat. All of them sleepy but thrilled to be going to pick up their big brother. They'd sleep over, and come back on Sunday through Banff, making a long wide loop through Red Deer and Sylvan Lake, then west through Rocky Mountain House to the

Icefields Highway, and back down to Lake Louise. Lowell loved those long drives.

We were a family then; I see that when I look at photos, like the one of Lowell washing his nearly new car—the yellow-and-white station wagon with the fins, which my kids all laugh at now. Or the one of Pauline in the white vinyl go-go boots we got her. She'd go through the house singing Nancy Sinatra's "These Boots Were Made for Walking" with an imaginary microphone in her hand. Crooning, "One of these days these boots are gonna walk all over YOU."

But there were times too, when I cried alone. Will was and would always be my only son now. But the one who died was just as real to me, in some ways. Even to Emily, who always remembered him even though she seemed almost a baby herself, when it happened.

I'd got a man to roto-till the small garden patch, and I'd asked Nolan to buy plants for me. I planned a birthday party for Will on the Victoria Day weekend. Still, I moved between sheer joy and dread, sometimes in the same moment, wondering what it would be like to have him back home again. Wondering whether I'd be able to handle him. My mind raced backwards and sideways and into the future, where the dread was always greatest.

I'd missed Will terribly, but I knew it would be better if he went to live with his grandmother for a while. More than anything, I wanted him to go on to university, and she would help in ways neither Lowell nor I could. But Lowell said it was Will's choice, and we couldn't force him.

Pauline went off to work the day after Lowell and the girls left. I turned over the flower bed in the front of the house. Nolan and his new friend, Ali, drove up around lunchtime. The trunk of Ali's car was filled with geraniums, marigolds and pansies, worth far more than the twenty dollars I'd given Nolan. "Pansies," Nolan laughed sardonically, when he handed me a flat of them. I knew that he'd bought them just so he could make that joke, but the three of us had a planting party that afternoon. Afterwards, we sat on the patio in our shirtsleeves, eating sandwiches, drinking coffee and smoking.

Across the street, we watched my neighbours, Margaret and Jon, put in a garden too. Their son Deanie played with pieces of paper, shredding and tossing the coloured bits into the air. Then he'd watch them flutter to the ground, where the small fox terrier raced around snapping at them. Deanie howled with laughter. At age sixteen, he was already too spastic and large for his mother to control. She'd told me that eventually they would have to put him in a home. I watched Deanie's misshapen face, his great pink gums exposed in a contorted grin, as if he were smiling and in pain all at the same time. The little terrier teased him, rushing at him, and then pretending to hide as Deanie covered his eyes

Ali saw me watching Deanie and said, "My father calls them Allah's children. They are God's gifts to be treasured. My father says, in this country, we hide them—why is that? Everyone is ashamed? So much you hide."

I'd been caught staring at Ali as he stroked Nolan's hand, and I blushed. For the first time since I'd known him, Nolan was calm, without the manic energy that used to drive him from one joke to another. Ali encouraged in him a gentleness, which accentuated Nolan's generosity.

Nolan had finally confided in his mother about his sexual orientation—in anger, at first, he told me. She had cried, and that had broken his rage.

"I knew a long time ago, Nolan. By not believing it, I only made things worse for you," she'd said to him.

Nolan followed me to the kitchen, where I began clearing up the dishes. Outside, Ali swept the sidewalk, looking out of place in his white shirt, sports jacket and hand-sewn loafers. His father had opened Ali Baba's House of Carpets around the corner from the furniture store Nolan's parents owned.

"Let me help with the dishes," Nolan said.

"Has your mother met him?" I asked.

"No. I will, I will." He didn't look up from the dishes.

"Don't surprise her. And don't do that to him either."

I never had a brother, nor had Lowell. Nolan had become one to both of us. Lowell even let him drive the panel truck one night. They had a hoot. The neighbours must have wondered about all the unusual visitors, but our house was the one the kids all came to, sitting around our big dining room table, the pot of tea always on. The rule was, if they smoked at home, they could smoke here. My kids were always bringing home someone for dinner, and I never minded. We didn't have a lot, but we had enough.

As Ali and Nolan drove away, I wondered about what Ali had said. That Will was a gift for all of us, like Deanie, like all the children on the blue bus. Maybe. But I know that there were times when Deanie's mother felt otherwise—when he exploded, and she couldn't restrain him. I no longer felt strong enough to fight for Will. There were still times when I slept too long, and just wanted to go on sleeping. Guilt, confusion and anger all wove into a tangle that I couldn't keep straight. Pauline was enough of a handful. I didn't think I could deal with Will, and his own quiet rage.

After I baked Will's birthday cake, I lit one of the candles and made a wish.

Trout

As the sun rose on Kootenay Plains, the mountain sky was dense turquoise, ringed by white snowcaps. The windsock at the end of the grass runway hung parallel to its pole. Shelagh had breakfast ready. The rangers had already eaten. Trout sat down to his porridge alone. Roald Vickery leaned over his maps in the office, with Jack beside him. Trout could see the surveyor's yellow trucks already waiting in front of the ranger station.

After breakfast, Vickery's Jeep led them towards the logging bridge and Whiterabbit Creek. Jack and Trout followed him in the truck. Trout watched the surveyor's convoy in the side mirror, dust pluming behind them. At the logging bridge, the Jeep pulled aside. Jack picked up speed until they reached the Whiterabbit fire road, where he stopped the truck and swung open the white-striped fire gate. The Jeep roared by, the yellow trucks behind it.

Jack caught up to them at one of the creeks running across the rough road, where the Jeep was stuck in the slippery gravel, water up to its bumper. Jack drove around and up the other side of the creek. He stretched the winch cable out to the Jeep's bumper. When he got back in the truck, his boots and pants were soaked, and Trout could see that Jack's face was taut.

At Charlie's cabin, the convoy stopped. Vickery spread his maps on the hood of the pickup. The survey boss and Jack huddled together, talking in low voices. What Trout couldn't hear, he pieced together from the movements of Vickery's lips.

"Don't want the same mess we had on the Brazeau Dam. All of it will be logged." Jack thumped the map, and the surveyor nodded.

The surveyors' trucks crawled past. The road ahead dropped to a trail, and brush whipped the trucks' mirrors as they disappeared up the mountain. Vickery turned towards the cabins and tried the unlocked door on Charlie Moses's place. Trout followed his uncle to the cabin, which was bare except for firewood, a wooden chair, a tin basin and a bucket.

Vickery walked across the trail to the second cabin, which Jack and Trout had used a few weeks earlier, and went in. When he came out again, he walked to his jeep and unlatched the jerry can from the rear bumper. He struggled under its weight and lugged the can to the porch of Charlie's cabin. He placed the gas can at Jack's feet and gestured towards the cabins.

"Torch 'em."

Jack looked at his nephew, at the cabins, and back at Vickery.

"Let's do it." Vickery jerked his chin at the gas can.

Jack shook his head. "Not this time, Roald."

The chief ranger stared at Jack blankly.

"We shot their horses, but I'll not be burning their cabins," Jack said. Trout thought he could hear the Scottish accent rise in Jack's angry voice.

"Then, get out of my way." Vickery lifted the gas can.

Jack moved to block the door. "These cabins can be moved, Roald. I'll do it on my own time."

Vickery stepped past him and trickled gas across the porch and into Charlie's cabin.

"Let's go, Trout." Jack stepped off the porch, and climbed into the truck. His jaw tensed as he switched off the two-way. Jack watched Vickery pouring gas. "That not how it's done. He's gonna blow himself up if those vapours catch a spark. Idiot!" Jack snapped.

As the Ford lurched forward and spun gravel, flames exploded in the cabin's interior. Within seconds, the roof was engulfed. Jack turned the truck around and sped out of the Stoney camp. In the rearview mirror, Trout saw Roald Vickery standing by his jeep. Arms folded, he watched the cabin burn. Trout was sickened, and his throat closed with bile. Jack's eyes were fatigued and furious. So much had changed on Kootenay Plains that morning.

"My father liked to say, *It takes a man to stand up to a fight, but it's takes a far greater man to walk away and make his peace,*" Jack said. "I didn't understand what he meant, until now." Trout saw tears in his uncle's eyes. "I wish you could have known your great-grandfather, Trout. And I wish he could have known you."

By the time they crossed the logging bridge, a pall had risen in the windless sky over Kootenay Plains.

Shelagh met them in the yard, her eyes questioning. Jack shook his head.

"No. God, no." She touched Jack's arm, but he pulled away. "Not Charlie's place? Good God, man."

The smoke on the other side of the river climbed

against the green base of the range, and the smell of the old wood cabin's burning filled the closed valley.

Shelagh sent Trout outside with his lunch. An hour later, Vickery's jeep raced past the ranger station, his face grim and pale behind the wheel.

After supper, Jack went to his office and sat in front of the typewriter for a long time. His files and maps lay open beside him. He sat with his chin in his hands, his elbows propped on the arms of the chair, and smoked his briar pipe.

When Frank Jones drove in from Nordegg, four days later, Jack handed him the letter.

"You sure about this?" Frank pushed the envelope back across the table. "I talked him out of firing you. You'll get a reprimand put on your file. I've got it here." Frank took a letter from his pocket. "I need you, Jack." Frank put the letter in front of Jack. "I won't take your resignation."

"I don't ever want to see him here again. So help me, I'll shoot the son of bitch," Jack said.

"I didn't hear that." Frank shook his head. "Either he does it his way, or, as I told him, we can do it your way. Move the graves and the other cabins in the valley to high ground." Frank spread his hands and shrugged. "Clearing's gonna get done in any case, Jack."

Jack waited before he replied, "I have to think about it."

"You do what you need to do." Frank looked to Shelagh. "There's one more thing."

He took a copy of the Rocky paper out of his briefcase and handed it to Shelagh, who opened it and spread it out on the table. The headline read: Ranger Burns Historic Cabin.

"Good grief, it's got your name in it, Jack," Shelagh said, as she read the news story.

"Son of a bitch."

"I know, Jack. We all know." Frank got up. "Think about my offer."

Jack looked at the letter of reprimand and said, "Jesus Christ, Frank."

When the back door closed behind Frank, Jack went into the bedroom and came out dressed in his town clothes. His letter of resignation lay on the table where Frank had left it.

"I'm going to the Bighorn," he said. He didn't ask Trout to come along. "I'm going to see Silas and Charlie." Jack went to the sideboard drawer and retrieved the stone pipe Silas had made him. "I'm not deserving of this."

The letter Frank had brought also lay open on the table, with the government seal on top, Vickery's signature on the bottom, and REPRIMAND in the subject line. Shelagh opened the drawer of the sidetable and placed the letter on top of the Cree Bible. The letter of resignation, she put into her apron pocket.

"You've got lessons, dear boy," she said to Trout.

Trout took his correspondence lessons from the shelf where they sat beside his dictionary and textbooks. He was glad that Frank hadn't accepted Jack's resignation.

As Trout bent over his lessons in the dining room, he watched Shelagh kneading bread in the kitchen.

Her mince, made with onions and spiced ground beef, simmered in a cast iron pot on the back of the stove, filling the room with warm comfort, ready for Jack whenever he returned. Trout wasn't sure about anything anymore, but he was certain that a rugged love, like his aunt's for his uncle, was something good. Not reverie or rapture, but true as anything of which the poets spoke.

On Saturday after supper, Shelagh leapt up first. "They're here," she said. Trout watched his father's De Soto pull into the yard, its sides muddy, and its grille bug-matted from the trip from Calgary. Against the backdrop of the mountains, his father's car seemed as alien as a Martian space craft, yellow, white and garish. His father sized him up and nodded in approval. Trout said nothing. His dad seemed awkward and overcome with emotion. Fortunately, Emily ran towards Trout. The twins, Chris and Liz, lagged behind. Emily hugged Trout, who bent down to hug her. But the twins stood awkwardly, like their father.

Trout's father explained why they were late, as Shelagh sat them down to eat. He described the mudhole near the end of the new highway construction. The station wagon sank to the wheelwells, and he had gotten a grader operator to lift the car gently by its bumper, shifting the weight and freeing them. They were lucky—they had been sixty miles from a tow truck or a gas station.

"Gonna have to patch the tank before we go. Grader blade gashed it," Trout's father said tiredly.

For the first time, Trout saw him, not as a father, but as another man. The lines on his father's face crossed when he frowned, and then again when he grinned, as he worked out this problem of how to fix the car. He drank and joked with Jack—they were both men who navigated with their hands. For a moment, Trout was jealous of his father's ease with his hands, of his ease with men like Jack.

After supper, Trout and his father tapped in the tent pegs with the axe, and strung guy ropes for the huge green tent that slept six. Like his father's car, the tent stood bright and brash here. Unlike the white cook tents of the Stoneys, or the dusty trucks of the backcountry, everything his father owned said City, said Loud. As the sun went down, his father backed the station wagon into the garage. Even Jack grunted in admiration as they watched Trout's father siphon the contents of the gas tank into empty gas cans, and remove the metal bands holding the tank itself under the belly of the car. Then, he wrestled it into the light where he could see the gashed metal. Taking his cutters and blowtorch from the toolbox he carried everywhere, Trout's father cut a metal patch and welded it to the tank. By ten, the gas tank was back under the car and refilled.

The girls slept in the tent. Jack poured rye, and Shelagh made late night sandwiches. Trout's father scrubbed his blackened face and hands. Trout went down to the fallout shelter one more time. His books and clothes lay ready on the bed. His journal sat closed on his desk with the conch beside it—the last things he would pack. Under the conch, he found a cheque from Shelagh with a note attached to the hearing aid brochure that Jack had picked up in Rocky.

"Happy Birthday, Will (Trout). A down payment on your future. Love, Shelagh and Jack."

They hadn't much money he knew, and Jack couldn't retire without both of them working. As Trout sat at his desk, the kitchen light warmed the bottom of the stairs. Occasionally he heard laughter. He wrote in his journal, "The future . . . ?" using the ellipsis Shelagh had taught him in her relentless grammar drills. "The colon is two eyes, the semi-colon is a wink, the ellipsis is the understood, and the unspoken between us," she'd said. Trout sat up, not wanting to sleep, knowing it would only bring morning and with that, his departure. Eventually, the bursts of laughter upstairs gave way to murmurs. He knew, by the loud punctuation of his father's guffaws, that Jack was telling stories.

Jack had come back from the Bighorn saddened, but still carrying the soapstone pipe. Only Silas understood what had really happened. Some of the Stoney people were angry that Jack could do nothing to help them. He promised them that not a tree more than was surveyed would be taken, so long as he was in the valley. Jack told them he'd help them move their ancestors' graves, and dismantle the remaining cabins and move them to higher ground. Trout wondered how his uncle could even stay on Kootenay Plains.

And Trout knew he would never see Carrie Moses again, for his father would take his sisters and him home the other way, west over Whirlpool Point, through Banff.

Their father slept late the next morning, so Trout and his sisters fed the dogs before breakfast. Aware that everything he did, he was doing now for the last time, Trout's chest ached with sadness and impatience. For he wanted this waiting to be over, and yet he couldn't bear to leave this place.

After breakfast, Trout cut up carrots and apples for his sisters to feed Babe and Belle. They ate with their whiskered lips extended, nuzzling through the corral fences, grazing treats from his sisters' hands. The girls held out their palms with their fingers together and flattened, as Jack had once shown Trout, so the horses' big velvet lips could reach the food.

Before lunch Trout and his father had the car loaded. With the tent roll on top, Trout threw a diamond hitch to lash it, and brushed past his father to tighten the rope. His things in the back took up too much room, so Trout had reloaded the car compactly, as Jack had taught him to do with the packboxes. Shelagh invited them to stay for lunch, but Trout's father was anxious to get back.

At the back door, Shelagh clasped Trout in her arms, and he felt her lips on the back of his neck. Jack said nothing, but he shook Trout's hand firmly and then went out to the forestry truck. Junior, who was already in the back of the truck, wagged his tail and woofed at the girls.

The heavy station wagon rumbled out of the ranger station yard, with Trout and his father in the front

and the girls in the back. They headed out to Kootenay Plains. Scree slides and flatirons towered over
them. Jack followed the station wagon closely—he'd
told Trout's father to keep the automatic transmission in low on the approach to Whirlpool Point. Re-
membering Jack's strong opinions about impractical
vehicles, Trout was sceptical now about the station
wagon's ability to take them over the point.

As Trout crossed the plains for the last time, aspens
were beginning to unfurl and their sweet syrup mixed
with the chalky glacial flour of the road. He tried to
memorize this afternoon, to take it with him. Deer
and elk herds driven west by the blasting roamed the
fringes of the plains now, but as his sisters pointed
them out, Trout remembered how, a year ago, all this
had been new to him. Jack's truck dropped behind
as the big De Soto kicked up gravel and raced past
the logging bridge. Charlie Moses's burnt cabin lay
across Whiterabbit Creek, and the stench of its burning would stay with Trout for a long time.

At the Whirlpool Point approach, Trout's father
stopped and checked under the car. The patched gas
tank was secure. Jack shook their hands and leaned
in the car window to say goodbye to his nieces, while
Trout gripped Junior's collar and hid his tears in the
big dog's fur. The St. Bernard's brow bunched over
his woeful eyes and his ears flopped forward. Both
he and Trout were pups. Junior knew he was not going with Trout, and Trout knew he'd never see the
dog again. His uncle called Trout aside and slipped
a fifty-dollar bill into his hand. "Look out for Mom,

okay?" Jack pulled his nephew towards him in a quick bear hug.

The De Soto's engine gunned as Trout's father mashed the pedal; its tires smoked on the bald rock. Trout watched Kootenay Plains fade in the rearview mirror. The valley ahead opened up to the headwaters of the upper Saskatchewan on the Great Divide in Banff Park. On the other side of the point jutted sheer limestone cliffs, dotted with limber pine, squat and wind-torn. At the summit, the De Soto fishtailed around a car that had stopped in the middle of the road, overheated, with its hood up. There was barely room to pass, and Trout's father cursed, knowing that if he stopped, they'd never make it. The car swung sideways, its fins cutting the air over the green whirlpool, before they descended to Thompson Creek and the national park boundary. Trout did not look back—his throat felt heavy and tight. His father drove towards Banff, and his sisters slept, their small heads tilted toward the sun. Trout drifted off to the steady hum of tires on the Icefields' Parkway.

They stopped at Saskatchewan Crossing, and his sisters lined up to have their picture taken by a gas jockey. The five of them stood in front of the De Soto. Trout's father squinted in the sun and cupped one hand over his eyes. All of them wore glasses now, even little Emily, who sat on the hood with Trout's arm around her.

His father stopped once more for gas at Fort Chiniquay. The service station had a teepee and a worn-out chuck wagon outside. They were now near Morley flats, where Silas's grandfather led his people to

Kootenay Plains in 1892, over the Dolomite Pass. Everything here was tinged with history, and history was tinged with memories of Carrie Moses. It was an ache Trout couldn't help, and knowledge he wasn't sure he wanted. Shelagh had snapped at him once. "You mustn't brood, dear boy. It does not a stitch of good. Now get out and get some fresh air." But it hadn't done him a stitch of good. Fresh air only worsened the longing.

As rain pummelled the car on Morley flats, Trout rubbed a circle in the fogged side window and saw the names of the Stoney children from the reserve spelled out in stones placed in the cutbacks along the highway: Daniel. Sarah. Joseph.

The engine revved on the last hill after Bragg Creek, rising above the plains. But Trout's father didn't stop, and they raced across the foothills that circled the city. As the streetlights came on, the rain slowed, and his father drove along Memorial Drive, across the lower deck of the Centre Street Bridge, inches from the iron girders. Then over past Scotsman's Hill, the Shamrock Hotel and the stockyards, where Trout breathed the smell of ripe cowshit. When his father stopped at the Mohawk gas bar for cigarettes, the reek of malt from the distillery, wheat from the mill, and diesel reminded Trout they were on the road home. Aroma Avenue, Kenny had called it.

The car slowed for the deadman's curve at the Ogden bridge. As they passed the Esso refinery, Trout's father watched him staring at the white tanks and cracking towers. Trout blinked and rubbed his eyes.

"You glad," his father said, hesitantly, "to be back,

403

Sunshine?" Trout knew what his father wanted him to say.

"Yeah, Dad." The tightness in his throat was gone now. "I am." And Trout was glad.

As they drove up to the small white house with the green roof, he saw his mother silhouetted in the window. She opened the aluminium door and stepped out under the single bulb, tapping out her cigarette on the toe of her high heeled shoe. Trout was startled to see the changes in her frail, beautiful face. Somehow, she'd become smaller in the year that he'd been away. She'd dressed up, and her bright turquoise dress made her impossibly pale skin seem unreal, especially when he compared it to Shelagh's weathered lines and freckles.

As his father parked the car, Trout recognized the blue Chevy in the garage as the truck from the general store. His father's ladders were on top of it now. Trout read the lettering on the truck: L.C. Dunlop and Son.

He was home.

Clare

I made Chinese food for Will's birthday, knowing
that, at Shelagh and Jack's, he'd had nothing but roast
all the time. Winnie Fung, who ran the store on the
South Hill, gave me some new recipes to try. Everyone called her store the Chinaman's, though Winnie
was a woman and her husband was never around—
just her daughter and two sons. Her youngest two
went to university, and the oldest boy terrorized the
main drag in a jacked-up car. Before she bought the
store, Winnie had run a restaurant. After work I went
through Chinatown, bought a wok, and found the
ingredients for the recipes she'd given me. One dish
I loved just for its name: Green Jade and Pink Coral.
It had ginger root, broccoli and crabmeat, with baby
shrimp, all stir-fried in a wok. No one in our neighbourhood owned a wok then, but Eirene had shown
me how to use it. With Winnie's recipes, I planned a
birthday supper.

Lowell and the kids arrived home from Jack and
Shelagh's that night, and Will walked into the house
with his bags. As he dropped them in the living room,
he and Pauline stared at each other. He managed a
shy grin. Pauline gave him a quick squeeze and said,
"Hello, stranger." He blushed and went out the door
to help his father unload the car. Pauline gazed after
him and said, "Mom, he's tall!"

Will's arms were wiry and tanned. Even his neck
and face were dark, although it was still early spring,

long before most people had any colour. Will reminded me then of my uncles, lanky and sinewy, their faces sunburned from being outdoors at the ranch, or in the oilpatch.

When all the kids' things were in, I finally hugged Will, though his eyes wouldn't meet mine—as if he had a secret to hide.

The next day, when we sat down to his birthday supper, he tucked away the egg rolls and egg foo young without slowing down. "Thanks, Mom. Real nice."

Our eyes met. Will had always been able to read people's eyes. I'd known that about him ever since he was a wee little boy. When Eirene met Will, she said he watched the people around him—not their lips, she noticed, but their eyes, their faces. I told her I was worried about him—he missed so much sometimes, answering questions no one had asked, with long thoughtful answers that left everyone baffled.

"Don't you worry," Eirene said. "With Will, what he doesn't hear," she paused for a moment and smiled, "he fills in with his heart."

After dinner, we had not one but two cakes: angel food, and a pineapple upside-down cake. We sang 'Happy Birthday,' and Emily brought in the gifts. Lowell had made Will a toolbox, and filled it with tools. Some of them were new. Others had belonged to Lowell's grandfather, old wooden-handled ones. "It's a start," Lowell said.

Will seemed surprised. He focused on the box, turned it, and fingered the riveted corners and crimped seams. "Thanks, Dad," he said, in the same voice I used when my kids got me presents I didn't want. But Will seemed touched by his father's handiwork. That was where his attention lingered, lost for a moment in the details of how the toolbox was made.

Most of our gifts for him were clothes, shirts and socks, since Shelagh had warned me that he'd grown a lot. Lowell also got Will a new tape measure, and later gave him his old workboots. I remember those boots: Will's and his father's, side by side at the back door. Both pairs bowed, the heels worn down on the inside. They were two very different men, even then, but destined to walk the same way. Will's voice had deepened and his speech was clearer than it had ever been.

I can't remember everything clearly now. Certain things I can't remember at all anymore, but most things that happened that spring, I remember in slow frames of grey and black, although the colour comes back if I put it in. Like a silent movie—I can add the piano, or the sound, but with a wobbly flicker. Sometimes I can see the individual pictures. After everything that happened that year, I went back and tried to keep all the memories intact—never realizing how much everything would change.

Trout

Trolleys rattled down 17th Avenue trailing sparks as the carbon rods arced on the overhead wires and the pavement trembled under Trout's feet. The high school's sandstone arches and green lawns were bordered with caragana and cottonwood. For five days, Trout and three hundred other students sat in the airless gymnasium writing the provincial examinations, test booklets open on the blonde wooden tables. Trout's sweaty shirt stuck to the steel-backed chair. The gym was electric with adolescent concentration. Trout's own focus was so intense that the pencil callus that formed on his forefinger stung long after. At the end bell, the students rushed through the doors, heading for the small park across from the Prairie Dog Inn, where they smoked and flirted under the poplars, riotous with pent-up energy and lust. Shyly, Trout walked past them, although he ached to join in.

Shelagh's lessons stayed with him and, as he walked to his grandmother's house for lunch, Will thought he had done well. All that month before the exams, he had studied and slept in the small room that had once been his grandmother's, and was now his. All traces of his beloved auntie were gone. The old house smells of oiled wood and wax were so strong that the exotic single Belvedere cigarette his grandmother allowed herself during the Sunday night poker game she and Hattie McLay played against Ida Beck and Merna Clipsham seared his nostrils.

On Friday night, after the last exam, Trout's father came to take him home, and together they loaded the panel truck. At home, Trout made sandwiches with his mother: thick slices of Spam out of the keyed tin and pink salmon on Wonderbread. She made neat squares of waxed paper, that in the morning would be stacked inside his father's old tin lunchpail with their shared name on the end. The mouth of his father's new plastic jobbie, as he called it, gaped too, and would be filled with fruit and sandwiches. The line of plaid Thermoses, with their silver mouths, yawned for coffee.

Trout slept those weeks, grateful for the cold air from the mountains that cooled his bare back, inhaling the scent of fresh flowers that his mother had planted. Before six o'clock, and long before his sisters woke, his feet found their shape in his father's boots. Trout's work gloves lay on the kitchen counter beside his lunch pail, their fingers curled around an invisible hammer. While he thought of Carrie and Kootenay Plains, this was the life he'd come back to. If her life was on the Plains, his was here. There was no escaping it, and there was never any discussion of another choice for him. Trout's friends and their fathers followed their fathers' fathers into the family trade, in a line that reached back to ancient Glasgow and the Highlands. Apprentices and journeymen in the craft guilds, banging tin and armour plate for the kings' armies and palaces. Before that, they laboured over the stone forges of the Iron Age. That's how it was.

Trout went to work as a helper on his father's crew, carrying scaffolds, pipe and insulation. During breaks, he was the coffee boy. He took the men's orders and their change, scurrying across the alleyways from the coffee shop, with a box of coffee cups and sandwiches. The cashier at the coffee shop flirted with him. Trout stammered when she winked at him, and he hurried back to the open cage that ran sixteen stories up the outside of the skeletal building. His father's crew sat with their lunch pails, their legs dangling out over the open top floor, facing the mountains.

Each Saturday morning at a quarter to seven, the panel truck, with L. C. Dunlop and Son painted on its side, carried Trout to the small jobs his father found—usually ripping out furnaces in the houses of older people that his grandmother referred to them. Jobs, his father said, that didn't make them much money, but they were building a business. The jobs would get bigger and then they could work together all the time, if Trout wanted.

Trout handed his father a hammer or the drill, lifting and buttressing the forms with his shoulders. They worked without talking. Trout learned the ways of metal, which was more supple than wood and contained and exerted great force. His father crimped creases and folds for added strength, and he warned Trout to look out for the slivers that flew into hands or eyes in a careless second. Trout's back was strong from the year of hauling wood and hooking hay bales. His hands were agile and his arms hard-muscled. Even his adolescent legs, most days, co-operated with each other. He could match his father's stride from ladder to scaffold, pacing single file along the high catwalks over the floors open to the sky, and a great distance from the ground. His father's crew worked without safety ropes. Trout was mindful always of where he stepped, after a pipefitter's ladder plummeted sixteen floors down. The man grabbed a sprinkler pipe that saved him—his feet swung over the street, saved by another man's job done well enough to hold him.

Just before the Stampede, Trout's father won a bid on a big job. He had gotten the contract to replace the furnaces and chimneys in a tenement near the Stampede grounds, owned by a rounder he knew from the King Eddy.

With his new learner's permit, Trout now drove to the job downtown. At the end of the day, he came home for a quick supper before he and his father went back to work three more hours at the tenement, tearing out old furnaces. Trout and his father carried load after load up the narrow stairs, to the panel truck, and out to the dump. They returned home just long enough to sleep, then went back to work again early the next morning. Trout worked without thinking, and he slept without dreaming, those days of early summer.

One Friday afternoon, work slowed as the crew waited at the day job for a shipment. Trout slipped away to the Natural Gas building. He'd seen an advertisement in the Herald for the hearing aid Jack had showed him—the one that was so sleek and tiny—and taking his new chequebook along, he ordered one. The money Shelagh had given him, and his own small account, would not be enough. The young woman at the desk told him he could buy the hearing aids on credit. They cost more money than he'd ever had in his life.

"Dirt on your hands looks honest," the hearing-aid lady laughed, as she took the impression of his ears, slipping a plastic needle as large as his mother's turkey baster into his ears, filling them with cold foam. She tugged a string from each ear after the foam had set, and slipped two pink moulds into a box.

"Should take about six weeks. Just in time for school. You'll be able to hear all the girls!"

Trout blushed. Someday, he wanted a girl as pretty as the hearing-aid lady, and as smart.

Her hands too, he noticed, were quick and nimble as she twisted the dial and printed the audiogram for him.

"This is you." She showed him a line like a mountain's peak, dropping off the edge of the chart, well below a box that said Normal.

"Is it that bad?" Trout asked.

The hearing-aid lady touched the arm of his jean jacket. Her eyes were violet. "I think I can help you," she said.

All that afternoon, as Trout worked, he saw her violet eyes, but the only word he could remember was "think". Doubt rang in his ears. Distracted, he banged the hollow ductwork and brought the hammer down on his thumb. Later, its tip turned black. Tired and embarrassed, he hid it from his father.

That Saturday, Trout woke at sunrise, as he always did. His room was filled with light, and he'd tossed the sheets off his bed in the restless sleep of summer.

The cat lay heavy beside him, her grey belly tipped to the sun, ignoring the birds outside.

After the drive downtown that morning, Trout and his father assembled the pile of scaffolding stacked against the vacant Swansea Block. Trout's father climbed the scaffold that rose alongside the building. Using a rope, he pulled the sections into place and he jammed himself between the brick and the scaffold to hoist the next piece on top. By nine o'clock, both Trout and his father were covered in sweat. Along Twelfth Avenue, two blocks away, the first traffic moved towards the Stampede grounds. Some walked, carrying costumes in dry-cleaning bags. Others drove by in pick-up trucks. White mounds of poplar seeds trailed them like dry snow.

The scaffold's metal skeleton soon stood three storeys above the street, with a plywood platform and ladders on top. As Trout and his father climbed it with their tools, the Swansea's roof provided a view of the fairgrounds to the south and the city to the north. Their weekday building's red iron skeleton dominated the sky between Elveden House, once the city's only skyscraper, and the new Husky Tower, between the Herald building and the Palliser Hotel's grey ghost.

Trout's father hoisted their toolboxes and a chain saw by rope to the platform, and then up to the roof. Trout used the knots he'd learned from Jack to lash the tools. His father was impressed. He squatted on the roof's peak, smoking a cigarette, and pointed out the buildings to the west. Trout, meanwhile, crab-walked over the roof on all fours. He fell sometimes, if he got up too fast. His balance was affected by his deafness—a secret he kept to himself.

"Keep your rear end up, that'll keep you steady," his father warned. "Like Spider Man."

Trout didn't reply—his back was already soaked with sweat as the temperature climbed. His father wanted to be done before the heat of the day became unbearable. After two more hours, they climbed down for a break and sat in the Chevy panel truck, which was parked in the shade. While his father smoked and listened to the country music station, Trout swigged icy Coke that seared his throat. He admired the scaffolding that climbed the building.

Earlier that week, Trout had found an hour between jobs to go to Western Outfitters to buy a pair of boots and Lee Rider jeans. His old jeans were too short to wear to the Legion's pancake breakfast. A day off was rare for Trout, and he looked forward to the Sunday outing. The Anderson girl would be there, his mother had promised. Art Anderson was the bus driver on the Ogden run. "You like her, don't you?" his mother had asked. Trout knew his mother was testing him and waiting to hear his stories. Someday, he thought, he'd tell her about Carrie.

The bus driver's daughter was two years ahead of Trout in school. She had never noticed him, until the day she spotted Trout at the lunch counter at Eaton's, where he was sitting with his new boots in a box beside him. "How's the workingman," she'd teased. Trout had blushed and stammered. The older girls never went out with the younger boys, always choosing the ones with cars, and with jobs on the railroad or in construction. Still, she'd noticed him and asked him, teasingly, "You going out with anybody?"

Trout's father switched off the radio. Break was over. Trout moved his tired legs, and tried to keep his muscles from cramping. He hadn't wanted to work today. But he followed his father, hand over hand, up the crossbraces of the rented scaffold.

When they'd gone to the Rent-All yard to pick up the scaffolding, his father had balked. "This all you got?" his father had said to the owner.

"Everything's gone, for seats at the Stampede Parade." The man paused. "I'll deliver it for you."

Back in the truck, Trout turned to his father. "Dad, it's all rusted."

"I know." His father shook his head. "We'll buy our own one day."

Trout was grateful for his gloves, for the metal was nicked and scabbed with masonry mud. Four metal chimneys needed to be replaced. Big job, his father said, okay money, but there would be more jobs, when word got around.

"We'll do it in stages. Cut it, lower it," his father said.

Trout's father gestured with his hands, and Trout silently handed him a cold chisel or the three-pound sledge. Trout roped in each section of the chimney so they could lower it to the scaffold.

"We'll get the bottom pieces from inside. Later." Sweat dripped from the end of his father's nose. "Gettin' too goddamn hot to work up here." But his father didn't slow down. They walked each pipe to the ladder, where his father climbed down, guiding the load as Trout lowered each section off the roof. His father took the weight onto his arms and shoulders.

As his father nailed a square of plywood over the open chimney hole, Trout squatted on the roof and watched the traffic beside the Stampede grounds, already backed up along Macleod Trail. Past that was the green patch of the Burnsland cemetery, not far from the Burns packing plant.

Trout's Grandma Dot had taken him there once. "Your great-grandfather knew them all," she'd said. "Pat Burns, and Art Cross, two of the Big Four. And you know the Lougheeds?" Dot pronounced it Lowheed, not Law-heed like everyone else he knew. "Senator Lougheed's buried two rows from my mother," Dot had said. "And then there's Bob Edwards, who wrote the *Calgary Eye Opener,* and the McClungs."

Dot had taken him once to see the McClung house, around the corner from her place. "Nelly McClung's niece lives there now. Don't know what all the fuss was, about that woman." His grandmother rolled her eyes sharply. "Auntie was just as good at cards."

Sweat dripped from Trout's forehead now, and splatted on the asphalt roof. His hair was soaked under his hard hat.

"Two more, Sunshine and we'll quit for the day," his father grunted, before he headed down the ladder, his face streaked with grime and sweat. But as Trout lowered the pipe onto the platform, the plywood lifted off the scaffold and the stacked pipe rolled. His father blocked the rolling pipes with his boots, but the scaffold tilted again under the shifted weight. His father looked up, the whites of his eyes visible as he grabbed at the slack rope. But the scaffold lurched from the wall and the ladder plummeted to the street. His father balanced on the teetering platform for a long, awful moment, and then the scaffold tipped. Pipes hit the ground first, and bounced on the sidewalk.

Trout's father jumped clear of the falling scaffold. His hard hat landed in the pipes around the Chevy. He spread his arms in a dive, and hit the ground hard. His glasses lay shattered beside him and his arms were askew. Trout stood on the edge of the roof with the rope in his hands, feeling terrified and helpless. He tried to shout, but his throat was dry. His father hadn't moved.

A few minutes later, a man with a blanket ran to help Trout's father.

Trout looked around. There was nowhere to fasten the rope. He couldn't get down from the roof. The balconies below him were tucked too far under the eaves. He'd never make it. He squatted with his head between his knees, as vertigo and nausea overcame him. His hard hat slipped over his face and fell, bouncing off the truck beside his father.

Trout gagged, and slipped on the roof. He felt his ankle snap under him. As he slid down the roof, the sharp shingles tore his knees. His toolbelt caught and dumped in the street. He spread his weight and slipped again. His nose rasped on the hot grit of the roof. Blood seeped down his pants. Trout clawed at the shingles. He could hear people shouting from the street. His shirt had caught on a nail, stopping his fall. He held his breath and his whole body trembled.

His shirt tore, and gave way. Trout slid to the edge of the roof. His feet dangled in the air. He pulled in his good leg, and wedged his boot in the eavestrough. Then, he heard sirens. He prayed, overcome with fear, knowing his foot was all that kept him from falling.

Trout lay face down on the stinging asphalt roof, dazed. He heard shouts above and below him. Hands secured him with a rope and turned him over. For a moment, he was weightless as he was lifted from the roof. Two firemen squatted beside him. "You're gonna be alright, bub. We got ya," one of them said to Trout. A ladder was lowered beside him. One of the firemen carried him, and grunted with each step he took down the ladder. At the base of the ladder-truck, more hands passed Trout over to a gurney. He slipped in and out of consciousness. His loose hearing aids whistled until someone took them out of his ears. Now, all sounds were muffled, except the rising drone of another siren.

He was in an ambulance. He strained to hear what was happening. A hand turned his face away from the tinted windows, and then he felt the flat hum of the siren. Trout fought the urge to gag again. He could make out shapes: a man in white, another in fireman's blue. The bass purr of a voice vibrated through his spine. Trout knew that voice. His step-grandfather, Ian, tapped a finger on his lips, and silenced Trout as he tried to speak.

At the hospital, Trout couldn't make out the distant buzz of conversation between the nurses and the doctor who stitched his nose after the freezing took effect. A nurse brought X-rays. Another doctor wrapped his wrist and straightened his ankle. A policeman arrived. Lips moved and bubbles floated out of them like cartoons, but Trout couldn't see the speakers' eyes or lips. He felt his step-grandfather's bass voice again, and Ian's hand pressed his arm.

Trout's hearing aids lay spotted with blood on the table beside him. A tube fed into his arm and splints supported his wrist and his ankle. Hushed tones came from the other side of the curtains around his bed. He couldn't reach his hearing aids. He fell back on his pillow, groggy from the tablet the nurse had given him.

When he woke, he was alone in the room. Moments stretched into hours. In the morning, stethoscopes and charts floated around him. Tones without words tormented him. Daytime followed him into sleep, where he kept sliding, tumbling on the slippery roof, waking up in mid-air to sirens, and to the memory of his father's eyes. A nurse came and gave him morphine and he fell into a dark deep sleep, where he chased the Stoney horses into the gap but couldn't overtake them.

When Trout woke hours later, he had no sensation in his arm. He'd fallen asleep on his splint. A nurse lifted him and massaged his arm until the circulation returned.

Trout's mother came into the room with his grandma, Ruby, and his step-grandfather, Ian. Trout watched their eyes. His mother's were swollen. She fumbled with his glasses, and he tried to help her put his hearing aids in. But as he sat up, the splint on his wrist tangled in the intravenous and he knocked himself in the face.

"It's okay. Let me." His mother seemed calm in a brittle sort of way. "I came last night, honey, but you were sound asleep." Her voice was tentative, sometimes breaking, telling him more than she realized.

"They're taking good care of your dad," Ian said softly.

No matter what the adults said to him that day, their eyes told a different story. Trout knew they were protecting him.

Over the next two days, his mother, grandmother, and step-grandfather came to see him morning and night. On the third morning, no one appeared. That afternoon, Ruby and Ian came to Trout's bedside.

"You're going home tomorrow," Ian said, looking away. Trout saw that his grandmother's eyes were red and she chewed her lip as Ian spoke.

For the first time in his life, Trout referred to his father by his name, and that was the name he would use for him ever after. "Lowell's dead, isn't he?"

No one would ever call him Trout again.

"Yesterday," Ian nodded. "It was his heart, the doctor said. It could have happened at anytime. It wasn't the fall."

"Oh, honey." His grandmother leaned over the bed, exhaling sorrow.

After she left, her lipstick stayed on Trout's face for a long time, waxy and sticky, as did the smokiness of her breath.

Trout needed a wheelchair to get to Ian's car the next day. Ian lifted him over the porch of his grandmother's house, and brought him magazines and comic books, which Trout devoured. He was glad for this temporary escape. There would be time to think later, of that he was certain.

Clare

The week of the Stampede Parade, Lowell promised me he'd take Sunday off, and we'd all go to the Legion's Stampede pancake breakfast on Prince's Island. I'd gotten Emily a square-dance dress, and buckskin moccasins that matched mine. The twins always wore jeans, like their big brother. Pauline turned up her nose at the event, although now she's the biggest country and western fan. Teenagers didn't go to Stampede breakfasts.

Lowell and Will were working on a job near the Stampede grounds that Saturday. I'd sent them off early that morning with full lunch pails. Will took four meat sandwiches, but I knew he'd still come home ravenous. I filled the camp cooler with pop cans and ice water, as the wind was already hot. Will and Lowell were going to be working on a roof—their arms were already tanned as dark as teak. Pauline's girlfriends now eyed Will when he worked in the garden, stripped to the waist, hoeing the rows of cabbages and potatoes in the cool air when the sun went down.

Usually I kept the radio on the country station during the day, listening for the news, something all the Ogden wives did then. But it was Saturday, and my girls were busy around me. There was mostly music on the radio—Johnny Cash, and sometimes Dolly Parton, and Hank Williams. I'd heard somewhere, if country music had a Shakespeare, it was Hank Williams. I thought that Patsy Cline and Loretta Lynn were its Bronte sisters. Somehow, I'd missed the midday news.

Just after twelve, the doorbell rang. I was making sandwiches for the girls. The kitchen was steamy and hot from the potatoes and eggs I was boiling for potato salad. The first radishes were ready, in the garden. I'd bought a ham, so we could stay on at Prince's Island and have a picnic lunch. Lowell needed time off, and God knows, we didn't need the money that badly. Will was paying room and board now, from his wages on construction. But Lowell had his dreams and so did I. We'd lie in bed, talking. When we have money, he'd say.

I heard the doorbell ring. No one in our neighbourhood, except salesmen, rang the doorbell—and they didn't usually call on Saturdays. My neighbours just knocked and yelled before walking in. I wiped my hands and went to the door. Through the screen, I saw a fireman in uniform. I recognized the captain of the Ogden firehall, who'd given the girls apples when I'd taken them there once on a tour. He had his hat tucked under his arm. His head was down, like he was trying to put words together. He told me there'd been an accident. At first, I thought it was my stepfather, Ian MacGrenaghan. Then he told me it was Lowell.

"No," I shook my head.

"I'll drive you to the hospital," the captain said.

I stepped out on the porch, and my neighbour, Margaret, came running from her yard. I wiped my eyes with my apron. "No," I said again. And then, "What'll I do about the girls?"

"I'll watch them. Go," Margaret said.

She brought me my purse. The girls stood at the screen door. Years later, when we talked about it, they said they knew then what had happened. Margaret told me she'd heard the news on the radio just before the captain's car pulled up.

On the way to the hospital the captain told me that Ian MacGrenaghan had called him at the Ogden fireball from Firehall Number 10, and asked him to take me straight to the General. Ian had heard the rescue call go out on the radio and knew right away by the location who it was.

"I'm here to see my husband, Lowell Dunlop," I said to the nurse, when we got there. The captain waited with me until Mom arrived at Emergency.

"He's in the operating room, Mrs. Dunlop. We'll let you know when he comes out."

"What about my son?" I asked the nurse.

Mom arrived just then and interrupted me. "Ian's at the Holy Cross with him now. He'll call, honey."

"I need to phone Lowell's mother," I said, fumbling with my purse.

"Let me," Mom said.

I shook my head. I couldn't find any change, and my make-up case landed on the floor, shattering the mirror.

Mom said, "I'll call Dot."

The doctors wouldn't let me see Lowell, even later that night. Everything that day seemed like something I'd already lived through. Yet, for all my premonitions—the shadows and dread that had haunted me for so long—I still hadn't seen this coming.

The doctor finally came out with the surgical mask still around his neck. "We've done everything we can," he said. His eyes met mine. "Go home and get some rest, Mrs. Dunlop."

The next day, Lowell's eyes were shut and his arms, braced by steel plates, reached out in front of him, as if to stop something coming at him. I put my head on his pillow. I whispered to him, calling his name over and over, telling him the names of his children, telling him that I loved him.

Lowell lived three more days. His arms, the doctors said, had telescoped, and were shattered. Both his lungs were punctured, but that still hadn't killed him. Lowell died of a stroke from a small hole in his heart that the doctors hadn't known about. All the men in his family had died of weak hearts, his father and his uncles. Lowell had outlived them.

He never woke up, but when I sat beside him, holding Pauline's transistor radio to his ear and telling him we loved him, his fingers gripped my thumb and wouldn't let go. He had such beautiful hands—calloused, small and delicate, for a man—with half-moon cuticles and slim fingers, and the strength that came from his work.

Lowell had once cut a man loose from a motorcycle wreck we'd come upon, driving home one night. The police were already there, waiting for the ambulance, but the man's leg was tangled in the spokes of the front wheel and he cried out in pain. Lowell ran to our car, and with his tinsnips cut the man's foot free, so the ambulance could take him away.

As Lowell closed his fingers around mine in that

hospital room, I don't know what he whispered, but he spoke to me for the last time.

Dot insisted on taking over the funeral arrangements. She told me that he would be buried beside his father. And he was. I wish I'd fought her about the funeral. But I didn't have the strength. I wouldn't let the girls go to see Lowell in the hospital. But they rode beside me through the gates of the cemetery, from the cathedral, past the fairgrounds, on the last day of the Calgary Stampede. Already the mid-way train was loading the rides for Klondike Days in Edmonton. The crowds rushing along Macleod Trail stared as we passed them on the hill to the cemetery. Lowell, like his mother, was proud that his father and grandfather were buried with the good people, the important people. But Lowell had always laughed, calling Mount Royal "Mortgage Hill." That's where the real crooks live, he'd said, one day, and pointed in the paper to the name of someone he'd gone to school with, who'd got caught swindling millions from retired people.

"Now he's hiding out on a golf course in Arizona," Lowell had said.

The funeral procession crossed Macleod Trail and parked in the lane beside the open grave where everyone had gathered: my mom and Ian, my four girls, Nolan and Ali, Eirene and her boyfriend, the priest Lowell's mother worked for, and some of her friends. My uncles: Jack, Bob, Charlie and Bill, and their wives, all stood behind me. Jack and Shelagh had driven down from Rocky. It was hot and humid—there'd been a thunderstorm earlier—but I dressed all in black, borrowing a black jacket from Mom. Despite the heat, I shivered as I pushed the girls out in front of me to say good-bye to their father. I'd already said whatever I'd needed to, to Lowell.

After the priest finished his prayers, the coffin was lowered, and it made a little splash. But the rain that morning was good for the crops, and the grass fires. One of the pallbearers, someone Lowell worked with, cast the first shovelful of wet clay, and the others followed, my uncles and Ian taking their turn. We buried Lowell behind his father. John Dunlop 1901-1947, his father's stone said, with a space on it for Lowell's mother. Beside it, the grass was newer, and the plot sunken where, little more than a year before, we'd buried Auntie beside her husband, Hiram.

Martha Bell (Golding) Worden 1865 - 1964
Hiram G. Worden 1855 - 1929

Her sister's grave was next.

Lavinia Francis Begg nee Golding
"Our Beloved Bean"
b. Dec. 5 1875 d. Oct. 12 1918

On the other side of the family plot, under a lilac bush, lay Lowell's grandparents: *Jack Dunlop 1879 – 1916*; and *His Wife, Jane Dunlop 1876 - 1953*.

From cradle to grave, the priest said. I thought of how the year had arrived with so much promise. I'd wanted to read a poem I loved, "Do Not Go Gentle Into that Good Night." It was one I'd given to

Will after Auntie died, but I knew there would be no place for poetry with Lowell's mother in charge of the funeral arrangements. During the funeral, I'd kept the poem folded in my purse, just in case there was a moment—one bloody moment—that wasn't choreographed.

Everything went exactly as Dot planned, until I made the mistake of taking off the jacket I'd borrowed. We'd all started back to the cars when Dot spotted me. My blouse had a dart of red stitched below the shoulder. I had on black shoes, a black skirt, even a black hat, and all Lowell's mother saw was that splash of red.

My daughters love to tell this story now to their friends. And sometimes, when I buy something extravagant, they call me the lady in the red dress.

Lowell's mother exploded. "How dare you!" She breathed so deeply, spitting out each word, that each word fell on me like a slap. Emily started to cry. For my kids' sake, I'd held back my tears. I wanted to be strong for them. But Lowell's mother wouldn't stop, and she lunged at me.

"You trollop! How dare you! You dirty little tramp," she said. Her friend, Mr. Jones, pulled her away, and Ian stood between us.

"She's scared," Pauline said, taking my arm. "It's not your fault, Mom."

Pauline was right. Everyone Dot loved lay buried there, among the important people. Good people— all of them gone: her mother, her auntie, her husband, and now, her son.

The priest took Dot to his car, and came to comfort me before he left. "She doesn't mean it," he said. But I knew that she did mean it. All that rage. He just didn't want her to mean it.

The priest put his arm around me. "God give you strength, Clare. Go to your family."

Trout

On the day of his father's funeral, Trout went to the cathedral, where his grandmother was parish clerk and where he had once loved to hear her sing. A rich man's church, his father had called it, but his father was given a service there anyway. The priest had offered on his secretary's behalf.

Old Lawson Leggett, the janitor, recognized Trout and went to ruffle his hair, as he used to do when Trout was a boy. Lawson caught himself and extended his hand instead, before he returned to the business of the church, placing the hymnals and wreaths. Trout sat behind the pallbearers—Ian, and a man his father knew from the Legion, and four of his father's crew—broadbacked men whose bodies were made from working. All of them stoic until the priest said, of Trout's father, "Some men do not go to churches, as others do." His rich voice boomed through the microphone.

"But they are makers of them. It is with their hands that they worship."

The row of men, some in new suits, fisted the tears from their eyes. Then they rose and lent their rough hands once more to carry Trout's father. Trout stood with them, and supported his weight on the back of the pew.

The final hymns swirled in the air, humid after the morning rain, and heavy whiffs of candle smoke suffocated Trout. He collapsed onto the wooden bench beside his mother.

When the procession went to the cemetery, Trout stayed behind at Dot's place, sitting in the shade of her windowed porch, his injured leg propped on a wicker chair. He had seen enough.

In the remaining weeks of that summer, Trout spent most of his time on his grandmother's porch. Once in a while his step-grandfather, Ian, drove him to Ogden to visit his sisters and his mother.

Ian assured Trout the accident was not his fault. The fire chief had examined the scaffolding and, while it was damaged, there was no way of knowing if the cross-braces had broken before or after the collapse of the scaffold.

Trout knew that neither his mother nor his grandmother could afford to carry the mortgage on his parents' small white house. On those trips to Ogden, Trout avoided anyone he knew. The shame he felt was too great, and for a long time he blamed himself for his father's death. Everything around him was coloured by his father's absence.

The panel truck was towed home by a neighbour. It languished in the driveway and its sign, L. C. Dunlop and Son, leered at him each time he visited the house, until his mother gave the truck away. It was too old and too slow to bring them any money. His father's tools, including the dented toolbox he'd made Trout, were laid out in the garage. Trout filled the toolbox with some of his father's things and took it with him. A few neighbours and tradesmen came by to look. Most left without buying anything, but his mother gave them beer anyway. Some of his father's crew, and others from the Legion, came and paid her too much for his father's remaining tools. Trout knew they were jinxed. But his mother took the money, even when she knew that the men would throw the tools away. No one wants a dead man's tools.

A month after his father's funeral, Dot's phone rang. Trout's new hearing aids were ready. He'd forgotten all about them, but life went on—factories continued to make plastic facsimiles of ears. When he walked down the halls of the Natural Gas Building with his new hearing aids, everything startled him. The faint whirr, shirr, clack, was new to him, until he realized that the sound came from the typists at their desks, who reached and pecked in a rhythm of work that ended with a carriage thrown, thumping to an offbeat drummer.

On the curb outside, as Trout waited for the traffic light to change, the rush hour traffic roared past him. Trout was dumbstruck by the sounds he could hear, and he did not know whether he wanted to hear them. His ears stung and his head throbbed with the reverberations of cars and heavy trucks racing down the road.

At his grandmother's house that night he could hear, for the first time, whispers of sound, but he still couldn't catch the words. The sketchy buzz as Dot spoke on the phone. And the cat upstairs, crying to be let in. At first he had wondered at this new sound, until he saw the brown tabby nuzzling his leg, and her rusty meow scratched at him. The small devices hidden in his ears now required that he buy new temples for his glasses. He folded the old heavy dark ones, full of transistors and wires, into his drawer. The ear moulds dangled by clear tubes. Their frames were still scratched from the accident.

Trout listened for the robins in the apple trees, and he saw their beaks move, but even when he strained, no sound came from them, and he cursed.

"Can you hear the birds?" Dot asked Trout at supper. Her excitement was so great that he lied and said yes, knowing that her need to hear him say this was greater now that Lowell was gone. Trout was learning to tell the necessary lies of adulthood.

After the Labour Day weekend, Dot packed Trout's lunch and waved him off to school before she went to the parish office. Trout walked to school from her house, which would always be, for him, four doors down from Nelly McClung's. Nelly McClung was long gone, but his family's brief association with her was a source of pride. Trout needed that, as a tradesman's son, now going to school amongst the children of wealthy Texas and Oklahoma oilmen, and the sons and daughters of university professors.

Passing the groomed lawns and cotoneaster and caragana hedges, Trout entered the sandstone arches of the school at the base of Mount Royal, with its football field sheltered by cottonwood trees. In the front foyer, trophy cases gleamed with cups and plaques. As he walked the gauntlet of blonde-helmeted boys, he saw that they too were as pretty, in their way, as the girls they flirted with. All of them in club jackets—Delta Roe, Sigma Phi, and Delta Phi—wearing tan and cream saddle shoes, schoolbooks proudly parked under their arms. The fraternity boys flirted with vivacious girls from his mother's old sorority, Sigma Omega Sigma, all dressed alike in kilted skirts, crisp white blouses and alpaca sweater-vests. The girls shouted to each other, excited at the first day of school. They had such confidence, greater than Trout's parents, more even than his grandmother's. Inherited pride, passed onto the sons and daughters of the men who hired his father and his uncles to haul and build. Trout didn't know whether to hate them, or imitate them.

Trout found his homeroom, 10-A, to which he had been assigned based on the results of his departmental exams. The bell rang, and the stairways filled. A blonde boy kissed a girl with hair past her waist, raven-plaited and thick over her shoulders. Her pleated kilt and blue stockings exactly matched her sweater-vest. She slipped ahead of Trout into the classroom. He surveyed the front rows and realized that his bag lunch set him apart from the others, as did his new salt-and-pepper jeans and the black desert boots that his mother could ill-afford, but that she'd insisted on buying for him.

Taking advantage of the crush of students milling about in the room, Trout bolted down the hall, pushing against the crowds coming up the stairs. He would leave school forever.

"Hey." A hand tugged at his elbow just as he reached the stairwell. "It's alright." The girl with the hair down her back faced him. "I wanted to do the same thing. First day jitters. We all get 'em," she laughed. "Come to class, sit beside me." She seemed sincere. Her eyes were two hazel sparks.

Trout followed her into the classroom and found a seat beside her. He saw another boy from his old neighbourhood, a friend of Kenny Dawes. "Adrian Carp's got a real brain, not like us," Kenny used to say, tapping his head. "Speak for yourself," Trout had said at the time. Kenny now went to the vocational school up the road, as did most of the kids from his old neighbourhood. Trout's father had told him once, "Might as well quit school, as go there. Better off starting your apprenticeship and making decent money."

Once the class started, the teacher called out their names. The long-haired girl's name was Iris. Trout almost didn't answer when the teacher called out, "William Dunlop?"

Finally, he stammered a belated response.

"Is it Bill?" the teacher asked.

Trout shook his head. "It's Will, sir." The teacher marked it down. Will's neck was crimson.

A girl in the class smiled at Trout. She was tall, and he'd noticed that she walked with a limp—one leg turned inward. He smiled in return and, as she pushed her hair back behind her ear, he saw that she wore the same tiny hearing aid that he himself wore. Now, when he saw her in the hall between classes, he nodded to her. They were conspirators together, he thought. Her face was slender, and her grey eyes were soft and sensitive. Too shy to approach her, Trout waited for Divine Coincidence to bring them together, but classes kept them busy, and after school the halls emptied.

That was when the kids with candy-apple red

Chevy Malibus and tangerine-coloured Road Runners drag-raced each other up Seventeenth Avenue. The Ogden kids took one of the World-War-Two-vintage school-buses home. The Mount Royal kids went off to music lessons and football. A few, like Iris, went to cheerleader practice after school.

By the end of September, the splint was off Trout's wrist. He practiced the confident strut of his classmates in front of his grandmother's floor-length mirror. Leaning on his crutch, he canvassed both sides of Seventeenth, applying for jobs. He kept his nerve, even when each of the shops turned him away. Finally, he tried a place his mother knew—a restaurant across from the school, run by a large Lebanese man named Al, who looked worried most of the time.

Al looked at Trout's crutch and pointed to a dishwashing machine. "Can you run that?" he asked.

Soon, Trout was working three nights a week. He used the money he earned to pay for his hearing aids and help out his grandmother. She'd already taken in tenants upstairs, and hadn't asked Trout for money. But Dot's silence told him what he had to do. Each day after school, Trout scrubbed dishes and pots at Al's restaurant, sometimes slipping down the backstairs to the poker game, which was supervised by an aging Chinese woman. Trout brought platters of spicy food for the gamblers who sat at the round, felt-covered tables. A smoky haze swirled around the single light bulb hanging over each of the tables.

"You're alright," Al told Trout, before sending him

down the unmarked stairs to the hidden gaming room for the first time.

When business at the restaurant was slow, Trout ate a hamburger with his new boss, and a bellydancer, the Beautiful and Exotic Addi, whose real name was Melissa. She performed in the downstairs lounge—her glossy picture on a small brass easel in the front window.

After weeks of jagged sleep, Trout's dreams finally returned, but he didn't dream of Addi—of her pearl-smooth navel, or her plunging velvet dresses with their strategically placed tassels. He dreamed of sweater-vests, and of the girl with the brown hair who wore only one hearing aid, and whose father, he learned through Iris, was a rockhound.

"A geologist," she had said, as she tutored Trout in math at the study hall. "Absolutely fabulous find," she whispered, between equations. "Stumbled on it. Wildcat well. Struck it rich, rich, rich. Unbelievable."

After school, sometimes, Trout and Adrian Carp followed Iris to the school fence, where she smoked and they listened to her talk.

"Everybody in the oilpatch's heard about Buddy Petrasuk," she said, snorting smoke. Then she ran off to her job at Super S Drugs.

Trout and Adrian started going to the poolhall above the car wash, across from the school. They ate their lunches there most days, playing pool for a quarter a game. Adrian racked the balls, and broke. He dropped a lucky shot on the pink in the corner pocket, but scratched on the orange.

"Just ask her out. You're both deaf, you got that in

437

common." Adrian lined up his shot. "I also heard she goes to piano lessons after school. Maybe she could teach you."

"Adrian, how do you know all this?"

"She's in my Latin class. Why don't you sign up?"

"Gee, with advice like that from my friends, who needs enemies? I can barely speak English."

"She doesn't want you for your voice. You still got those seashells you used to bring to school? She likes scuba diving."

"Lena Petrasuk lives in the biggest house on Sifton Boulevard, with a turret, Iris says. Four cars in the driveway, and you want me to talk to her about my sea shell collection I had in Grade Three?"

"She's from Winnipeg, for godsake, Dunlop. How stuck-up can she be?" Adrian picked up his books. "Come and visit me on Saturday. I'll find out if she likes you. The library's got a new l.p. collection. Everything, even rock. Stereo headphones, so even you can hear."

"Don't tell her anything, Carp."

That Saturday, Adrian introduced him to the stereo record section of the downtown library. The headphones wouldn't work with his new hearing aids, which whistled with interference. But if he took out his hearing aids, Trout could turn up the volume full blast without bothering anyone. At lunch, he and Adrian went to the Billingsgate Fish Market for clam chowder. He followed Adrian back to study, glad to be out of Dot's lonely, tidy house.

When he listened to the blues, Trout was transported right back to Kootenay Plains, and to Carrie.

First, Trout discovered Sonny Boy Williamson, whose notes that New Year's Eve had infiltrated his dreams. Then, he listened to Otis Spann, whose left hand walked the bass and boogie lines on the keyboard, while his right hand ran wild with the highs, which were still beyond Trout's hearing. But Trout knew where those notes lived now, and Otis Spann knocked large on all their doors. Big Mama Thornton, Bessie Smith, all the Chicago boys and girls in their dark suits and shiny dresses, their stagey fedoras, with their amps and chrome Telefunken mikes. Howling Wolf, and Mississippi Fred McDowell, whose name rhymed with growl—and he did. These were the singers and players whose songs carried Trout that fall.

Trout played them so often that he memorized the tunes, unaware that he was humming them until a librarian shushed him. Trout would not have gotten the courage to speak to Lena Petrasuk, if it hadn't been for those songs that taught him to walk tall. One day, he found the moment, in the school library. Lena was reading a field guide to the coastal waters. Trout walked towards her, and as she turned to him, she smiled. She'd been waiting too, as if she knew he was coming. There was a small gap between her two prominent front teeth. Trout burbled something, tossed out the names of his shells, a Latin name or two mispronounced. Despite his stammer, his red face, and against all his hopes that the earth would open and reclaim him before he finished, her breath pushed softly towards him in an airy echo.

"Yes, yes, yes," he later told Adrian Carp, sitting in the front booth at Al's. "Okay, she said one yes. But it was a long yes. Maybe it was 'sure'," Trout gushed. "I'm taking her out for coffee. Here, at Al's."

"Hey, big spender, you work here. The coffee's free. So, when?"

"She knew my name."

"I know. I told her you liked her. So when's the big event?"

"Damn it, Carp. I asked you not to."

"Dunlop, you need all the help you can get. I pleaded your case, said you had a terminal illness and three months to live." Adrian grinned. "She said you have a nice smile. So, when?"

"Next week? I should go. Got supper tonight with my mom and my sisters."

Otis Spann played grandly behind Trout, and Big Mama Thornton crooned low as he stepped to the beat. Trout hopped on the bus and got off at Eleventh and First. His route took him past the Swansea Block, with new chimneys on its high-peaked roof, new windows and doors on its front façade, and a sign:

Suites—Occupancy December 1
Inquire Within

Trout crossed the street, and cut over to his mother's new place, four blocks from the Stampede grounds. Trout watched the crew who came off shift, men like his father, packing their tools into their cars and trucks at the end of the day. He walked on, like the bluesman sang: *Walk on, walk on.* And that was the beat he kept that fall. Walk on, walk on. He hummed it, deep down, until it crushed the lump in his throat, a low down growl that reverberated through his jaw to his inner ear.

But Trout was never far from his father's death. All around him were the buildings his father had worked on, including the Baptist church. Its steeple was topped with a steel ball, onto which Trout's father had placed pennies before he'd welded it shut. It was a secret Trout shared with his father, and it cheered him whenever he saw that steel ball glinting in the sun. Trout hummed the walking bass of the bluesman: *Walk on, walk on.*

A couple of days later, Lena Petrasuk stopped him in the hall and apologized, saying she couldn't make their date. Some other time, she said. An agonizing week followed, before Trout finally got up the courage to ask her out again. She said yes, and she wouldn't let him buy the coffee.

Lena was direct. "How'd it happen?" she asked, and tapped her ear as she looked at Trout. He told her, and asked in turn, "You?"

"Congenital. Born that way." She laughed. "But I can carry a tune. Go figure."

All that winter he waited for her after school in the sitting room of her music teacher's big Mount Royal house, where he studied while she played. With her one good ear, Lena had perfect pitch and Trout's lessons were interspersed with Bach, Bartok, and Tschaikovsky. The bass lines and the low notes were mostly clear to him, since they were carried by the acoustics of the dark wooden floors and high celings of the old house.

Lena told Trout to play his harmonica in the shower, and when he did, the notes carried back to him, supple and clear—even the the high ones. When he didn't have to work, he walked Lena home over the crest of Mount Royal, overlooking the grounds of the Glencoe Club with its guard at the gate and its heated pool. She took him swimming there after Trout finally confessed that he'd never learned to swim. But he had no fear of water, and Lena supported his body underwater with her fingertips. She pulled him towards her as he floated, suspended and guided by the soft touch of her hands under him.

Afterwards, their hair froze as they walked to her parents' grand home on Sifton Boulevard. Lena showed Trout her father's library with its cherrywood shelves and hundreds of books. Each room in the turret was full of treasure: her bedroom held her scuba tanks, spear gun and diving mask. In the music room, there was a baby grand, and her father's hi fi with tall speakers, and stacks of complicated amps, tuners and tape recorders.

"Stand here." Lena motioned towards the piano's open top. As Trout stood with his head above the soundboard, she played for him. He watched the hammers ripple along the metal strings as her hands glided over the keys. Sound washed over him in waves. The hairs on his arms stood up. Lena's shoulders ducked as she dove into the music, and she flipped her silken hair over her shoulder, teasing the keyboard. The room resounded in crescendo as her muscular fingers rippled down the keyboard, as if she might rock the piano on its legs.

Later, Lena played him Beethoven on the stereo and opened up her father's bar. "What do you drink?" she asked. "Scotch," Trout replied. "Neat."

Lena looked impressed. They clinked their glasses, and she stood between the speakers.

"Lie down right here." She pointed to the floor. "I'm serious."

When Trout laid down, she turned up the speakers and laid on the floor beside him.

"Such power," Lena said, taking Trout's hand. "Dad bought a place on Gabriola Island. We want you to come with us next summer." Lena kissed Trout's cheek.

Slowly, the recurrent dream began to subside. The one in which Trout startled awake in the middle of a slow, endless plummet. Where he slipped from the slick roof, his father's eyes before him again, his father's shattered glasses on the pavement. And the unending shame, the feeling he had that he'd somehow failed, began to lift. When his grandmother went out, Trout stood in the tub and wailed on his harmonica, wild and mournful, the notes bouncing off the ceramic tiles and blown back at him, along his jaw. Walk on, walk on, the bluesman blew. All that pain, pouring into the air, like water, like rain.

Trout always took Lena's hand now, when they walked. All that winter, her mittens warmed his gloves, and she slipped barehanded from them in the spring. And as summer came, Lena took Trout to a sandy beach below the hill in Mission late one night, with a bottle from her father's bar. The water was warm. It was Stampede time again, and the crowds were elsewhere that night, so the beach was deserted. Lena and Trout could see the fireworks at the fairgrounds, as they sipped their Scotch. Trout finally told Lena about his father and the accident. She listened with her good ear near his lips, her chin on his chest. As Trout talked, she stroked the reddish hairs of his sun-bleached arms, and his brown hands that never came clean, from his work as a gardener at the Botanical Gardens. She kissed his tears, and he held her until he was calm.

One day they waded out to a sandbar on the river that was hidden from view. Lena reached for Trout's ears and took out his hearing aids, holding them in the palm of her hand. Once again deaf, Trout watched her take the one from her ear, and put them all in the pocket of her blouse. Whether she said it, or her lips moved silently, as he and Kenny used to do in their secret language, he heard her. "Tell me what you hear," she mouthed.

Her fingertips opened up to his. He matched each fingertip of hers with his own, and felt her strength, as she began to move them, round and round in small circles. He thought of all the poems he'd read, rapturous and true, and said: "Around me, I hear wind. Behind me, I hear water. Under me, I hear the earth. Always, I hear you."

Trout's earth-stained fingers slipped between hers. Lena pulled him towards her, and her blouse slipped from her shoulders. Carefully, she folded it, protecting the tiny plastic ears inside. He kissed her and she kissed him back. "There is nothing to stop us now," she said. He unclasped the clip at the front of her bra, and she shrugged it to the ground. Lena stood before him, her body a soft work of light. He didn't think about the house on Sifton Boulevard, or about her father, or about anything else. He knew this was inevitable. This reverie. Trout shivered. It had nothing to do with the wind that curled around his back, after Lena brushed her hands through his unbuttoned shirt. Lena's fingers smoothed over the small hairs on his chest, and glided over his ribs and around to his bare shoulders blades. She teased him with her tongue, and gently bit his lower lip. He kissed the gap in her teeth, as he had wanted to do ever since he'd met her. Her piano-player's hands cupped his head, and her fingers rippled through his hair and he felt small sparks. He lifted her breasts, and weighed them in his palms. With the soft pads of his thumbs he caressed her nipples, rotating outward to the dark radius in awe. He did this for a long time.

She was not his first love, she knew. Trout was not hers, Lena told him. And she would not be his last, she said, once she heard from the university in Vancouver. But none of that mattered just yet, as he slipped from his clothes, and she loved him.

Afterwards, they dove into the river, and as she had taught him, Trout swam. How he swam for her.

Clare

I couldn't watch as the real estate agent hammered in a For Sale sign on our front lawn. Lowell's mother—my kids always called Dot their "other grandmother"—had listed the house. I couldn't carry the mortgage. Nor could she, we'd both agreed, our conversations terse. The house became the focal point for our conversations; we never talked about Lowell, only about the damn house, as if it were him.

"You need to get on," Dot would say to me. "Do what you need to do." I think now she was really talking about herself, because that's exactly what she did. She got on.

When the agent drove away, I went to the garage where Lowell's tools lay, dumped there with the ladders. The scoutmaster had agreed to take the truck. I was trying to sell everything, and the truck wasn't worth much. But it was the same type my father drove for the dry-cleaning company. I couldn't be mad at Dot, who had grown up without a father or a mother, herself. I understood more than she ever knew. That was some of what pulled me to Lowell, I'm sure. The two of us lost, without fathers. Although, we didn't ever talk about it that way. We made our family and a home, filling a huge hole in each of us with work and children. Lowell and I were always hungry for love, but nothing quite satisfied us.

It wasn't the funeral, or the scene with the Dot at the cemetery, that finally broke me down. It was that damned sign spiked in the lawn, stating to everyone who walked down our street: It's Over. They're Gone.

I'd sat in the cab of the truck after the agent left, listening to the radio and smoking. The sun warmed the cracked seat. That smell of cigarette smoke and sun on the leather, and the stink of gasoline, made me think of one of the last things I ever did with my father. In the fall of 1939, just after the war broke out, Uncle Jack had ridden down to Calgary from the reserve where he was an Indian Agent. Mom got a call saying Jack couldn't get his horse to cross the Centre Street bridge, because of the streetcar tracks. My dad shook his head and laughed. "Your family," he said to Mom. We didn't have a car. But Dad took the truck home at night sometimes. Mom and I drove with him to get Jack, in the dry-cleaning truck full of suits and jackets and white cloth laundry bags.

Dad smoked too, and it was hot that day. We drove with the truck windows wide open. I'd always liked the sharp creases, the brand new smell of jackets and skirts waiting for their owners, swinging in the back until their owner's bodies filled them, and they'd step out to a glamorous time. We climbed through Chinatown, past the twin lions on the Centre Street Bridge, by the big houses on Crescent Heights, and found Uncle Jack with his horse tethered to a fence in a vacant lot, his blanket and saddle drying in the sun. Jack didn't have a car, and he was far too stubborn to ask my grandpa for a ride, but he'd call Mom. My dad gave him a ride to the recruiting station at Mewata Armouries. Uncle Jack was told to settle his affairs and report back in a week, ready to go. Dad drove him to our house for supper. Uncle Jack worried the whole time about his horse, although the lady who owned the vacant lot said she'd watch him. It was odd even then to think of my family crossing the Centre Street Bridge on horseback. Some of my cousins didn't have electricity or running water on their farms until the fifties. Jack told us he used to ride to town and camp at the top of Crescent Heights overlooking China-town until 1929, building a fire and letting his horse graze above the city.

When we got back to the horse, Jack boosted me onto its back and led it around the lot. It was an acre-age really—one of those farms that the city swallows up for houses, just as our house in Ogden had once been someone's farm. I'd dug up a horseshoe one time, with the nails still in it, lost in mid-gait, and another time, a crowbar with a missing tooth jammed the tines of the roto-tiller. Mom hugged Jack before he rode off. That was the last time I ever heard of anyone crossing the Centre Street Bridge on a horse. Not long after, Dad too shipped out, then my uncles, all of them coming around to say their goodbyes. Our little kitchen would be full of smoke, and bottles of rye lined up on the table, brand new uniform jackets and hats filling the front hall. I lay awake in bed listening to the laughter, and then the hush after they left—a hush that lasted five long years, until they came back. Well, at least my uncles came back.

For a long time, Lowell and I, before we went to sleep, always said we loved each other. I'd insisted at first, like the rapid now-I-lay-me-down-to-sleep, I-pray-the-Lord-my-soul-to-keep, I said as a little girl.

Then we were too tired and we forgot, once or twice. After awhile we stopped altogether. My father had said goodbye to Mom and me, before he shipped out. Although, none of us realized then that it was for good. I wonder if he did.

But that day the agent brought the sign—after he drove away, I wrapped my hands around the truck's big steering wheel, as if I might find something of Lowell's grip, the oil from his hands, anything. And I bawled. I pounded the wheel. I must have hit the horn, because it started up, a long blunt wail going on and on, until my neighbour Margaret came out of her house and found me. Her husband, Jon, lifted the hood, as I had seen my husband do at an intersection once, pulling at wires until the horn stopped honking.

I read somewhere that when people lose an arm or a leg, the body remembers the missing part, twitching and itchy, and phantom pains set in. Jon had silenced the horn for me, although I hadn't really wanted him to. Margaret took me to her house and made me coffee. On the counter, a row of cream puffs stood cooling. We ate them, and smoked. I've always been cheated of my goodbyes, Margaret, I told her. She said nothing, but rocked me in her arms like a mother.

That night I laid in bed with Lowell's place empty beside me. A phantom pain ripped through me. For a long, long time afterwards, in my sleep, I'd feel Lowell against me, and I rolled towards him. But in the morning I woke, clutching a fistful of sheets, the pillow against my chest, my mouth dry, and my eyes damp from crying in my sleep.

It took a long time to sell the house. One of the neighbours bought the station wagon.

Once the house was sold, we moved to a place near the Stampede grounds—the top half of an older house—with two bedrooms. Pauline slept on the couch in the living room, Emily slept in my room, and the twins slept in bunkbeds in the back room. The people downstairs fought sometimes, and my girls were frightened. Still, we did all right with what we had. We managed to keep the television set, and Pauline painted some of the old furniture from the ranch in bright hues of yellow and purple. We needed that colour then, even though it ruined the furniture. Dot would've had a fit if she'd ever come to visit.

Will went to live with Dot. It was closer to the school, and I wanted to give him a chance to go on to university. I'd sold our double bed and bought myself a cot, one that cradled me in its canvas mattress. I didn't want a bed with an empty place next to me anymore.

One day Emily asked me, "Are we poor Mom?" She couldn't have been more than seven. She knew. The people downstairs were poor. Some of the people in the rented houses beside us were poor, too. I brushed Emily's hair from her eyes, wanting to make everything better. "No, we're not, honey. We have each other. To be poor is to be without hope. We still have hope."

She, of course, doesn't remember that, but she was the kind of kid, like her brother, who watched.

By that time, the twins were coming home cut and scraped from fights with the kids at their new school. They fought with their backs to each other, facing out into the world. Pauline quit school and went out to work in a restaurant, lying about her age.

Eventually, Pauline left, and then the twins moved out too. Emily and I stayed together. When she married, I rented the basement suite in her house.

One day, Emily walked into my living room with a sheaf of papers that she'd brought home from the public library. I was having tea with Pauline, who'd come over to visit. Emily had always asked me questions about her dad. My answers had never satisfied her. She spread the photocopies across my dining table.

One headline said: *Unofficial Truce. Ground Fighting in Korea Over. War Continues In Air and At Sea. Tuesday, November 9, 1951.* Below it was a smaller headline: *Northside Gang Found Guilty in Affray. Jury's In: Ringleader Gets Two Years Hard Labour.* The other paper read: *7 Convicted in Brawl. Judge Slams Gang Violence.*

"The past's the past," Pauline said, glaring at Emily. "Why are you digging up all that stuff?"

After Pauline left, Emily sat down beside me. "Tell me, Mom. What was Dad like?"

I shook my head. What was there to say?

Emily touched my arm. "Mom?"

I pointed to the headlines in the *Calgary Albertan,* that day in 1951. "This one was in red. It won't show up in the microfiche, but I remember—it was red. And I wasn't weeping in the courtroom when your

451

father was sentenced to two years hard labour. That's the reporter's imagination. I was wondering what we would do, your unborn brother and I."

"Tell me what it was like," Emily said.

I couldn't tell her what she wanted to hear—not then. I wasn't ready. But I took the clippings to bed that night. I'd long given up smoking by then, and had gone back to reading in bed, like I used to do.

When I can, I write, but mostly I make watercolours. The colours soothe me in a way words never did. But I wanted to tell my daughter the story of us, all of us.

Late one night, the phantom pains came. I'd woken into that clarity that comes before sunrise, and disappears after the first cars appear on the streets. So I picked up my pen and began to write in a notebook, like the ones I'd bought for my kids years ago. For nearly three months I wrote, recalling as much as I could, or dared. Then I showed the notebook to Emily.

"Finish it, Mom," she said.

For a long time, I was so hurt by that—not daring to ask her, finish what, or how? But last summer, I took those notebooks—I'd filled four of them—and I started to write more stories. When the kids came to visit, I passed my notebooks across the table for them to read. Thy argued about how things had really happened. Even the twins disagreed, sometimes—Liz taking one side, and Chris, the other.

Will lives down east now. When he came to visit and I showed him my stories he said nothing, at first—just passed the book back to me. But one night,

Pauline came over for supper. We opened a bottle of wine, and Will began to tell stories about the year we had sent him away.

"You're exaggerating," Pauline said.

"I'm not," he said, flushing. The grey in his beard, his fading red hair, reminded me of my grandfather.

After Will left, I found one of his notebooks among my things, and used his words to help me write mine. He phoned me from time to time. Once, he spoke of Lowell. It had been a long time since we'd mentioned Lowell's name.

"The world is getting younger, Mom. And we're not," he said.

I knew what Will meant. When I go out on the bus or down to the Kerby Centre for my senior's group, I don't recognize the city anymore. And sometimes, when I turn down a street I used to know, it takes a long time to remember where I am. I want to jot down everything, before it's all gone younger on me. What I can't remember, I sometimes make up.

Pauline was there for so much of it. "That didn't happen, Mom," she'd say. "You didn't say that." She never says that in front of her brother and other sisters, only to me.

I do remember something Will said, one day on the phone from Ontario. "What if it had happened this way instead of that, Mom?"

I wondered for a long time. What I might have said, what I should have said to Lowell that morning before he died. Would it have affected the outcome? I don't think so. But I would have gotten to say good-bye.

Acknowledgements

First, Oliver Sacks's book, *Seeing Voices,* provoked memories that led to a journey through a world I thought I knew.

Earlene Wasik for sharing her stories and those of the mothers of deaf, deafened and hard of hearing children. Wendy Caswell for her talents and insights as a "contraption lady" extraordinaire.

Many sources were instrumental in writing this book, but I would like to particularly acknowledge: Dr. Howard Adams, Kathleen and John Elliott, Robert Elliott, Ben Gadd, Edwin and Wayne Getty's 1975, *A Case History and Analysis of Stoney Indian— Government Interaction with Regard to the Big Horn Dam,* The Glenbow Archives, Grant MacEwan, Andrew Nikiforuk, modern day missionaries, Karen and Rodger Rinker, for pointing me towards the Bighorn people, Jane Ross and Daniel Kyba, Maggie Siggins, Chief John Snow, and Walking Buffalo, or George Maclean.

I thank all those who have so generously lent me their ears and their stories in the making of this one: Ian Adam, Billy Brass, Fiona Bain-Greenwood, Cynthia Chambers, Burke Cullen, Barry Dempster, Ken Dyba, Pam Knott, Irene Kanurkas, Robert Hilles, Marlene Lacey, Keith and Ellen McArthur, Pete Miller, Charles Noble, Jon Redfern Barb Ritchie, Ken Rivard, Sonja Skarstedt, Winston Smith, Richard Stevenson, Jeff Stewart, Rosemary Stewart, Pat Stirton, Wendy Struthers, Christine Thomson-

Hunter, Herman Van Reekum, Terry Watada, Barry Wood.

And finally I'd like to thank Oolichan Books, especially, Ron Smith, who discovered me the first time, and Hiro Boga, my editor, who discovered me the second time, and who patiently saw this book through to publication.

Author photo credit: A. Edgar

Bruce Hunter is the author of three books of poetry and a collection of short stories. Deafened as an infant, he worked in blue-collar jobs for nearly fifteen years, including variously as a labourer, Zamboni driver and gardener before and after attending Malaspina College. In his late twenties, he studied with W.O. Mitchell at the Banff School of Fine Arts and attended York University.

For the past twenty years, he has taught English and Liberal Studies at Seneca College as well as stints teaching Creative Writing at the Banff Centre and York University. In 2002, he was the Writers' Guild of Alberta's Writer in Residence at the Banff Centre. In the fall of 2007, he was Writer in Residence for the Richmond Hill Public Library.